STUDIES IN GERMAN LITERATURE,
LINGUISTICS, AND CULTURE

VOL. 19

STUDIES IN GERMAN LITERATURE, LINGUISTICS, AND CULTURE

VOL. 19

CAMDEN HOUSE
Columbia, South Carolina

DANCES OF DEATH

Die schwarze Dame.

Alfred Kubin, *The Black Lady* (circa 1900) as illustration to the line from *Erdgeist,* "Jetzt kommt die Hinrichtung."

Dances of Death

Wedekind, Brecht, Dürrenmatt, and the Satiric Tradition

EDSON M. CHICK

CAMDEN HOUSE

Set in Garamond type and printed on
acid-free Glatfelder paper.

Copyright © 1984 by Camden House, Inc.
Drawer 2025
Columbia, South Carolina 29202
Library of Congress Catalog Card Number: 83-70286
All Rights Reserved
Printed in the United States of America
First Edition
ISBN: 0-938100-24-6

Acknowledgments

This study began as a topic for a Dartmouth College freshman seminar; members of the Dartmouth Humanities Colloquium heard and criticized an early version of Chapter Three; and a Dartmouth faculty development grant gave me three months to write a first draft. Some years later a Williams College sabbatical leave coupled with a Fulbright research scholarship made possible the completion of the penultimate version. In this connection I owe thanks to Dr. Ulrich Littmann of the Fulbright Commission, Bad Godesberg, and to the faculty and staff of the German Seminar at the Technical University of Berlin, especially to Professor Horst Enders and Renate Weniger. Egon Karter of the Reiss Theater Agency, Basel, kindly opened their Dürrenmatt archive to me; and Dr. Walter Huder of the Berlin Akademie der Künste gave me free use of the Georg Kaiser archive there.

I am indebted to Williams College for help with printing costs, to the staff of Sawyer Library for all kinds of assistance, and to Rosemary Lane and Eileen Sahady for their encouragement and skill in putting the manuscript into shape. I am grateful to Gunther Holst for valuable suggestions regarding the final form of the manuscript. Finally, my thanks to James Hardin for taking the project seriously and for his morale-building criticism.

Friedrich Dürrenmatt's Tower Construction IV is taken from Dürrenmatt, *Bilder und Zeichnungen,* copyright 1978 by the Diogenes Verlag AG Zurich, with the kind permission of the publisher.

Contents

For Ed, Judi, and the Kids

If the term satire designates an inner form that expresses itself in various ways through history, then the concept must be repeatedly reformulated.
Jürgen Brummack

Introduction

ONLY WITHIN THE PAST fifteen years or so have scholars and critics of modern German drama begun to accept and apply the concept of satire in their treatment of the major plays of this century. The term has now begun to acquire the breadth and flexibility it has long had in the Anglo-American tradition. I want to contribute to this process by examining in detail a few plays—for German satire has found its strongest expression on the stage—in the light of this broader and more productive set of categories. To this end I have chosen to concentrate on five pieces by five dramatists, to refer, sometimes at length, to other works by the same writers, and to adduce from a variety of sources, literary and nonliterary, information that will contribute to the understanding of these topical and tendentious plays. The authors are Frank Wedekind (1864-1918), Carl Sternheim (1878-1942), Georg Kaiser (1878-1945), Bertolt Brecht (1898-1956), and Friedrich Dürrenmatt (1921-   ).

Without speculating on differences in national character and in attitudes toward irony, I believe the German reluctance to accept and affirm satire as a respectable literary mode can be attributed to two obstacles: a longstanding one on the right, and another more recent one on the left. The former condemns satire on aesthetic grounds.[1] Following the course laid by Jean Paul and Friedrich Hegel at the beginning of the nineteenth century, ruling opinion has denied satire any enduring artistic value. Indeed some authorities have viewed it at worst as hostile to the humanistic principles of true art and literature and at best as a propagandistic genre not worth serious study. Hegel and Jean Paul installed humor as the ideal form of comedy, by which they understood a temperate and objective view of the world's folly and confusion taken from an Olympian standpoint, reconciling earthly contradictions, and so making us serene and free.

One consequence of this was that, until recently, the only satiric works to find a place in the German canon of worthwhile literature have been eighteenth-century Enlightenment and Rococo pieces, often in rhymed verse and couched in witty, graceful, and overtly didactic tones. In the light of all this it is no wonder that the most vigorous satiric dramatists of the past eighty or ninety years have been loath to accept that designation. Friedrich Dürrenmatt, in his impatient, contentious way, says that in German culture satire and the comic in general are thought of as second rate. "Spirit," he writes ironically, "is expressed either through pathos or—a form peculiar to these climes—in a strange, imbecilic cuteness held, it seems, to be *esprit*. Theatrical comedy is suspect, isn't taken seriously as something for adults.[2] ·

The obstacle on the left is newer and arises from firm beliefs concerning the determinants of history, society, and human nature. I refer here to the Marxist cant that has colored literary studies both east and west of the Elbe. Even scholars of the first rank, when dealing with satire, sometimes suffer lapses of perception and style. Volker Klotz, for instance, sees in the plays of Wedekind above all a socioeconomic statement on the condition of the world. Wedekind allegedly shows us "the unfree society of the capitalist free economy preserved and secured in an imperialist state which exerts the right of the stronger in its foreign policy and at home."[3] The observation is legitimate; but when it pretends to sum up Wedekind's strongest convictions, then it leads to distorted judgments and smug, I-know-better criticism that brands Wedekind politically naive and ignorant of the laws of production and class struggle, defeating himself by playing into the hands of the capitalist enemy.[4]

Only one of our five playwrights earns the approval of this school of criticism: Bertolt Brecht; and that is because his earlier, satiric plays are passed over in favor of his later, doctrinaire pieces. Critics in the East condemn Georg Kaiser because he concentrates on moral questions and does not penetrate to the true material source of our ills. According to this view, his late-bourgeois, false view of reality blinds him to the true nature of the capitalist social order.[5] And according to Erich Kühne, Friedrich Dürrenmatt is altogether on the wrong track. In *Der Besuch der alten Dame [The Visit]* he should have directed his satiric attack not at the petit bourgeois morality of the citizens of Güllen but at monopolistic capitalism. To make matters worse, Dürrenmatt is pessimistic; he presents the Gülleners' moral collapse as a predetermined, inevitable event.[6] Equally damning is the fact that the play is set in a fantastic fictional milieu quite divorced from the real world of European history.[7] In other words, Dürrenmatt, according to this view, fails on several counts: he is unrealistic, formalistic, fatalistic, and ahistorical. Marxist criteria, as developed and applied in recent years, reduce satire to a form of direct cultural criticism, to diatribes against greed, urban rot, and the like. In effect it puts a number of pieces of good literature in a class with the products of crackpots like Philip Wylie, Paul de Lagarde, or Julius Langbehn.

Dürrenmatt fends off the insistent demand that he and other authors are morally obliged to declare and demonstrate their political persuasion. "The writer," he contends, "can fulfill his task only if he is an anarchist. He must attack but remain aloof. The one place he belongs is between two stools."[8]

Finally, the charges of insufficiency directed at Dürrenmatt and others partake of Marx's own "failure to ground the central element of political life, *power*, in the elemental soil of human nature."[9] His treatment of political man is inadequate because it lacks a psychological core. And this same shortcoming in Marxist criticism is a fatal weakness when dealing with plays by Wedekind and Sternheim, for instance, where the psychology of power—*Realpsychologie* is Wedekind's word for it—is of crucial significance.

The other side of this coin is that a Marxist play with satiric intent is often misunderstood in the West, perhaps because psychological insight is lacking. Audiences in Zurich saw Brecht's *St. Joan of the Stockyards* as an attack not on capitalism as a whole but on some of the system's evils, abuses that might well be corrected to make society more humane.[10] That is, the intended moral is evident only to those who already think right.

The Zurichers's perverse but innocent misapprehension points to a paradox in the way satire seems to work. The greater the satire's realism and verisimilitude and the closer it adheres to real historical and social conditions, the weaker its effect will be. Satires that are embedded in a fantastic fiction make their point most effectively. There is, for example, at least a general consensus on the impact and message of Swift's *Gulliver's Travels*. The fantastic vision is, for satiric purposes, the sharpest; and to paraphrase an often quoted Dürrenmatt dictum, grotesque fantasy is the only way we have nowadays of being precise.[11]

This truth is embodied in the two improbable female satiric figures that frame this study: Wedekind's Lulu and Dürrenmatt's Claire Zachanassian. Both are bigger than life, inscrutable, protean composites of the phantasies and daydreams endemic in their time. Lulu: the Marilyn Monroe of her day, an erotic prodigy built to excite men of all persuasions and some women as well. Claire Zachanassian: the composite of the celebrity worshiper's idols, a kind of grotesque Jackie Onassis, rich and powerful beyond human capacity to conceive, dominating the jet set, and living the beautiful life.

The best satire strikes this right combination of the weird and the familiar, the fictional and the topical. This mixing is a basic stylistic principle of satire. Sternheim, for instance, puts the farcical, mundane, and cruel action of his *Die Kassette* into the mold of a traditional five-act tragedy with numbered entrances and exits. The plot is constructed out of trite comic conventions distorted to aggressive ends.[12]

In recognition of the pejorative connotations of the word in the minds of his countrymen, Carl Sternheim repeatedly and vigorously disavowed all satiric intent in his writing. And until recently, literary studies have lent him support by arguing that, far from launching ironic attacks, he apotheosizes his protagonists and propounds through them his optimistic Weltanschauung. W. G. Sebald, in his recent book, is not so kind. He senses the outrage that informs Sternheim's drama but then rejects author and work as neurotic and morally irresponsible.[13] Finally, and most commonly, the force of Sternheim's work is vitiated simply by calling it second-rate. Supposedly, he writes badly, is unpoetic, is insufficiently dialectical, and provides no properly satisfying resolutions to his plays.

In all these instances Sternheim's angry irony goes unmarked. Academic criticism, until recently, remained inflexible; it seemed compelled to mend or reject the fragmentation that satire is and represents. Students of Sternheim clove to the surface meaning of his drama and cited his occasional authorial pronouncements as corroboration for their readings.

Frederick Crews offers a psychoanalytic explanation for this effort to dampen the discomforting effects of literature in his essay on "Anaesthetic Criticism" suggesting that "our reaction to a work of art will be a compromise demanded not only by the work's conflicting signals but also by the habitual bias of our ego."[14] Misreading, he argues, is a natural defense mechanism. "All literary criticism aims to make the reading experience more possible for us, but anaesthetic criticism assumes that this requires keeping caged the anxieties that the artist set free and then recaptured. The effect is often to transform the artist from a struggling fellow mortal into an authority figure, a dispenser of advice about virtue and harmony."

Wayne C. Booth uses more old-fashioned language to say much the same thing. He notes that each of us likes to think our own reading of an ironic statement is the correct one and explains further why irony, and that acrimonious irony we call satire, is such a sensitive and troublesome issue:

> An aggressively intellectual exercise that fuses fact and value, requiring us to construct alternative hierarchies and choose among them; demands that we look down on other men's follies or sins; floods us with emotion-charged value judgments which claim to be backed by the mind; accuses other men not only of wrong beliefs but of being wrong at their very foundations and blind to what these foundations imply—all of this coupled with a kind of subtlety that cannot be deciphered or 'proved' simply by looking closely at words: no wonder that 'failure to communicate' and resulting quarrels are often found where irony dwells.[15]

Charles Witke sees the problem in a positive light and suggests that the satirist works by irony and indirection, withholding any statement of an ideal norm, because he wants his audience "to go through the strengthening exercise of finding it for themselves."[16]

One pervasive source of confusion is that satire is strictly speaking not a literary genre. Almost all modes of literature are congenial to it. We can speak generally of a work "imbued with the satiric spirit" or one that employs certain satiric techniques.[17] It is a way of writing.[18] The concept is so loose that it can embrace the works of Aristophanes, Swift, and Karl Kraus.

I do not propose to develop a coherent or definitive theory of satire. That has been done well and often, particularly in the past decade or so, by a number of German, English, and American scholars. Rather, I should like to build onto their insights with a view to suggesting new and illuminating readings of plays by Wedekind, Sternheim, Kaiser, Brecht, and Dürrenmatt.

For purposes of orientation, I would like here to offer an open and suggestive formulation based on the concepts Jürgen Brummack has distilled from his reading of satiric literature from antiquity to the present.[19] According to Brummack, it has always been accepted, and has, in fact, become a cliché, that the spirit of satire was born with the human race. In his "Essay on Satire" (1693) John Dryden writes: "If we take satire in the general signification of the word, as it is used in all modern languages for an invective, it is certain that it is almost as old as verse; and though hymns, which are praises of God, may be allowed to have been before it, yet the defamation of others was not long after it. After God had cursed Adam and Eve in Paradise, the husband and wife excused themselves, by laying blame on one another; and gave a beginning to those conjugal dialogues, which the poets have perfected in verse."[20] As a literary technique it first bore fruit in early Rome.

From a general anthropological standpoint satire originates in a basic human way of feeling. That feeling, the first of the three primary characteristics of satire, may be private irritation, savage indignation, or delight in aggression. Second, the satiric attack serves a good social purpose. And third, it makes use of almost any literary form: epic, essay, novel, or drama. Satire is, in short, aesthetically socialized aggression; and *a* satire is a work that gives it expression.[21]

The aggressive impulse is not sublimated; it is palpably present in the text. Satire is traditionally presumed to be older and less civilized than comedy; it may inveigh against living persons, including the audience, or against accepted forms and ideas.[22] The satirist may attack openly and leave no doubt about his intentions. Or he may, for the sake of emotional or aesthetic effect, or perhaps to hoodwink the censor, renounce invective and deliver his denunciation by indirection of varying degrees: through burlesque or irony. Like Perseus, he may resort to sly contrivances to save his own life and still kill the Medusa.[23]

It is indirection and the fictions employed in satire that make it art and also what complicate the work of reader and interpreter. All the plays to be examined here are examples of indirect and hermetic satire. To cite Sternheim once more as an example, it was precisely the seeming ideological neutrality of *Die Kassette* that in 1961 incited particularly younger spectators to loud protests and altercations with other members of the audience.[24] These incidents were presumably the sort of quarrel which, according to Wayne C. Booth, is often found where irony dwells. Satirists use ironic fictions, constructing frequently insane and intricately organized worlds that function in themselves like clockwork. The best modern dramatic satire attacks covertly with the weapons of irony. And irony, in the rhetorician's definition, is an attack using the partisan vocabulary of the opposition.[25]

Yet its hidden meaning asks to be discovered. The satirist transmits signals to his audience through inconsistencies or implausibility, through grotesque or ironic deformation that there is more here than meets the eye. These signals mean that to understand fully the reader must first identify the intent of the work and then strive to reconstruct its true meaning. Ideally the reader or audience will be provoked to work at the reconstruction of the work's true meaning. The more outlandish the disguise, the greater will be the intensity of response.[26] In modern satire, and particularly in satiric drama, the work of interpretation is further hampered by the absence of a consistent and recognizable authorial voice. Also, if it presents the positive contrast to a deficient reality, it does so only by implication. It presents no explicit norm of behavior, nor is it governed by discernible aesthetic standards. Nevertheless, some strong family resemblances help identify certain works, including dramas by Wedekind, Sternheim, and the others, as essentially satiric. Tone, theme, patterns of action, aggressive irony, travesty, expansive rhetoric, and the capacity to aggravate an audience are some of the things they have in common.

Broadly speaking, the monstrous threat that looms behind these plays is nothing less than the dehumanization of our existence. The works themselves necessarily partake of this inhumanity; they are at bottom expressions of the very death instinct and aggressive drive of which they warn us. Their central symbol is violence: suicide, murder, mutilation, war.[27] The dehumanized world is a given, and the satirist feels no need to disguise it in any fashion. Before pronouncing his lethal laws of human happiness, Brecht's Paul Ackermann announces, "Oh, Jungens, ich will doch gar kein Mensch sein" (Oh, but boys, I don't want to be human at all).[28] Wedekind, Sternheim, Kaiser, and Dürrenmatt make similarly unambiguous statements.

Heretofore, radically satiric drama, as distinct from comedy with satiric overtones, has often been lumped together with the genre called tragicomedy or dark comedy. Writing about tragicomedy, Karl S. Guthke argues that Dürrenmatt's plays must be tragicomic and not satiric, for "the satirist in his contempt for what is, knows, by contrast, what and how reality *should be*. This, in turn, means that his criticism [...] is leveled at reality from an unshakably firm standpoint; from a sure knowledge of form and ideal."[29] On the other hand, by positing the validity of the concept of figural satire, whose firing platform is movable and often hard to locate, and by accepting Brummack's formulation: satire is aesthetically socialized aggression, we can identify a number of important plays in a well-defined tradition and propose more fruitful readings of them.

Modern German satiric drama is theater of an unusually intense and acid sort.

It not merely manipulates and embarrasses its audience through dissonances and contradictions; it is militantly ironic and takes up arms against uncanny, intangible, and deadly forces. It aims to revolt, disillusion, and frustrate the spectator, to shock him into awareness, and to enlist him ultimately in the forces of right and humanity.

Because of his aggressive tone and his cold rationality, it has been observed that "the satirist runs the double risk of being unpopular in his own time and of being forgotten by later generations."[30] Not only does he show the ideological foundations of our Weltanschauung to be false and inhuman, but he carries out his exposé without feeling, in an intensely logical and cerebral way. His work lacks the music, the emotion, the inspiring hymnic qualities of true poetry. Its effects are obviously contrived, the structure clearly calculated. Satire views all with icy intellectuality.

The life of a satire in the annals of literary history is almost invariably a short one. Satirists draw on the idiom and fads of the times. Their travesties, or fantastic visions, if they strike the public fancy, are quickly taken out of context, made commonplace, and absorbed in the vocabulary of a blander essayistic cultural criticism. At worst the satirist may see his work adapted to the service of forces he meant to destroy. And at best he can take some cold comfort in the oft noted fact that "the satirists who regard the absurdly horrible as always possible seem to be better prophets than the serious commentators."[31] But the satisfaction of having been right fades in the face of the galling fact that history and reality rapidly overtake and mimic his ugliest fictions. "Mir fällt zu Hitler nichts ein," wrote Karl Kraus in 1933 as the lead sentence to *Die dritte Walpurgisnacht* (published posthumously in 1952). As so often occurs, a grotesque and deadly actuality has outstripped the satiric imagination.

In the opening monologue of his *Traumstück* (1922), Kraus lets his poet persona complain, with more pathos and self-pity than a satirist would normally allow himself, of his Cassandran role. He is, he says, condemned,

> unsägliches
> zu sagen, Unerhörtes taubem Ohr
> noch einmal anzutun und immer wieder.
> Und immer wird zum Inhalt solcher Botschaft,
> daß eine Welt, die sie empfangen soll,
> sie nicht empfangen will, wenn sie's vermöchte.
> Verirrter Drang, die Seelen aufzureißen
> mit einem Schrei, daß sie verschlossen sind!
> Was Menschen sind, verhindert sie zu hören,
> daß sie nicht Menschen sind. Nur mich allein
> verhindert's nimmer ihnen es zu sagen.
> Und labyrinthisch immer angelockt,
> find ich zum Ausgang nicht und nicht zurück.[32]

(to say the unsayable, to impose once more the unheard of on deaf ears and over and over. And the contents of such a message turns out to be that a world that should receive it does not want to receive it, even if it could. Errant urge to open up souls with the cry that they are locked closed! The qualities that make them human prevent them from hearing that they are not human. I alone am never prevented from telling them that. And lured ever onward over labyrinthine paths, I don't find my way out or my way back.)

Kraus overstates the case. To be sure, good satire may not have changed the world, but it has always found an audience. And I hope to show, by reading the dramas treated here as intended satire, that they and others like them have a hitherto unsuspected power and import.

The five playwrights are all considered modern, but I have found that their work can be discussed using critical terms others apply to Neidhart von Reuenthal, Ben Jonson, and Jonathan Swift. In fact, I have relied heavily on the work of others for guidance.[33] For historical and critical orientation on matters of genre definition I exploited Brummack's thorough overview of the concepts and theories of satire from Archilochus to the present. His "Forschungsreferat" is far more than a good summary; it evaluates, defines and points the way for further study. Another basic source, Wayne C. Booth's *A Rhetoric of Irony*, clarifies concepts and discusses how the open deceptions of satire work, from the author's and the reader's standpoint. Northrop Frye's *Anatomy of Criticism* told me I was dealing with satire of the high norm and provided a clear set of identifying characteristics. Matthew Hodgart's *Satire* offers a valuable and thorough introduction to the whole topic and in Chapter Six gives an overview of satiric drama. Hodgart also develops some critical terms, of which "travesty" is the most important. He extends it to mean the fantastic vision, or what might also be called the outlandish fiction, of a satire.

The initial inspiration for this study I drew from Alvin B. Kernan's *The Plot of Satire* with its clear enumeration of structural tendencies: jumbling, magnifying, diminishing. Kernan provides criteria for identifying a work as satire as well as a framework for its analysis. His study is nicely complemented by Ronald Paulson's *The Fictions of Satire* which deals more with the material, images, and symbols found in the genre. Paulson draws attention to satire's central symbol of violence and to the connections between crime, guilt, and punishment, all of which, together with Brummack's definition, suggested that the theme of aggression could serve as the axis of this study. Robert C. Elliott's *The Power of Satire* also pointed me in this direction. Elliott approaches satire from an anthropological angle and looks for its origins in magic and ritual. His remarks on the malefic power traditionally attributed to the satirist's hatred and on the audience's, or scapegoat's, fear of death by ridicule helped me organize some ideas about the relation between satirist and society and the way satire affects theater audiences. One more primarily theoretical essay I drew on was Karl Pietzcker's article on the grotesque, in which the defeat of expectations by a hostile reality, absence of authorial direction, topicality, use of wild fictions, aggression, in short many of the characteristics of what others called satire, are listed as the identifying marks.

Ulrich Gaier's *Satire* is both historical and normative. His concluding outline of a definition of satire uses examples from Dürrenmatt's *Der Richter und sein Henker* [The Judge and his Executioner, 1950]; and though it tends toward existential overstatement, speaking of the satirist's verbal battle for liberation against the dread faceless force of reality, it presents a vivid picture of the battle and the rhetorical weapons he uses to neutralize the threat: synecdoche, metaphor, irony, hyperbole, and grotesque distortion. Gaier also makes good use of the term "figural" to characterize much of the satire written over the past hundred years. The figural mode of narration is one in which the author's standpoint is obscured and the story tells itself, so to speak, through the medium of one or more characters. In whatever genre, figural satire projects figures and systems which have to do with casts of mind and consciousness itself but which have more than one possible valid meaning. It does not pass judgment but rather works through mimicry. Gaier broadens and deepens the concept of satire so that it can be used to advantage in discussing not only Dürrenmatt but all the other dramatists this study focuses on.

Jörg Schonert's *Roman und Satire im 18. Jahrhundert* also draws generalizing conclusions from a historical investigation and reinforces many of Gaier's points. He writes of satiric mimesis and indirect, representational satire, his term for what Gaier calls the figural mode. Schönert also notes that anticlimax is essential to the structure of satire, where forces defeat each other and themselves ("sich aufheben"). His conclusions are in turn supported and extended by Gerhard Hoffmann in an article on Ben Jonson's *Volpone*. Hoffmann chooses the word "hermetic" to express the idea of figural satire and remarks on how the satirist—that is, the satiric speaker: e.g., Swift's Gulliver, Wieland's Democritus, Grimmelshausen's Simplizius—is absorbed into the play as one or more of the characters. In addition he mentions some of the conventions of theatrical satire, in particular the device of a play within a play.

In *Swift and the Satirist's Art*, Edward W. Rosenheim makes the observation that serious, Swiftian satire is an expression of anger at the corruption of the human intellect and spirit and links this anger with the aggressive nature of the satirist and his characters. More important in determining my approach was Rosenheim's specification of the two essential ingredients of satire, which he defines as an attack by means of a "manifest fiction based on discernible historical particulars." That is, satire is very topical and is also couched in a "wildly original imaginative conceit," which is, incidentally, the rough equivalent of Hodgart's travesty and Dürrenmatt's "Einfall" (bright idea).

Closest of all to my project is Peter Uwe Hohendahl's *Das Bild der bürgerlichen Welt im expressionistischen Drama*. It covers much of the same ground I do. It is far more than a sociological investigation and in its perceptive observations concerning Wedekind, Sternheim, and Kaiser provides valuable material for any book on modern dramatic satire.

> *Great satire has always reflected the*
> *problematic quality of its attitude.*
> Jürgen Brummack

1

Frank Wedekind and his Lulu Tragedy

THE NAME FRANK WEDEKIND (1864-1918) is well-known to students of drama and teachers of literature, but his plays are seldom read nowadays. Theater audiences find them dated and obscure. His most controversial and ambitious pieces, *Erdgeist* [*Earth Spirit*, published in 1895] and its sequel, *Die Büchse der Pandora* [*Pandora's Box*, first performed in 1904], are more familiar to opera-goers than to readers and theater audiences thanks to Alban Berg's operatic adaptation, *Lulu* (1937).

Many of Wedekind's twenty plays seem ill made, wordy, occasionally pompous, and chaotic in structure. They owed their early popularity in part to Wedekind's notoriety, to the tumult they excited at premières, to appreciative treatment by Germany's finest theater directors—Max Reinhardt and Leopold Jessner, among others—and to the support of influential critics: Alfred Kerr, Herbert Ihering, and Siegfried Jacobsohn.

Wedekind was notorious and interesting. He wrote dramas that seemed freighted with great literary and ideological import. His obsession with sex, his satiric political poems in *Simplicissimus,* one of which earned him four and a half months in prison for *lesé majesty,* put him in trouble with censors and made him all the more appealing to liberal intellectuals. It was a challenge to stage and interpret his works because of their opacity and scandalous reputation.

More important for theater people and reviewers was the recognition that Wedekind was writing a new kind of unliterary, or even antiliterary, drama which demanded new styles of directing and acting. He had grafted the lively and popular Parisian arts of cabaret, revue, and mime onto the "problem drama," as cultivated by Ibsen and Hauptmann, that dominated the contemporary literary scene.[1] He not only brought new life to the German stage, he also created modern dramatic satire in Germany. The best writers for the German theater in this century—Sternheim, Kaiser, Brecht, Dürrenmatt—all learned from him and improved on his inchoate ideas. They all have acknowledged their debt, and Wedekind's influence has thus become a literary-historical truism.

Wedekind was the first in a line of critical, intellectually—rather than mysti-

cally or aesthetically—inclined German dramatists who sensed something catas-
trophically wrong with their times and took up the weapons of satire to combat
it.[2] He filled his plays with topical material critical of contemporary mores and
culture: Victorian attitudes toward sex and sex education, the school system, censors, the institutions of marriage and family, women's emancipation, Neo-
Romanticism and Naturalism in art and literature, journalism. On a cursory reading he seems to have scattered his shot so that it had little effect. The impact of
his attack is also seemingly vitiated by ambiguities in his treatment of sexuality—a
curse and at the same time the only source of salvation—and the vitalistic philosophy ("Lebensphilosophie") of the day. Wedekind's public pronouncements
only cloud the picture further. Some he made to hoodwink the censor. Others
don't seem to fit the play in question. Yet it is possible to give the Lulu Tragedy—
and other Wedekind pieces as well—a reading which integrates what appears a
jumble into a coherent and powerful whole, and that reading is best conducted
under the assumption that it is a satire.

Wedekind thought of the drama as his *magnum opus* and never ceased in his
effort to get it past the censor and before the theater public. When in 1894 his
prospective publisher objected that his five-act *Erdgeist: Eine Monstre-Tragödie*
was too long and diffuse for the stage, Wedekind broke it in two and added one
act to each half. The first play of the pair retained the title *Erdgeist: Tragödie in
vier Aufzügen* [Tragedy in Four Acts], and the new act was sandwiched between
original acts two and three. The sequel, completed a few years later, he called *Die
Büchse der Pandora: Tragödie in drei Aufzügen* [Tragedy in Three Acts]. For
this he composed a new act one as exposition and preface to original acts four and
five. For convenience and in accord with usage I will refer to the pair of plays as
the Lulu Tragedy.

Of his twenty dramas it is first and foremost these two that were to serve as
model and inspiration for the dramatists to follow. Though they may never
recapture the stage, they will stand as monuments to their author's cold, sharp
eye. They contain his most effective attack on the evils and follies of the time and
of the human condition. They employ the devices and incorporate the perceptions of all great satire.

Stephen Spender gave his collection of Wedekind plays in translation the title
The Lulu Plays and other Tragedies of Sex.[3] And that sex is the leading metaphor
in almost all Wedekind's work is a reflection of an admitted personal obsession.
He writes to Georg Brandes in 1909, "But everyone has something odd about him
and is occasionally driven by the desire to understand that oddness. I readily
admit that I owe everything to this one [illegible]."[4] It is clear on the surface of it
that Wedekind uses his Lulu, as he does female figures in later plays, to demonstrate that sensuality is not a redemptive source of pleasure. It makes fools and

criminals of human beings. It has much the effect of money, another conventional satiric metaphor. I use the term metaphor because there is reason to believe that behind it lies a more elemental threat that is not easily described in a direct way.

In *Erdgeist* three men first get what they want, then what they deserve: Lulu and a violent end. In *Die Büchse der Pandora,* Lulu becomes a diseased predator like the others, and her express desire for death at the hands of a maniac is fulfilled. Words become active forces and metaphors become reality, which is to say that Wedekind takes the world at its word and draws the disastrous consequences. "I have never misrepresented the consequences that accrue to a person from his actions. Everywhere I have always demonstrated them in their inexorable necessity," says the chief character in *Zensur* [Censorship, 1908], speaking for the author.[5] At the same time, when the plays are viewed from the standpoint of the satiric mode in general, *Erdgeist* can be seen as the unmasking of the aggressive male in his suicidal folly. *Die Büchse der Pandora,* on the other hand, attacks the female of the species, as have satirists since Juvenal's time.

The Lulu of *Erdgeist* is beautiful and presumably naive, the realization of every man's erotic dream. "Sie beschämen die schönste Phantasie" (You put the most beautiful phantasy to shame. I, 390), says Dr. Schön. On the negative side, she owes this universal appeal in part to her utter lack of human sentiment. And she has no personality beyond what suits her master and victim of the moment. Costumed as a Pierrot or as a ballet dancer, under the name of Nelli, Eva, Mignon, Lulu, Countess Adelaide d'Oubra, or Ragapsischimulara, she reflects the wishes of others and evidently aims to please. But the outcome is always the same: her men grow soft and find they lack the strength to cope with her. In the face of her impassivity they sense their own folly and impotence, fall prey to delusions of persecution, and bring on their own demise. The major episodes in the dramatic action follow a course parallel to that of the male figures moving through a sequence of repression, release, and failure or anticlimax. This dramatic rhythm informs smaller units as well as the longer sequences which end with sudden death.

The action of *Erdgeist* can be outlined briefly. Dr. Schön (his character belies the name), newspaper publisher, business tycoon, and cold-blooded psychological realist, wants to make an advantageous marriage, and so tries to suppress his feelings for Lulu and get her out of his life by coupling her with other men. But in the end he succumbs, marries her, and proves to be the greatest fool of all. In a fit of paranoic madness he so frightens her that she shoots him. When Lulu fires the pistol at his back, she provides the ultimate demonstration of his failure and impotence. The irony is that he has created Lulu, literally picked her up off the streets, educated her in the ways of the world, and kept her as his mistress. By the time he finds he must deny her, she proves superior even to him in the art of dominating others.

Schön's marriage and death in act four complete the overarching action of the play. They constitute the most violent event in a series of similar dramatic events from which Lulu emerges ever stronger. Wedekind writes that he intended her to be "a magnificent example of a female as it emerges when a creature, whom nature has endowed with rich gifts, can develop unfettered in the society of men, to whom she is far superior in natural intelligence" (I, 867).[6] In the hilarious and bloody last act of *Erdgeist* six admirers, one a countess, are dancing attendance on her.

In her childlike, instinctive manner, Lulu beats her men at what they think they do best: dictating to others. Wedekind writes with facetious equanimity of *Erdgeist:* "Instead of the title *Earth Spirit* I could equally well have written *Realpsychologie,* in the sense of *Realpolitik.* In writing the play I wanted especially to eliminate all such logically untenable concepts as: love, loyalty, gratitude. The two main figures, Schön and Lulu, have subjectively nothing to do with these concepts, she because she has had no education, he because he has overcome that education" (I, 945).[7] On a mechanistic level, love, loyalty, and gratitude may indeed be logically untenable concepts; but in the end the deeper logic of Wedekind's satire uncovers the true nature of *Realpsychologie.* In *Erdgeist,* Dr. Schön is its main practitioner, and he is also the primary scapegoat and target of satiric attack. He dominates the play, sets the rules of the game, and endures the consequences. In *Die Büchse der Pandora,* Lulu assumes this role, likewise suffers repeated defeats, and meets an even bloodier end at the hands of Jack the Ripper. Each brings out the worst in others and becomes the victim of his own machinations.

Lulu's victim in act one of *Erdgeist* is Dr. Goll, the medical commissioner, an apoplectic, senile sadist with a penchant for pubescent maidens. Goll is content as long as Lulu—he calls her Nelli—dances for him to the tune of his violin and lash. Yet he can suffer from spells of mad jealousy. He is already uneasy as he watches her pose in Pierrot costume for the portraitist Schwarz. Both he and Dr. Schön inflate themselves and belittle the painter, first by suggesting his work is inadequate and then by making vulgar comments on his overall inadequacy. Joining the game, Lulu says, "Ein Maler ist doch eigentlich kein Mann" (A painter is really no man. I, 392).

When Goll is lured away to watch some young girls rehearse for the ballet, Schwarz casts off all restraint and tries to prove his manhood. After a wild, slapstick chase, Lulu surrenders and sinks onto the ottoman. In the anticlimactic, absurd love scene that follows, Schwarz seems paralyzed. He goes no farther than to kiss her hand and declare his love. Lulu answers his ardor with cool chatter about an earlier lover with twenty-four dueling scars, plays with Schwarz's watch, and refuses to address him by the intimate "du." She acts the thoroughgoing *Realpsycholog* and shows emotion only when she fears violence from the disillusioned painter. "Bringen Sie mich nur nicht um!" she cries (Don't kill me! I, 399). As if in answer to these words, old Goll smashes down the door, comes at both with raised stick, and dies on the spot of a stroke. Passion and revenge have been foiled, and Dr. Schön's scheme for rendering Lulu harmless has failed. Lulu and, indirectly, Schön have succeeded only in bringing out Schwarz's criminal proclivities (I, 401).

The remainder of act one shows Schwarz acceding to Lulu's proposal that they should marry, even though he fears the consequences: "Es ist zu spät für mich. Ich bin dem Glück nicht gewachsen. Ich habe eine höllische Angst davor" (It's too late for me. I can't cope with this happiness. I have a hellish fear of it. I, 403). This final episode is staged like a *danse macabre* around Goll's corpse.

In act two, Schön sets out to repair the marriage between Schwarz and Lulu, intending again to keep Lulu out of his way. The union is breaking up because Schwarz is too weak-willed and naive:

Lulu: Er liebt mich.
Schön: Das ist freilich fatal.

(Lulu: He loves me. Schön: That's a nuisance of course. I, 414). Aiming to make him an illusionless *Realpsycholog* and a domineering husband, Schön only drives Schwarz to despair over his own inadequacy and to a gory suicide by cutting his throat with a razor. Dr. Schön has defeated his own ends and would be altogether ruined by the scandal were it not that a revolution in Paris fills the newspapers.

In act three Lulu turns the tables and overpowers Schön with the same brutal methods of manipulation he used on Schwarz. Through applied *Realpsychologie,* she forces the manipulator of public opinion and of the financial world abjectly to confess his weakness:

Lulu: Seien Sie doch ein Mann.—Blicken Sie sich einmal ins Gesicht.—Sie haben keine Spur von Gewissen.—Sie schrecken vor keiner Schandtat zurück [...] Sie erobern die halbe Welt.—Sie tun, was Sie wollen—und Sie wissen so gut wie ich—daß [...]
Schön *ist völlig erschöpft auf dem Sessel links neben dem Mitteltisch zusammengesunken:* Schweig!
Lulu: Daß Sie zu schwach sind—um sich von mir loszureißen [...]
Schön *stöhnend:* Oh! Oh!du tust mir weh!
. . . .
Lulu: Er weint wie ein Kind—der furchtbare Gewaltmensch!

(Lulu: Be a man.—Look at yourself—You haven't a trace of conscience.—You

shrink from no disgraceful act [...] You conquer half the world.—You do what
you want—and you know as well as I that [...] Schön *has collapsed in complete
exhaustion in the armchair next to the middle table:* Silence! Lulu: That you are
too weak—to tear yourself away from me. Schön *groaning:* Oh! Oh! You're hurt-
ing me!

. . . .

Lulu: He's weeping like a baby, the fearsome brute! I, 441).
She then, in a travesty of a scene from Schiller's *Kabale und Liebe* [Intrigue and
Love, 1784] dictates to him a letter breaking off his engagement to a respectable
and wealthy young woman. He signs it as his own death sentence (I, 442).

The fourth and last act begins with the frivolity of a bedroom farce and ends
when Lulu eliminates her third husband, Dr. Schön, by firing five bullets into
him. He has surprised her in the arms of his son Alwa and discovered five more
admirers: a circus strong man, a schoolboy named Hugenberg, the coachman
Ferdinand, old Schigolch, and the lesbian Countess Geschwitz, hiding under the
table and behind curtains. His last attempt to be rid of her fails when she fittingly
turns his own weapon on him and shoots in self-defense. "Es ist mißglückt" (I
have failed. I, 457), he moans. And when he asks for water, Lulu brings him
champagne. Schön, the villain, has been transformed into a cuckolded fool. When
Lulu once again exposes his insufficiency, he reacts just as Goll and Schwarz did.
He becomes paranoid, violent, and suicidal.

Despite the up-to-date cast of characters and background of *Erdgeist*, satiric
conventions and emblems from the distant past emerge clearly. Lulu is a close
relative of the winged Venus who delivers the verses of Chapter 13, "Von Buol-
schaft" (On Amours), from Sebastian Brant's immensely influential bestseller
Das Narrenschiff [*The Ship of Fools*, 1494]. The illustrative woodcut shows the
winged Venus elaborately clad in a long dress with train and controlling by
means of ropes a cuckold, an ass, a monkey, and two fools. Behind her stands the
bony figure of death. The whole configuration is an emblematic representation
of Lulu at the height of her career. Frau Venus boasts, "Ich züch zu mir der narren
vil/Vnd mach ein gouch vss vem ich wil" (I attract many fools/And make a fop of
whom I wish). Whoever is struck by Cupid's darts, "der kumbt von witz,/Vnd
dantzt har noch am narren holtz" (he loses his wits and dances thereafter under
the fools' yoke).

Even Lulu's downfall is prefigured in Brant's masterpiece, not merely by Death,
who threatens everyone, but by the allusion in the text to the burning lust that
brought low Dido, Pasiphaë, and Phaedra. But it is the image of woman current
in Wedekind's own time that gives Lulu her specific traits. She is the embodiment
of that paradoxical quality Wedekind mentions in the prologue: "des Lasters
Kindereinfalt" (the child-like simplicity of vice. I, 383). She is at one and the
same time a *femme fatale* and a *femme enfante*, a fusion of the two female types

that most obsessed the writers of the turn of the century. She becomes increasingly lethal as the play progresses, bringing death to others in many different ways, until she finally brings about her own.

Through the fate of Schön and his predecessors, *Erdgeist* demonstrates the deadly consequences of *Realpsychologie* and of the dream of sensual bliss. *Die Büchse der Pandora* does the same on the example of Lulu herself. In the second play all her conniving and exploitation of others leads only to personal disaster. All that remains of her earlier naiveté is her portrait in Pierrot costume. She has in fact become the capricious, vicious, modern incarnation of that medieval emblem of sin and evil, Frau Welt (Dame World). Though unaffected by it herself, she carries venereal disease. The world around her is diseased as well; in act two it is a gambling hell and bordello where she plays madam. Naked lust and self-interest have completely replaced the outmoded concepts of love, loyalty, and gratitude.

Having created this predatory environment, she loses her power and becomes a slave to her own sexual urges and the victim of swindlers and extortionists. Her physical beauty counts for nothing in this jungle, whose denizens are not merely heartless but also depraved. Adolescent girls and handsome youths hold greater charms here. Trapped by her own machinations, she flees her Parisian salon and takes refuge in a Soho garret.

As *Die Büchse der Pandora* nears its end, Lulu suffers the consequences of her exploitation of others. What had once been the source of her power, namely sex, has now consumed her, leaving her a nymphomaniac prostitute. Barefoot and wearing a tattered black dress, she leads three outlandishly ludicrous customers—Herr Hunidei, Kungu Poti, and Dr. Hilti—up the stairs from the street. Only with the first does she transact business. The second kills her protector, Alwa Schön, and the third is discouraged by the presence of Alwa's corpse on the bed. The fourth visitor is Jack the Ripper.

The sex murder at the end of *Die Büchse der Pandora* sums up both plays and gives them their memorable profile. First, it is poetic justice. Lulu gets her just deserts, and in a Dantean sense, the punishment fits the crime. As she preyed on men, so a man mutilates and slaughters her. Second, it fulfills her long held death wish. "Mir träumte alle paar Nächte, ich sei einem Lustmörder unter die Hände gekommen," she says in fairy tale tones in act one of *Die Büchse der Pandora* ("Every few nights I dreamt I had fallen into the hands of a sex murderer." I, 492). What Dr. Schön inflicted on the painter Schwarz by means of words, Jack accomplishes with a knife. Satire regularly makes its point by turning thoughts and words into actions. Third, the final episode brings love and death, lust and horror together into a striking event. Fourth, in Jack the Ripper, Wedekind has embodied the greed, impotence, perversion, and violent aggression that characterize other males in the two plays. And finally, the conclusion is a travesty of Wagner's "Liebestod;" Lulu's yearnings are fulfilled in the bitterest literal fashion. The

"Ripper's" deed lays bare the modish emotional cliché of the turn of the century, the idea that one achieves *unio mystica* through death and emotional transport. The fact that ecstatic fulfillment fails to take place is altogether consonant with the play's—and satire's—rhythm of purpose, passion, and anticlimax.[8]

Jack excises the source of Lulu's power, the thing that attracted and cowed her men: namely, her sexual organs. He reduces her to these alone and treats them as a curiosity. In an early, unpublished version, the "Monstre-Tragödie," he crows in his native tongue over the trophy: "I would never have thought of a thing like that.—That is a phenomenon, what would not happen every two hundred years.— —I am a lucky dog, to find this curiosity [...] When I am dead and my collection is put up to auction, the London Medical Club will pay a sum of three hundred pounds for that prodigy I have conquered this night. The professors and students will say: That is astonishing!—"[9] This final grotesque twist is the mark of Wedekind's satiric style: to suggest that Jack is motivated as much by his bourgeois collector's pride as by his insane lust.

Wedekind has been building all along on the human susceptibility to the lure of power and sensual thrill. Dr. Schön, master of *Realpsychologie* and public relations, commands the minds and hearts of Europe. He can sell a second-rate painter and a mediocre dancer to the public by appealing to the propensity to daydream. Lulu too takes advantage of that human weakness in her various guises as Pierrot, Goll's Nelli, Schwarz's Eva, and young Alwa Schön's Mignon; and her weapons prove stronger than Dr. Schön's. She is so good at the game that she is capable, in act four of *Erdgeist,* of entertaining a half dozen suitors in the same room at the same time.

As the play moves toward its denouement, Lulu progresses through a sequence of transformations: flower girl, child bride of an aging sadist, discreetly adulterous artist's bride and model, grotesquely promiscuous magnate's wife; then penitentiary inmate; directress of a sporting house; and finally syphilitic, nymphomanic streetwalker in Soho. Wedekind suggests that the last metamorphosis is the reality behind the earlier fictions. The elaborate costumes which grow ever more stylish and garish are suddenly gone. The painting of Lulu in Pierrot costume is still there, hanging unframed on the garret wall, but its colors have darkened so that the added light of an oil lamp is needed to study it.

On the male side, Wedekind starts with the relatively cultivated and refined Dr. Schön and moves to Rodrigo, the circus strong man and extortionist, to Puntschu, the unscrupulous stock speculator, to Jack the Ripper. Jack acts out the wishes and aggressive instincts repressed or sublimated in the others. Dr. Schön has committed a psychic murder and Lulu has commissioned the killing of Rodrigo, but there is nothing cerebral or mediated about the play's ultimate confrontation. Jack's blade and Lulu's genitals are Wedekind's reification of the phantasies of the age.

To *Realpsychologie* and the dream of immediate gratification, Peter Michelsen adds a third object of Wedekind's satire: the world of capitalism, governed by laws of supply and demand. He writes:

> Capitalist society is least capable of positioning itself as the opponent of the imme-
> diacy of carnal pleasure. Immediacy, understood as mere instinct, is a bourgeois
> ideal that can best be realized in a world governed solely by supply and demand.
> Having renounced all ties, the human being sees himself, in his intercourse with
> others, confined to the most 'elemental' as well as to the most 'abstract' relation-
> ships, in both of which the complexity of social communication has shrunk to a
> minimum. The connection between sexuality and money does not involve a perver-
> sion of the former. On the contrary: the abstractness of the banknote is altogether
> appropriate to the banality of naked sex.[10]

What then is the moral? Or better, what is the basic plot of this satire? The following emerges from a close reading of the play: Ruthless assertion of power brings retribution in the form of despair and painful death. In like fashion, unbridled sensuality becomes malignant, murderous, and suicidal.

In the overall action the same, or similar, events follow on one another, each crueler and more concrete than the last. The final act then presents it all again in phantastic, Grand Guignol style. Here the events of *Erdgeist* are repeated as the train of grotesquely comic suitors passes in quick review. And then Jack appears as the sum of all the depraved and threatening men in *Die Büchse der Pandora*, as Lulu's Nemesis, and ultimately as Death, who has been there all along standing behind Venus. Wedekind recapitulates the action of his *Lulu* in the grotesquely distorting and deadly accurate mirror of satire, showing us at one glance, with the aid of the portrait, the naive Pierrot of *Erdgeist,* act one, and the diseased prostitute and masochistic victim.

Wedekind's use of costume reinforces the impression we gain from the action. Lulu is a quick-change artist in more than one sense. From street clothes she changes to the Pierrot costume. Later she appears in housewifely negligee, in dance costumes, in the simple but elegant clothes of a rich man's wife, in the most stylish products of Parisian *haute couture*. And then, just as abruptly, she appears barefoot and in rags, and all illusions are stripped away.

The play's ending seems violent enough, but it provides no resolution. Lulu's murder brings none of the ecstatic release she yearned for. And Jack's words and actions give the last scene a comically banal quality. He is outraged at the fact that there are no towels in the garret and at the presence of Countess Geschwitz, on whose slip he finally wipes his hands. The curtain falls on a darkened stage, three cadavers, and Countess Geschwitz's dying whimper: "O verflucht!" (O damn!) which echoes the cries of despair heard at the end of earlier acts.

The Countess is Wedekind's satiric spokesman in the last act. Like Schigolch, she is an outsider, condemned to see the truth but powerless to do anything about it. She perceives the vice and folly around her but is herself helplessly caught up in the dance. Alone on the stage she speaks:

Die Menschen kennen sich nicht—sie wissen nicht, wie sie sind. Nur wer selber kein Mensch ist, der kennt sie. Jedes Wort, das sie sagen, ist unwahr, erlogen. Das wissen sie nicht, denn sie sind heute so und morgen so, je nachdem, ob sie gegessen, getrunken und geliebt haben oder nicht. Nur der Körper bleibt auf einige Zeit, was er ist, und nur die Kinder haben Vernunft. Die Großen sind wie die Tiere; keines weiß, was er tut. Wenn sie am glücklichsten sind, dann jammern sie, dann stöhnen sie, und im tiefsten Elend freuen sie sich jedes winzigen Happen. Es ist sonderbar, wie der Hunger den Menschen die Kraft zum Unglück nimmt. Wenn sie sich aber gesättigt haben, dann machen sie sich die Welt zur Folterkammer, dann werfen sie ihr Leben für die Befriedigung einer Laune weg.—Ob es wohl einmal Menschen gegeben hat, die durch Liebe glücklich geworden sind? Was ist denn ihr Glück anders, als daß sie besser schlafen und alles vergessen können?—Herr Gott, ich danke dir, daß du mich nicht geschaffen hast wie diese.

(People don't know themselves—they don't know what they're like. Only someone who's not human knows them. Every word they say is untrue, a lie. They don't know that because they are one day this way, the other that, depending on whether or not they've eaten, drunk, or made love. Only the body remains for a while what it is, and only children have reason. Grown-ups are like animals; none knows what he's doing. When they are happiest, they moan, then they groan, and in the depths of misery they delight in every tiny morsel. It's strange how hunger robs people of the strength for misfortune. When they've sated themselves, then they turn the world into a torture chamber for one another, then they throw away their lives to satisfy a whim.—Have there ever been human beings who have been made happy by love? What is their happiness but sleeping better and being able to forget everything?—O Lord, I thank You for not having created me like these. I, 533-34).

This is the message of the Lulu Tragedy and of other Wedekind plays to be discussed in this chapter: the flight from boredom and the chase after ever greater power and excitement lead to gratuitous violence and self-destruction. Lulu and Jack were meant for each other, according to the logic of satire.

The final scene and the piece as a whole are mixtures—*saturae*—of elements that don't blend: stilted rhetoric and slang, slapstick and pathos, bad jokes and blood, sentiment and cynicism. Wedekind makes us laugh at death. He gives us, in Alfred Polgar's words, a "hellish frolic." In *Ja und Nein* Polgar writes: "His [Wedekind's] poetic extract of the world is saturated with its farcicality and its misery. Its true countenance is revealed in a grimace."[11] Audiences in Berlin and in smaller cities laughed without restraint at the miseries of Lulu and her entourage in *Die Büchse der Pandora*, responding to their ludicrous aspects.[12]

This laughter must have been what Wedekind, in "Der Witz und seine Sippe" (Jokes and their Kin, 1887), calls "the mocking laughter of hell, the most magnificent triumph of frivolity. The movements of the diaphragm are slower and occur in fits and starts. Mouth and throat are opened wide, lips protrude so that the teeth are displayed in all their glory. The eyes remain calm and cold."[13] By frivolity Wedekind means satiric wit. In this early essay he treats it in imaginative detail but with a moral revulsion that suggests a guilty fondness for it. A few years later, in his plays, he does not hesitate to employ it in order, as he says, to belittle the sublime and besmirch the pure (I, 898-99).

In this same essay, Wedekind's comments on "der schlechte Witz" (bad joke or dirty trick) and its sister, the irony of fate, anticipate the pattern followed by the action of *Erdgeist* and *Die Büchse der Pandora,* namely: purpose, passion, anticlimax (I, 890-92). Bad jokes are sprinkled through the plays. Jack the Ripper makes one:

Jack: Du scheinst einen schönen Mund zu haben.

Lulu: Den hab' ich von meiner Mutter.

Jack: Danach sieht er aus.

(Jack: You seem to have a pretty mouth. Lulu: I have that from my mother. Jack: It looks that way. I, 536). When we watch the frustrations of a buffoon, an anticlimax, the collapse of a calculated effort at manipulation, or the self-defeating projects of fools, our feelings are divided. One derives a certain malicious satisfaction from observing these tricks of fate; they evoke that mocking laughter. Yet the human cost fills us with fear and terror (I, 891).

To achieve these effects, Wedekind concocts his mixes in a variety of ways. Generally he selects ingredients that work against one another and lead to a frustrating stand-off. Contradictory arguments may cancel each other out; or a character will say, for no apparent reason, the reverse of what he has earlier asserted.

This is one reason why theater audiences, critics, actors, and directors were slow to appreciate Wedekind. They were unaccustomed to farcical melodrama. Even when scenes were played for laughs, it was in the belief that the comic effects were superimposed on a uniformly serious text. "[The audience] considered the author naive," writes Julius Hart of a performance of *Der Kammersänger* in 1901, "and thought that he was making all kinds of inadvertent jokes. So it laughed at the things that are really supposed to be laughed at and thought that those things were intended to be serious [...]."[14] The cool, straight-faced quality of Wedekind's drama made his irony hard to detect. His audiences had had little experience with figural satire and were accustomed to laughing only on unmistakable cue.

Later, in 1919, laughter had become the normal response to the final act of *Die Büchse der Pandora.* But it was laughter of the "frivolous" sort, according to Paul Gunther, who played in over 100 performances. He comments: "But much depends on the tone of the laughter. It shouldn't be a liberated happy laugh but rather the more abbreviated, strained sort which is appropriate to this bizarre tragicomedy."[15] This explains why one production failed when the male characters did not expose themselves to ridicule.

One of the most perceptive of early Wedekind critics, Arthur Möller-Bruck, writes in 1899 of *Erdgeist,* act four, the high point and theatrically most exciting part of the Lulu plays: "Just as *Frühlings Erwachen* ended in supergrotesque fashion, *Erdgeist* was supposed to be intensified in its concluding pages to a comic distortion which completely neutralized the tragic effect and made the weightiness of the action seem farcical [...]."[16]

Early audiences as well as the spectators of the 1920s usually failed to see anything funny here, even when Albert Steinruck as Dr. Schön performed a *salto mortale,* falling down a whole flight of stairs after Lulu shot him. The reason for this, Albert Diebold surmises, is that the audience was not prepared to accept Wedekind's concept of *Realpsychologie,* or the assumption that humans are predators lacking any moral instinct.[17] Apparently, viewers empathized with him and were persuaded that his fate was tragic and not at all deserved.

The attributive most often applied to the character of Dr. Schön and indeed to the entire work, is "cold."[18] Wedekind believed the role of Dr. Schön to be far harder to play than Lulu; for he must be serious, calculating, ruthless, and at the same time look the fool because of little mistakes and his sexual enthrallment. He is repeatedly put down and made a fool of by an even cooler Lulu, who has no soul, no human sentiments, no humanity whatsoever. Similarly, Lulu is akin to that dead-faced dancing woman, Sphinx-like and often child-like, who appears in the drawings of Beardsley, in the works of Yeats, and in the guise of Wilde's Salomé.[19]

Wedekind the satirist cultivated a diagnostic manner of writing and of performance that has often been remarked on. In the preface of *Die Büchse der Pandora* he speaks in clinical terms of the intended effect of his satire, arguing that it is a homeopathic remedy, not poison, and reminding us, "Medicine differs from poison only in the way it is used."[20]

Wedekind's medicine is made up of potent substances, and it is the triumph of his art that they hold each other in check. Lulu's speeches and gestures in scenes of violence and bloodshed are weightless, cool, even frivolous. They stand in grotesque contrast to the eruptive furor and insane passion others display. Each of the Lulu plays culminates in a tracicomic scene in which dynamic and vital events are observed in their contradictory, multivalent quality. In speaking of the final episode of *Die Büchse der Pandora,* Paul Böckmann uses the phrase "*danse macabre* of sensual desire."[21] To put it conceptually, one sees repeatedly the mutual refutation of standpoints. Concretely, the painting of Lulu in Pierrot costume becomes an ever more eloquent object as the play progresses and as the evidence mounts that human sexuality is not sweet and natural but murderous.

This contradiction and the others like it are incapable of resolution. Wedekind contrives implausible combinations that accurately reflect the mind of his time, a mind which often did not distinguish between vitalism and aggression, innocence and depravity, economic liberalism and ruthless exploitation. So intractable are the oppositions that there seems to be no possibility of reconciliation or emotionally satisfying conclusion in Wedekind's cerebral drama. Since Ibsen, the traditional happy wedding has disappeared from comedy. Wedekind and the other satirists who follow his lead—Sternheim, Kaiser, Brecht, Dürrenmatt—work to accentuate the anticlimax. The happy ending may appear as travesty, as in *Die Dreigro-schenoper,* for example, a comedy with satiric touches. But in satire of the high norm, expectations are deceived, plans thwarted, and all ends in frustration, rage, and darkness. These playwrights do not merely withhold resolution; they see to it that fate plays a dirty trick (Wedekind) or that matters take the worst possible turn (Dürrenmatt). In his essay *Goethe und Tolstoy* (1932) Thomas Mann says that the ironic artist will refuse to move beyond the suspensive stage and will hold back the promised concord indefinitely yet in a playful manner that suggests he could, if he wanted, resolve the discord. Mann had Richard Wagner and Richard Strauß in mind when he formulated his ideas on irony. Wedekind's Lulu Tragedy was set to music atonally by Alban Berg.

Whereas comedy is a process, writes Peter Thorpe, satire tends to be static, despite its exuberance and all the energy spent.[22] Satiric works may end in explosive fashion, but the muddle and confusion of the body of the play are either sustained or aggravated. Rather than relieve anxieties and tensions, satire nourishes them. Despite the grotesque distortions and exorbitant fictions, satire gives us a highly accurate analogy to real life, in part because it refuses to solve problems or impose meaning on the confusion of our existence. The stage turns dark, but there follows no dawn.

Nor is there any relief or human warmth emanating from Wedekind's calculated use of language. The melange of styles keeps the reader or listener on edge. Each character has his own idiom or idioms. Alwa Schön is the worst or, satirically, the best with his supply of cultivated, arty clichés and hackneyed sentiments. Countess Geschwitz generates a lot of emotional heat with her overearnest moral sermons. Rodrigo overasserts his criminal virility through locutions drawn from the argots of the circus and the underworld.

In the case of language as well as action, the final scene presents a frenzied acceleration and exaggeration of what has gone before. To the modes of speech already introduced Wedekind adds sign language, Kungu Poti's pidgin German, Dr. Hilti's equally primitive sounding Zurich Schwyzerdütsch, and finally, in early versions, Jack the Ripper's stilted English.

Wedekind's directorial maxim for actors in his plays was: "step to the footlights and speak."[23] And it was well understood by the 1920s that Wedekind's plays, like all satire, were rhetorical in the extreme. It was clear that his speeches were to be delivered so as to draw attention to their diction. Many of them are couched in brilliantly polished "paper" German and larded with trite aphorisms. The manner is often painfully awkward because one hears artificial, Schillerian rhetoric from the mouths not of tragic heroes but from utterly unidealistic, often quite immoral figures.

This travesty on the language of classical tragedy is made all the more striking by the admixture of circus idiom, schoolboy clichés, financial and legal phrases, and crude locutions from the world of criminals. Wedekind's audience not only sees its own folly and villainy; it is forced to listen to itself talking and to hear the hollow sounding words that have long been part of its intellectual luggage. The whole conglomeration—including biblical phrases, lines from Shakespeare, malapropisms, quotes from dime novels—taken together is a reflection of the European mind in its vulgar, cruel, reality.[24]

Wedekind's theater with its stilted diction, overwrought and melodramatic gesture, and the garish glamour of its costumes is often extremely stilted and wordy and at the same time so low-brow and operatic that its effect is to revolt the spectator. The Lulu plays are therefore, in a perverse way, antiliterary theater and at the same time an attack on bad taste. Wedekind makes his case for plain speaking—the satirist is traditionally the plain speaker—by making us aware of the bad uses of language. To this end he merely cites and imitates what he has heard and read. The repellent effect derives from the unlikely juxtapositions and the mixing of uncongenial modes of speech.

The drama critic Kurt Aram wrote in the October 23, 1926 issue of the Berlin *Tägliche Rundschau:*

> In real life as well as in the theater Wedekind loved well constructed periods in a sometimes decorous German, always with formal mien such as hotel directors assume when dealing with illustrious guests, in order to suddenly interrupt with smirking sarcasms and well polished antitheses. The opposite of the naturalistic style of speaking. When his sentences are delivered as if in a realistic drama, they all sound artificial or stilted with all kinds of sarcasms almost involuntarily scattered through.[25]

Wedekind practices these stylistic tricks with a tightrope walker's agility. Again and again he seems about to lose his footing, only to regain his equilibrium again. The metaphor is Wedekind's. In his essay "Zirkusgedanken" [Circus Thoughts, 1887] he develops an aesthetic and philosophical system from the distinction between stable and labile balance. Stability, as in the mechanics of the trapeze, is for the single-minded idealist. Lability, as in the high wire act, is for the practical minded, who may perform closer to the ground but whose art requires greater skill and elasticity. On the near invisible wire, the performer seems to hover in the air (I, 882). He appears to strain repeatedly in varying ways to regain his balance. The satirist, I would interpolate, uses the same tricks to keep his audience at the same time insecure and involved. He seems to be engaged in a constant struggle to defy and control some monstrous, terrifying reality, which in this analogy would correspond to the force of gravity. He creates a realm of fascinating danger and uncertainty. And he maintains his balance by countering terror with mocking laughter.

Wedekind checks the sensation that we are falling into chaotic darkness by embodying the malignant forces in figures like Dr. Schön and Lulu. Thus he tames the unnamable, makes it into a bad joke, and lets it defeat itself. In so doing he tacitly suggests the ultimate victory of order and justice, however much events on the stage seem to deny it.

Countess Geschwitz tries to define the problem in one discursive, reflective monologue and pronounces only platitudes on the bestiality and blindness of human beings. (I, 533-34). Her efforts are inadequate to Wedekind's larger purpose. Ulrich Gaier explains why: "Satire goes into combat against that with which consciousness can't cope, against pure force and calamity; against a gap in the system of series through which chaos is erupting *(horror vacui)*; against a form of being that resists any functionalization; against reality in general, insofar as it frustrates all efforts to appropriate it."[26]

Wedekind reduces and belittles this reality by embodying it in stage figures prone to error and doomed to defeat. A glance at his casts of characters will indicate the immense range of his satire. In Dr. Schön he exposes the evils of bourgeois culture at the turn of the century and shows its cast of mind to be a pernicious, sometimes distorted amalgam of Nietzschean and Darwinian ideas. The schools of art and literature of the time find their representatives, as does the movement for women's emancipation. In Lulu and Jack the Ripper, however, Wedekind is pointing to something that rests far deeper in the human psyche and the order of this world.

The plays aim not only to make the audience aware of a threatening reality but also to set its mind free from paralyzing, half-subconscious obsessions with sex, power, and money. The devices of belittling, grotesque incongruity, and "frivolity" work to this end. When Jack returns from the back room to the stage, smeared with Lulu's blood, his first action is to lift a bowl from the floor and replace it fastidiously on the table. Lulu's first customer, the sadist Herr Hunidei, carries a book entitled *Ermahnungen für fromme Pilger* [Admonitions for Pious Pilgrims. I, 526]. These and countless other striking incongruities serve as signals to the audience and move it to look beneath the surface. When Wedekind avoids easy resolutions and leaves the spectator hanging, he is accomplishing the same thing.

It may be that his cipher is too complex and that he supplies too many ironic twists, inconsistencies, and interruptions. This is one reason that good critics arrive at opposing interpretations. The very titles of the plays serve to lead one astray. Does *Erdgeist* suggest, as does the motto taken from the second act of *Wallensteins Tod* [Wallenstein's Death, 1800], the concluding tragedy of Schiller's great trilogy, that the play warns against the corrupting forces of money and power? Or can the enigmatic apparition of *Faust I*, representing the uncontrollable, chaotic forces of all nature, be meant as well?[27] The figure of Pandora also invites contradictory interpretations. Robert Graves finds two conflicting versions of her myth.[28] The older, matriarchal one, the story of Phyllis and Demophon, contains a warning to men who pry into women's mysteries. According to Hesiod, on the other hand, Pandora was "as foolish, mischievous, and idle as she was beautiful—the first of a long line of such women."[29] The title, like the play, may be read to blame the ills of the world on the folly and vice of either sex.

Most probable, but still speculative and surely not the last word, is the theory that the title *Erdgeist* contains an allusion to the vitalist cult of the time, to the worship of sexuality and fertility that was summed up in the trope "heilige Erde" (sacred earth). This theory is attractive because it suggests the play's satiric intent and is consistent with attacks on these fads and daydreams contained in later Wedekind plays, especially *"Hidalla"* (1904), *Tod und Teufel* [Death and Devil, 1906] and *Frühlings Erwachen* [*Awakening of Spring,* 1891].

The title *Frühlings Erwachen,* incidentally, has almost always been taken at face value. The play has regularly been admired as a message piece siding with the vitalist party and reprimanding society for the cruel repression it imposes on the sexual urge in adolescents. This is one of the reasons it has remained Wedekind's most popular play since the censor released it for performance and Max Reinhardt staged it in Berlin in 1906. It was received then as a poignant and topical piece, written in a cause that progressive, right-thinking persons would have supported.

Wedekind said nothing to dim the play's success. But it is quite possible to extract an altogether different meaning from the text, supported by evidence found in other works by Wedekind. It can, for instance, be read as an antivitalist play attacking single-minded sexual reformers. It exposes their assumptions as false, for sex is shown not to be beautiful and pure, and growing up is nothing like the "awakening of spring." Quite the contrary; it is killing. Wedekind shows the cult of "heilige Erde" to be the product of aberrant, potentially dangerous phantasies. Sex is an unavoidably painful, maddening, perverse, sometimes lethal force. Teenagers are no happier than Lulu toward the end of her days. Concerning Lulu one may then ask: Is she a flighty, naive little flirt, or is she one of Lilith's offspring, called Lilim, those avaricious, seductive female demons who control the sex life of men?[30] It seems she is akin to Kundry in Wagner's *Parsifal* (1882) who is transformed from a creatural maidservant of the Grail into a demonic seductress and then dies as a redeemed Mary Magdalene.[31]

To anyone familiar with French literature and theater of the past century, Lulu's other, seemingly cute and harmless avatar, the Pierrot figure, suggests much more than the traditional scapegoat who exposes and outsmarts his tormentors through his guiltless simplicity.[32] The Pierrot of the Theatre des Funambules appeared in the 1820s variously as hermaphrodite, devil, orangutang, and later as "a neurotic profile, dogged by nightmare," making suicidal gestures and "nakedly illustrating the vice of men in this fin de siècle."[33] In Jean Richepin's play *Pierrot Assassin de sa Femme* (1883) and in poems by Laforgue and Verlaine, he becomes increasingly "inhuman, unearthly, and ultimately deadly."[34] Yet behind the morbid madness and frostly licentiousness that appealed to Aubrey Beardsley there remains some of the original innocence.

Lulu's white powdered face, to which attention is twice drawn, is a second Pierrot motif complementing her ubiquitous, heavily symbolical portrait in long-sleeved smock and loose fitting trousers (I, 390, 410). The mask is appropriate to Lulu because of its traditionally protean and androgynous quality—Sarah Bernhardt played the lead in *Pierrot Assassin*—and because of its "mysterious inscrutability" in French pantomimes of the 1880s and later.[35]

In these years Pierrot appeared often in literature, in the theater, and at fairs. Mimes and actors gave the figure the most varied interpretations. The classic nineteenth-century Pierrot at the Théâtre des Funambules is described by a contemporary as "Ingenious like a child, cowardly, crafty, lazy, mischievous by instinct, obliging, jeering, [...] ingenious in the arts that tend to the satisfaction of his tastes; he is a naïve and clownish Satan."[36] In short, Wedekind has endowed his Lulu with traits of a commedia dell'arte figure.

To add to the mystification, he has given her the characteristics and even the destinies of one or more of the great courtesans and actresses of Parisian and London society: Sarah Bernhardt, Lillie Langtry, Cora Pearl. These were pleasure-loving, ambitious women who employed their natural wit and sexual magnetism to dominate men and rise in the world.[37] An account of Cora Pearl's career reads much like a summary of the action of *Die Büchse der Pandora:*

> In March of 1858 she went to France, and a series of liaisons followed with various persons of influence under the second empire. Although large sums of money, with diamonds and jewelry, passed through her hands, she never became rich. She maintained a large establishment in the Rue de Chaillot, which her admirers called Les Petits Tuileries [...]. At one period when out of money, she made her appearance at Les Buffes Parisiens as Cupid in Offenbach's "Orphée aux Enfers." On the night of her debut the theater was filled to overflowing; certain of the boxes sold at 500 francs [...].[38]

Like Lulu, she died in a squalid, small room, though not under the same sensational circumstances.

Clearly, Lulu's traits are drawn from many models in art and real life, and her name itself suggests a piquant mixture of topical, contemporary, and mystic qualities. The sound evokes associations with Lilith, with Nabokov's Lolita, and with Marlene Dietrich's Lola Lola, Professor Unrat's Nemesis in the film *Der blaue Engel.* Gittleman, citing Kutscher, points to what was most likely Wedekind's immediate inspiration, namely, a pantomime performance in Paris by Felice Champsau and entitled *Lulu, une Clownesse Danseuse.*[39] But it is also quite possible that Wedekind's acquaintance with Lou Andreas Salomé (1861-1937) furnished some of Lulu's more bizarre traits. According to Rudolph Binion, who in turn cites Friedrich and Elisabeth Nietzsche, Wedekind, and Lou herself, Salomé was at twenty "sharp as an eagle and brave as a lion, yet a very girlish child."[40] Nietzsche saw her giving free rein to her feline "predatory pleasure-lust" and noted that she had "a brain with only a rudiment of a soul." He accused her of being "shrewd and fully self-controlled in respect of men's sensuality, heartless and incapable of loving [...]." Elisabeth Nietzsche, who was not known to be charitable in her judgment of other women, regarded her as a "poisonous reptile."

When she was introduced to Wedekind in Paris, Lou was married to the Goll-like Professor Andreas whom she was to depict "as the ultimate in demonic violence and intellectual disarray, domineering and weak-willed by fits and starts."[41] On meeting Wedekind, she agreed "to coffee in Wedekind's room [and] misled him into taking the follow-up for granted. 'Adventure!!!!!' she told her calendar." At this time, around 1892, she was alone with him on some fourteen occasions, and from the outset well in control of the situation. "He's already trained," she wrote.[42] It is tempting to surmise that, among other things, the final episode of *Erdgeist,* act one, retells the story of that first encounter: alone together in the atelier, the chase, and the anticlimax when Lulu asserts her domination and chill control over herself and Schwarz.

At the heart of it all rests Lulu, that medley of cosmic and banal components; she provides the governing fiction and phantastic vision that give the plays their force and profile. Is she a superhuman spirit? Is she old Schigolch's illegitimate daughter? Was she at one time his mistress? Did she murder her third husband's wife? Or is she a demonic, driven hetaera, the destructive, disruptive monster of Wedekind's "Monstre-Tragödie," as he designated the plays in their original form of a single five-act drama?

The text raises these and other questions but leaves them open. To answer them, one must have the courage to reveal one's prejudices. The misogynist, the cynic, the antibourgeois revolutionary, the sentimentalist will betray himself just as the men in *Erdgeist* expose their impotence and villainy through their treatment of Lulu. She says of herself and her plastic, protean nature: "Ich habe nie etwas anderes sein wollen, als wofür man mich genommen hat." ("I have never wanted to be anything other than what people have taken me for." I, 457).

In the past few years a number of opera directors have presented Alban Berg's *Lulu*. Heinz Josef Herbort suspects that German audiences have long been deprived of the opera because no one knew how to solve Wedekind's "equation with several unknowns."[43] One production makes Lulu into an aggressive beautiful beast, depraved and yet endowed with a certain dignity, and makes of the piece a serious social parable. Another sees her as a cool, sly, rather lethargic figure who accepts her doom silently. Sopranos in the title role have stressed her lascivious nature or have played her in intellectualized, disinfected fashion. The part defies any single consistent interpretation. Günter Seehaus complains that it is nearly impossible to write a history of the role relying on the reports of reviewers. Each critic has his own preconception and makes corresponding demands on the actress.[44] Peter Conrad rightly maintains that the problem of Lulu's identity in the eyes of her beholders forms the core of both plays.[45] Wedekind puts his characters and his readers in the same quandary, and the play consists in a series of efforts to capture and fix her image. Conrad writes:

> Lulu is an art object to those who pursue her [...]. Like dispirited twentieth-century artists, they all despair of catching the elusive spirit of life which activates Lulu, and they settle for oblique glimpses, replicas and models of her. She is perpetually being translated into images which are then marketed, and as she passes from the cool detachment of the early scenes, where she is the indifferent spectator of the images others fabricate of her, to her entrepreneurial selling of herself as a prostitute in London, the images are correspondingly cheapened and degraded [...].

The interpreters of Lulu fall roughly into two categories. The first group sees her as a mythic creature, an Undine, victimized and betrayed by the men in her life; and it views the play as antibourgeois, anticapitalist social criticism. The second school likewise holds that Lulu is something other than human but finds her demonic and ruthless in exploiting her power over men. The first group would have her a naive flower child: a pure, beautiful, natural, sacral or astral being who is desecrated by sadistic, rapacious capitalists.[46] This reading appealed so strongly to some interpreters that they were swayed to argue that it revealed Wedekind's own underlying intent, even though the plays themselves make quite a different statement.[47] No critic has yet seen in her the embodiment of pure evil, but the second group acknowledges the play's pessimistic tone and agrees that Lulu is as predatory and corrupt as the men around her.[48] A few characterize the work as a dance of death.

The one scholar to accept and stress Wedekind's mixing of dissonant, heterogeneous elements is Friedrich Rothe.[49] He argues rightly that it reflects the intellectual dilemmas of the age. To reconcile social abuses with faith in natural man is as hard as it is to fit Lulu's conniving bitchiness with her role as a modern Eve. Similarly, the Life Force has at best a remote connection with the issue of women's rights.

Whereas Rothe confines himself to the intellectual history of the *fin de siècle*, Friedrich Dürrenmatt goes to the opposite extreme, urging readers not to be distracted by ideological concerns and to appreciate the playwright in Wedekind. Twenty years ago, paying tribute to his seminal influence, Dürrenmatt suggested why Wedekind is insufficiently admired: "His problem, sexuality, is no longer the center of attention today. It would certainly be more agreeable than the Cold War. People have still not learned to see comedies in Wedekind; consequently he leaves most of them cold: they take him seriously, mistakenly. They see him still as a wild sexual reformer and evaluate his statements by standards of true or false; people should learn finally to see in him not a relationship to reality, but a reality, not so much what he reflects, but how he reflects."[50]

Dürrenmatt might put this differently today when in many minds the matter of sexuality obscures the Cold War. Though he seems to underplay Wedekind's topicality as he does that of his own dramas, he is actually urging readers to look beyond theatrical pronouncements on women's rights and the like to find what Wedekind's—and his own—plays really say. Anyone familiar with Dürrenmatt's essays knows that "comedy" ("Komödie") usually means satiric drama and that he arrayed himself and Wedekind in the tradition of serious literary satire couched in phantastic fictions, which he calls Aristophanic and in which he includes Rabelais, Cervantes, Swift, Gogol, Karl Kraus, and Bertolt Brecht.[51]

The controversy Wedekind aroused continues long after his death. His life, ideas, and works have been mocked, abhorred, and admired. Censors kept some plays out of the theater for nearly twenty years. During World War I, cultural patriots considered production and publication of his works tantamount to sabotage, indicating the danger they were felt to represent and the threatening power that resides in satire.

Wedekind's literary destiny testifies also to the frustration satire brings. Though kindred spirits, Karl Kraus, for example, supported him with all means at their disposal, the butts of his attack in the establishment understood him better than his friends. He became the *bête noire* of German *Kulturpolitik* and consequently failed to reach a wide audience, and the true significance of his work went largely unnoticed. Wedekind contributed to his own defeat by squabbling with censors and publishers and by dramatizing his personal idiosyncrasies. He played the fool and martyr in real life, and many of his dramas are weak because they serve as vehicles to express self-pity and personal resentments. Only after his death in 1918, which ironically coincided with the end of the war and with the lifting of all police and military censorship of the theater, did his work achieve popularity, but then mainly as a historical curiosity.

Yet as early as 1919 proto-Nazi groups began to revile him, in much the same way as churchmen and censors loyal to the Kaiser had done. Demonstrators forced the Munich Kammerspiele to drop *Schloß Wetterstein* from their repertoire, on political, not on moral grounds.[52] Wedekind once again became the scapegoat and symbol of decadence to a public which had little acquaintance with his writings.

Wedekind warns us in the prologue to *Erdgeist* that Lulu is a pernicious and contradictory figure. She makes her first entrance costumed as Pierrot and riding on the shoulders of a stagehand. With impudent, taunting irony, the master of ceremonies, an animal trainer, has already mentioned the connection between lust and horror (I, 381) and has practiced elaborate mystification with the terms "Tier" and "Mensch" (animal and human). He then calls for the snake, and Lulu is carried on. The trainer continues, in the tone of a carnival barker, praising natural diction in his rhymed iambs, and points out that this figure is snake, Eve, Pierrot, Pandora, all things to all men:

> Sie ward geschaffen, Unheil anzustiften,
> Zu locken, zu verführen, zu vergiften—
> Zu morden, ohne daß es einer spürt.
> *Lulu am Kinn krauend*
> Mein, süßes Tier, sei ja nur nicht *geziert!*
> Nicht *albern,* nicht *gekünstelt,* nicht *verschroben,*
> Auch wenn die Kritiker dich weniger loben.
> Du hast kein Recht, uns durch Miaun and Fauchen
> Die *Urgestalt* des *Weibes* zu verstauchen,
> Durch Faxenmachen uns und Fratzenschneiden
> Des *Lasters Kindereinfalt* zu verleiden!
> Du sollst—drum sprech' ich heute sehr ausführlich—
> *Natürlich* sprechen und nicht unnatürlich!
> Denn erstes Grundgesetz seit frühster Zeit
> in jeder Kunst war *Selbstverständlichkeit!*

(She was created to cause mischief,/To entice, to seduce, to poison—/To murder without the victim noticing./*Scratching Lulu on the chin*/Not so *mannered,* please!/Not *silly,* not *affected,* not too *complicated,*/Even though the critics praise you less,/You have no right, by meowing and spitting,/To dislocate the *primal form* of *woman,*/To spoil the *childlike simplicity* of *vice* for us/By foolery and making faces!/You are supposed—and this is why I speak at such length today—/to speak *naturally* and not unnaturally!/For the first basic law in every art since earliest times/Has been *matter-of-factness* [or: plain speaking]. I, 383).

If she follows Wedekind's detailed stage directions, the actress portraying Lulu will convey the impression through her light, carefree manner that everything she does is natural, logical, self-evident. But the spectator, accustomed to another kind of logic, will, to sneak in a Brechtian term, experience alienation when she speaks in the cheerful tone specified by the stage directions as she arranges a murder or when, with motherly affection, she reminds Alwa Schön, "Ich habe deinen Vater erschossen" (I shot your father. I, 515, 493).

The incommensurables and contradictions in the Lulu Tragedy and in Lulu herself belong, together with grotesquery, irony, and jumbling, to the arsenal of the satirist. The hostile satiric object has, by nature, internal contradictions, and all the satirist need do is to let it speak and act itself. Individuals, society, the representatives of ideologies, that is, will destroy themselves and each other. The reader and audience, alerted by the "alienation effect" produced by these devices, will recognize and reject the dissonant object. This object of figural satire, says Ulrich Gaier, is the broken figure that represents the threatening forces of chaos.[53] The term "broken figure" sums up what I have been trying to say with other words about the language, course of action, and characters of these two plays. Anticlimax, the bad joke, impotence and violence, self-defeating projects, and jumbling are all aspects of the same thing. Resolution, tragic or comic, cannot occur in this kind of literature.

The only hint of consistency and harmony to be found in the Lulu Tragedy and the dramas that follow comes as an ironic afterthought when the scapegoat, here Dr. Schön, accepts his ludicrous fate as deserved.[54] Even Lulu considers her end a matter of course, if not just. But from the spectator's standpoint the sacrificial death does nothing to alleviate a hopeless situation.

Even though the Lulu Tragedy is packed with topical references and populated with individuals and types well known to audiences of the *fin de siècle,* its full significance did not attract attention until many years later. Heinrich Mann, a friend and kindred (though less bitter) social critic, appreciated the prophetic satiric powers of the early Wedekind and paid him this tribute in a talk delivered in 1923:

> If in the year 1900 someone was writing as if it were 1914: who was to greet him with open arms! Positing a world of naked struggle at a time when people thought themselves totally civilized! Picturing everyone differently, more menacing than they pictured themselves back then; stripping bare, first of pretty words, moral pretense, finally almost of their flesh! And in the theater to boot, where people like to see themselves lovingly mirrored in a comfortable, sentimental life!
> This was the mission of the dramatic poet Frank Wedekind.[55]

One thing that allowed audiences to misread or censor this message was the satiric-dramatic idiom Wedekind chose, namely: topical matters, often of a very trivial or sensational nature. The play as a whole has the appearance of a medley of the fads and phantasies, prejudices and preoccupations of its age. A theater critic wrote of *Erdgeist* in 1901: "Among living German poets there is probably not one who gave such complete expression to the ways of thinking and feeling in our time as Frank Wedekind."[56]

By far the most colorful and deeply felt tribute to Wedekind's angry pen and cold eye for the unparalleled "menschliche Sauerei" (human swinishness) in the world about him comes from Carl Sternheim.[57] Using a metaphor he was fond of applying to himself, Sternheim sees Wedekind as a fanatically indignant, titanic surgeon carrying out a vivisection down to the kidneys and bone marrow on the notables of the time as well as on the living corpse of Europe and of the human race. "Thanks to him," Sternheim wrote, "Germany was continuously *au courant*. The average man's big shots were salted, peppered, and served up to him once more before they made him vomit, the statesmen, the Max Reinhardts, Paul Cassirers, the mentality and image counterfeiters, the prostitutes, pimps, pederasts, *haute volée* stood stark naked before the simple man so that he completely lost his fear of these ghosts and the poet-liberator experienced his jubilant laughter."

One sees in Sternheim's name-dropping how close satire can come to gossip and libel. The predatory entrepreneur Salzmann in the last part of Wedekind's *Schloß Wetterstein* [*Wetterstein Castle*, 1910] was identified by those in the know as Max Reinhardt. An infatuated schoolboy poet named Hugenberg, a role filled in *Erdgeist* by a girl, was in real life a rising right-wing industrialist and politician, Alfred Hugenberg (1865-1951), who served as chairman of the board at Krupp from 1909-1918. In the 1920s he manipulated German public opinion through the conglomerate of newspapers and wire services he had assembled. Sternheim both despised and feared him and his ilk, and this attitude may partly account for the fact that he became an enthusiastic supporter of Wedekind. Hugenberg delivers the final line of *Erdgeist:* "They'll kick me out of school." The speech is laughable, grotesquely out of place, yet true to life and characteristic of the Hugenberg we will see again later as he fits into Sternheim's satiric world.[58]

In the Lulu Tragedy the styles, psychoses, and ideological aberrations of its time and of the ensuing decades are made manifest. The play prefigures, and indirectly warns of, the paranoid system of ideas Otto Weininger (born 1880 and died by his own hand in 1903) set forth in *Geschlecht und Charakter* [Sex and Character, 1903] ten years after the completion of the "Monstre-Tragödie." Weininger was even more obsessed with sex than Wedekind and understood all human life in sexual terms. Human characteristics fall into one or the other of two categories: male or female. The female principle is pure sexuality; the male is the same with a small admixture of spirituality.[59]

Weininger's typification of womankind reads like a one-sided character study of Lulu. Weininger's prototypical woman has no memory, no relationship to the past, is unconcerned with death, has no capacity for logical or ethical thinking, has no ego. "Undine, the soulless Undine is the Platonic idea of woman," he asserts.[60] She is thoroughly mendacious, has no interest in objective truth or even in thinking at all. She is shameless, perverse, vulgar, and inclined to polyandry. She is by nature domineering: "Letting her instincts run wild and satisfying them almost defiantly, she feels herself to be mistress of all, and she believes it purely a matter of course that she should have power."[61]

The most powerful of all human beings is the creature Weininger calls "das Weib als Dirne" (woman as prostitute), the hetaera whose nature and behavior correspond closely to Lulu's.[62] Like her male counterpart, the Dr. Schön-like "Tribune" or demagogue, she is a talented *Realpsycholog,* able to manipulate others, concerned solely with reputation, rising and falling like a meteor. Her career is destructive and without meaning, and she is felt to be the scourge of God.[63]

Satisfaction eludes her, "for all the life she has she wants to feel concentrated in this moment [of orgasm]. Because this is impossible, the prostitute *[Dirne]* is never in her life satisfied, not by all the men in this world."[64] She is the *femme fatale,* witch, and temptress driven by an urge that grows malignant and morbid. Finally, as in Lulu's case, her aggressiveness becomes suicidal: "She wants to be destroyed and to destroy. She damages and ruins."[65]

Weininger is in paranoid earnest. He fears and loathes not woman necessarily, but human sexuality. And the pathological systematization in his book aims not merely to save men from entrapment by women but to encourage woman to emancipate herself by freely renouncing coitus. His answer to the "Frauenfrage" is to redeem both male and female from the tyranny of sex through repression and asceticism. By becoming perfectly chaste, men, and women too, can elevate themselves to the level of "pure humanity" where the curse of sexual differentiation is lifted.[66]

Though he admits to feelings about sex that look almost as obsessive as Weininger's, Wedekind maintains his artistic and ideological balance, suggests, at least, that sex has the potential for goodness and beauty, and lets the menace of perverted eroticism destroy itself. Wedekind is too realistic to contemplate seriously the dream of perfect resolution, redemption from the flesh, and the spiritualization of the human race.

Weininger's closely reasoned misogynist and anti-Semitic ravings—he places Jews in the female category—have the express aim of saving the world. This fact may help explain the book's phenomenal publishing history: thirteen editions by 1911, a 26th in 1926, and a "Volksausgabe" (popular reissue) in 1929.[67] Another reason for its success is that Weininger's ideas found a sympathetic and enthusiastic response; his book was the symptomatic expression of an intellectual, or ideological, epidemic that began in the 1890s. Two of Weininger's fellow Austrians, the artists Gustav Klimt (1862-1918) and Alfred Kubin (1877-1959), were in effect illustrating his book around the time it appeared. Kubin's crepuscular, grotesque depictions of woman as spider, as executioner, as slaughterer find their counterpart in Klimt's more brightly colored castrating female figures. The image of woman as a subhuman, exclusively sexual creature, insatiable and aggressive, seemed to reflect a widespread fear in men of impotence. Kubin's and Klimt's "erotic nightmare" corresponds in turn to the curtain speech that closes act four of *Erdgeist*. Lulu has forced Dr. Schön to break off his engagement, and he is now condemned to marry her. As he collapses under the pressure he says, "Jetzt—kommt die—Hinrichtung [...]" (Next comes the execution. I, 442).[68]

The sado-masochistic Expressionist statement on the topic of the relationship between the sexes, again anticipated in the Lulu Tragedy, can be found in Oskar Kokoschka's (1886-1980) *Mörder Hoffnung der Frauen* [Murderers Hope of Women, 1909] where aggression and love and the death wish are indistinguishable in the climactic mutual murder—or love-killing, as opposed to Wagner's love-death—of male and female.[69]

That Wedekind radically distorted and, by implication, rejected both feminist and misogynist ideologies does not mean that he was any less perturbed by the pernicious racialism that was the secondary point of *Geschlecht und Charakter* ("Geschlecht" can mean family or race as well as sex) and the main point of Huston Stewart Chamberlain's equally enduring best seller *Die Grundlagen des neunzehnten Jahrhunderts* [*The Foundations of the Nineteenth Century,* 1899]. Chamberlain's ultra-nationalism and crude social Darwinism were generally unexamined determinants of European thinking at the turn of the century. German neonationalists and captains of industry spoke of the survival of the fittest and the struggle for existence in business and international relations. The Lulu Tragedy shows the consequences that flow from applying social Darwinist principles to human relations.

Wedekind was bothered by his contemporaries' susceptibility to these ideas, and particularly by the widely accepted propositions that Aryan peoples are physically, morally, and mentally superior to others and that their propagation might be organized in more efficient and exciting ways in order to improve the species. The best formulation of this popular state of mind is Willibald Hentschel's *Varuna: Eine Welt- und Geschichtsbetrachung vom Standpunkt eines Ariers* [Varuna: A Consideration of the World and History from the Standpoint of an Aryan, 1902].[70] In 1904 Hentschel set forth plans for realizing his theories in a book called *Mittgart: Ein Weg zur Erneuerung der germanischen Rasse* [Mittgart: A Way to the Renewal of the Germanic Race]. Hentschel and his supporters, calling themselves the "Mittgartbund" (Mittgart League), proposed to found a rural colony where they could pursue the genetic selection of a human super-race. The community had a threefold appeal. First, it was to house solely members of the inherently beautiful Aryan race. Second, community law and order was to be based on the principles of struggle ("Kampf") and fitness for battle; individual combat was in the view of the League still the best way of deciding disputes.[71] The third and most sensational aspect was that there were to be 100 women for each one of the 100 men selected. The colony's governing council was to conclude a union between each man and the woman of the moment. This temporary marriage was to be dissolved as soon as she became pregnant. In this fashion the procreative powers of the males could be exploited with full effectiveness. Hentschel estimated that "three hundred such communities would produce an annual crop of 100,000 unbroken human beings."[72]

Wedekind responded to *Varuna* in 1904—the year in which *Die Büchse der Pandora* was published—with a drama entitled *"Hidalla" oder Karl Hetman der Zwergriese* (*"Hidalla"* or Karl Hetmann the Dwarf Giant). The play is thinly veiled vituperation and ridicule of prophets like Hentschel and their retinue, with some sideswipes at women's emancipation and the publishing business. Karl Hetmann, the anti-hero of *"Hidalla,"* proclaims to the world his new morality of beauty and eugenics. He is secretary and founder of the International Association for the Propagation of Thoroughbred Humans. His appearance stands in blatant contrast to his doctrine and makes of him a "broken figure" of the first water. That he is thin-haired, toothless, misshapen, and generally a poor specimen seems to detract not at all from the rhetorical impact of his message (II, 148). His profanation of Darwin and Nietzsche: the idea of the ennoblement of the race quickened by the institutionalization of free love, attracts wide attention, thanks to good publicity in the press. He finds himself surrounded by fatuous, frustrated women and villainous entrepreneurs aiming to exploit his idealism.

And yet Hetmann confesses he is no better than they, for he is both impotent and perverse, finding pleasure mainly in the effect his words have on others. The contradictions in Hetmann and in his program frustrate his every plan. He is jailed on the eve of the Association's great convention, and his plan to die an ecstatic martyr's death at the hands of a mob excited by his rhetoric goes awry when someone proclaims that he is insane and unaccountable for his words. The circus clown who excites laughter by tripping over the slightest impediment and getting places a split second too late is called a "dummer August," and that is what, by his own admission, Hetmann figuratively becomes. He might even have become a "dummer August" in reality if he hadn't succeeded in hanging himself, thereby for the first time accomplishing an end.

The psychological point the play makes about racists and eugenicists is that they, like everyone else, are motivated by selfish hedonism and do not hesitate to practice *Realpsychologie* in asserting themselves over others. Arthur Moeller-Bruck noted at the time that all Wedekind's works deal with applied egoism: "Notice how the actions begin, under what antiidealistic conditions and how logically they end: what lies between is regularly a classic example of our most vital urges, gastric, sexual, etc., and has their significance."[73]

There is no clown figure in *Schloß Wetterstein* (*Castle Wetterstein,* 1910), a pared-down, nightmarish version of the Lulu story, completely without cabaret frivolity. Because it lacks the irony and comic-grotesque humor that leaven the Lulu Tragedy, it is Wedekind's bitterest statement on human society and the relations between men and women. It lays bare the evils inherent in voguish views on marriage and love. In his review of the play, Herbert Ihering tries to find reasons for its harsh tone but provides only the psychological observation that Wedekind had no capacity for coping with the world and was unable to keep it at a distance. Experience had become terror, he notes, and writing a means of defense.[74] We will encounter the same phenomenon in Dürrenmatt's later work: In this dramatic world there are no broken figures, only perverse villains and their victims.

Wedekind remarks in his preface that the drama contains his views on the "inner necessities upon which marriage and the family rest" (II, 360). The facetiousness of these words soon dawns on the reader. Wetterstein Castle and the whole world of the play become a whorehouse. Not only marriage but human intercourse of all sorts are perverted through avarice, boredom, lust, and aggression. The pursuit of happiness ends either in vegetable dullness or in self-destruction as the dramatic action satirically refutes Rüdiger von Wetterstein's suspiciously high-sounding, very modern and enlightened speech on marriage: "Die Ehe ist für den Menschen da, nicht der Mensch für die Ehe! Ihr Glück, Ihre freie Entwicklung sind die heiligsten Ziele unseres Zusammenlebens" (Marriage exists for mankind, not mankind for marriage. Your happiness, your free development are the sacred goals of our life together. II, 379). These phrases are part of his marriage proposal to Leonore, whose husband he has recently murdered.

The drama draws the lethal consequences of Rüdiger's hardheaded, realistic psychology, expressed in statements like: "Unser Gefühlsleben besteht aus der Überschätzung menschlicher Beziehungen.—Jeder Mensch ist ersetzlich" (Our emotional life consists in the overestimation of human relationships. Every human is replaceable. II, 384). The ensuing events exemplify the abuse of the power each sex holds over the other and of the power residing in money. Each act deals with a psychic murder and a form of psychic rape, accomplished each time with greater finesse and in more perverse fashion, as prepetrators become victims.[75] In act one, Rüdiger, Baron of Wetterstein, wins the hand of Leonore von Gystrow, the woman he has recently made a widow through a series of deceptions. She knows he has murdered her husband but succumbs nevertheless when he argues to her satisfaction that, in the cause of women's emancipation, he is liberating her from outmoded bonds of marriage, family, and traditional propriety. In act two, Leonore, following the suggestion of her daughter Effie, drives the *Gewaltmensch* (person operating with brute force) Meinhard Luckner to commit suicide in her embrace. By artful dissembling she has robbed him of his manly sense of self-respect and so saves her husband for the time being from exposure as an embezzler.

In the third act, Effie, free of all compunction like her father and, like her mother, exploiting the power of her vitality, beauty, and seemingly infinite sexual appetite, reaches the pinnacle of success as the mistress—in both senses—of all in Karl Salzmann's household. Salzmann, a satanic, totally corrupt character, is the world's greatest entertainer, entrepreneur, and procurer, presiding over a group of specialists he has gathered in Castle Wetterstein. This group includes, among others, an anarchist constructing an atomic bomb in the cellar, a sadistic poet, a doctor with a genius for medical research, all drawn here by Salzmann's money and promise of power.

The fantastic figures of Effie—a self-conscious Lulu—and Salzmann are ultimately overshadowed by Chagnaral Tschamper, Argentine millionaire with strange tastes—Jack the Ripper in a new guise. He has paid Salzmann 200,000 dollars ostensibly for the pleasure of committing suicide in Effie's presence. Always on the lookout for titillating adventure and in need of her share of the money, she agrees to participate. Working with finesse on her sentimental proclivities—even Effie is vulnerable—and then breaking down her illusive recollection of an idyllic childhood, he commits the final psychic murder. She drinks the cyanide he had poured seemingly for himself. He finds his sexual delight well worth the fee: "Ach, das ist schön! Ach, das ist eine Wonne!/Dank dir, mein Kind. Dank dir. So süß war keine" (Oh, that's nice! Oh, that's ecstasy!/Thank you, my child. Thank you. None was ever so sweet. II, 433)[76]

The final scenes of this play, in verse that occasionally strikes lyric notes, constitute one of Wedekind's most striking formal travesties. They are quite inappropriate to their action and message. Yet they present the logical results of Rüdiger's ideas. Human dignity and conscience are atrophied; the chase after happiness takes on ever more perverted forms; and sensual pleasure becomes indistinguishable from death and horror. Castle Wetterstein, Wedekind's world in miniature, is at once bordello and charnel house.

The last of Wedekind's dramas which should be cited in order to throw more light on his Lulu Tragedy and its satiric qualities is *Tod und Teufel: Totentanz in drei Szenen* [Death and Devil: Dance of Death in Three Scenes, 1905], a satyr-play companion piece to the morbid *Schloß Wetterstein*.

Wedekind uses *Tod und Teufel* to express his most serious concerns; and though not as artful as the Lulu Tragedy, because the irony is more overt and rhetorical, the play is a satiric gem demonstrating the perverse mentality of western capitalism and of the human animal generally.

The play takes place in a fairly ordinary house of prostitution quite unlike Salzmann's castle. Fräulein Elfriede Malchus, morally indignant bluestocking, battler against white slavery and for women's emancipation, has just entered to confront the bordello owner, the Marquis Casti Piani (he ran the sporting house in act two of *Die Büchse der Pandora*). With the exception of one interlude in verse, a demonstration in the form of a play within the play, this short piece consists mainly of talk and speech-making reinforced by histrionic gesture.

Casti Piani and Fräulein von Malchus, the two main figures, have minimal libidinal energy and devote themselves to white slavery. She works against, he for this trade. Each is inspired with a sense of mission to save the world; and both claim to be fighting for women's rights, whose proponents and opponents Wedekind often ridiculed. Casti Piani argues with irrefutable economic and psychologically realistic logic that women disgrace their sex when they surrender themselves to men for no recompense. His thesis is that love and affection are mere excuses to satisfy baser urges; men have hypocritically fostered moral outrage at prostitution and sanctified the institution of marriage in order to rob women of their power. Men sense that feminine seductiveness is a "hellish danger for our culture" (II, 216), whereas the mark of a true culture is an ever expanding love market.

To the moderately perceptive person his points read like the arguments for cannibalism in Swift's *Modest Proposal*. The love market is Casti Piani's immodest proposal, and his case for it follows the tight reasoning of paranoid logic. The reader and the audience Wedekind had in mind should feel compelled to agree because they accept without question the premises: namely, that not merely animal and vegetable life but all aspects of human life—relations between men and women, the family, business, and the state—are governed by laws of supply and demand as well as by the principle of the survival of the fittest.

Specifically, Casti Piani maintains, woman's sexual equipment fits her to dominate man. All she need do is exploit her natural advantage. In this fashion, namely by shifting the focus to anatomy, Casti Piani solves with one masterful stroke the vexing problem of women's emancipation. His disquisition conjures up a beautiful new world where, by a seemingly logical extension of accepted premises, our self-understood scales of value are suddenly inverted. Prostitution is now, according to these lights, morally good. To combat it is to degrade womankind. In the course of his speech, Casti Piani moves from this logical development of illogic to ever more flowery and jumbled rhetoric. His sole listener, Fräulein von Malchus, is so transported that she melts at his feet and pleads to become his wife. Casti Piani has accomplished, unwittingly and to his dismay, a rhetorical seduction. His lecture was so effective that it defeated its purpose; Elfriede is moved to act against its moral.

But Casti Piani is not emotionally impervious either. For all his cynical pragmatism, he too is prone to lapse into sentimentality. Once his suasion has succeeded so well, he loses control and becomes vulnerable. He recalls his unhappy childhood and indulges in self-pity. His switch from hard-nosed man of business to weepy idealist coincides pretty much with the corseted Elfriede's conversion to belief in prostitution. Casti Piani is ripe for destruction. Wedekind does him in by

granting him a glimpse of reality and forcing him to see that his sole moral support—the belief in the natural beauty and goodness of sex and sensual pleasure—
is a delusion. This is accomplished by means of a play within the play. Casti Piani
and the audience witness a versified interlude played by two persons with strong
sexual instincts. In it the prostitute Lisiska demonstrates that sensual desire
brings only disappointment and pain. Once given free rein in a bordello, lust
becomes a hellish, consuming fire and turns to suicidal perversion. It is a "Men-
schenschlachterei" (human slaughter), a curse that drives people to masochism
and suicide (II, 229).

The bitter disillusionment, the destruction of a cherished belief of that time
and ours, brings Casti Piani to despair. And when Elfriede offers to make him a
gift of her virtue and her first night of love—as if he had never spoken of the love
market—that's the last straw. His extravagant and unexpected reaction is to
shoot himself in the heart. The play ends with this bad joke plus one more.
Elfriede, tears streaming down her cheeks, speaks these concluding lines: "Diese
letzte Enttäuschung hast du dir doch wohl in deinem furchtbarsten Weltschmerz
nicht träumen lassen, daß dir eine *Jungfrau* die Augen zudrückt" (In your worst
depression you could never have dreamed this final disappointment: that a virgin
would press your eyes closed. II, 232). We see now that Casti Piani was wrong all
around, and his once compelling arguments now fail to convince. Nothing works
for him, least of all human nature. The perverse logic of satire works to expose
the inherent limitations and folly of his mind and others like it.

The play provides a number of signals urging us to look beneath the surface of
the dialogue to find its true meaning. It is a straight thesis play and yet has
moments of high pathos. The action moves in abrupt shifts and weakly motivated reversals. The main figures change character with implausible abruptness.
The anomalous quality of the piece informs even small details like the decor of
the bordello. It is strikingly simple, consisting of two pairs of chairs separated by
two walls of ivy. Most remarkable are the whores, all dressed in austere white
smocks with white ribbons in their hair. Three of them appear at the close to
attend Casti Piani as he dies. He mistakes them at first for Furies, but they look
and act more like Vestal Virgins or maidens to be sacrificed in some cultic
ceremony.

Finally, the uncomplicated action of the play is almost obscured by the exaggerated, trite, melodramatic gestures—self-prostration, tears, the embracing of
knees—and by the unrealistic manner of speech which veers between stilted
paper German and an overblown pathos reminiscent of the young Schiller. Only
in the interlude, in the dialogue between Lisiska and her customer, is there
straightforward speech. Paradoxically, they talk in a rhymed verse form which
blocks the audience's empathy just as effectively as the artificial prose.

The satiric travesty of *Tod und Teufel* consists in the amalgamation of a set of
uncongenial beliefs: Social Darwinism, capitalist free enterprise, women's liber-

ation, and the dream of redemption through sexual license. These were the articles of faith of the intelligentsia of Wedekind's time. He incorporates them all in the sexually impotent prophet of liberation and sensual pleasure, the broken figure of Casti Piani.

The proving ground is the bordello, where all these ideas and dreams ought most easily to be realized. But efforts to put them into practice bring into evidence the reality principle, which is at bottom the nature of the human animal. Given unlimited license to fornicate, the prostitute finds that her life in this house is pure hell. She feels herself to be a "Teufelsbraten" (A devil's roast. II, 222). Confronted and defeated by reality, his folly revealed, Casti Piani sends his flesh the way of his ideologies by firing a bullet into himself. The abrupt and arbitrary suicide, makes his end laughable, as it should be in the case of any figure who serves both as satirist and as the butt of satire. The character that was satanic and fearsome goes under in a grotesque-comic scene, attended by prostitutes in nurse-like uniforms and mourned by a bluestocking virgin who tried to pay *him* for a night of love.

These are but a few of the ironic reversals and paradoxes that expose what Wedekind thought dangerous and foolish in two casts of mind one would suppose to be hostile to one another: entrepreneurial aggressiveness and sentimental idealism. The common denominator in *Tod und Teufel* is the seductive word "free" as in free enterprise, free love, and women's emancipation.

Wedekind used the term *Totentanz* not merely as a subtitle to *Tod und Teufel* but rather freely, as did several of his contemporaries, including Hofmannsthal. In 1902, for instance, Wedekind wrote in a letter that he had an idea for a ballet, "a modern *Totentanz*, naturally."[77] In fact the designation is apt, for it is the core idea of his best plays. Wedekind's work is close in spirit to those early representations in word and picture from the time of the Black Death in the fourteenth century.

The *Totentanz* has always been used to satiric ends. It attacks human vanity, unmasks the folly of human desires, and exposes the corruption of clergy and laity. In the presence of death, all men are equal; the mighty are brought low and the lowly raised. The earliest *danses macabres* arose from the fear of omnipresent death, and they deal with the bitter reality of human frailty in the face of an angry God and the plague. They aim to provide a foretaste of the tortures of Hell and point beyond visions of the cavorting dead to eternal damnation.[78] Drawn willy-nilly into the round by the half decayed corpses of unredeemed souls, the newly dead of all stations are compelled to dance about like lunatic fools.

Except for the inscrutable Schigolch—the name may be a twisted form of "logisch" or "psychologisch"—no one in *Erdgeist* or *Die Büchse der Pandora* stands outside the dance. All are caught and know they are damned. With terror and resignation, Schwarz, Dr. Schön, and the latter's son, Alwa, pronounce sentence on themselves and join in. Schigolch alone, at once a man of the world and a revenant (I, 407-410), remains aloof. He abandons Lulu shortly before her murder, for instance, and goes to a restaurant for some good English Christmas pudding and so escapes dying with the others (I, 533). Whether he is her father, a former lover, her mentor, or a poor, unredeemed soul returned from the grave is not clear. Wedekind is free with exciting hints which he undercuts with devices such as providing the old man with a mistress, the former wife of the King of Naples (I, 510). Though he does not obviously call the tune, Schigolch is a distant cousin of the minstrel Death in the *Totentanz* and much like one of those rotting bodies that lead the dance. The following exchange indicates the morbid cynicism of his vision which makes of him Wedekind's satiric spokesman. With fatherly concern he asks Lulu:

> Was bist du jetzt?
> Lulu: Ein Tier!
> Schigolch: Daß dich der!—Und was für ein Tier!—Ein feines Tier!—Ein elegantes Tier!—Ein Prachtstier!— — —Dann will ich mich man beiset-zen lassen.—Mit den Vorurteilen sind wir fertig. Auch mit dem gegen die Leichenwäscherin.
> Lulu: Du hast nicht zu fürchten, daß du noch mal gewaschen wirst!
> Schigolch: Macht auch nichts. Man wird doch wieder schmutzig.
> Lulu *ihn besprengend:* Es würde dich noch mal ins Leben zurückrufen.
> Schigolch: Wir sind Moder.
> Lulu: Bitte recht schön! Ich reibe mich täglich mit Kammfett ein und dann kommt Puder darauf.
> Schigolch: Auch wohl der Mühe wert, der Zierbengel wegen.
> Lulu: Das macht die Haut wie Satin.
> Schigolch: Als wäre es deswegen nicht auch nur Dreck.
> Lulu: Danke schön. Ich will zum Anbeißen sein.
> Schigolch: Sind wir auch. Geben da unten nächstens ein großes Diner. Halten offene Tafel.
> Lulu: Deine Gäste werden sich dabei kaum überessen.
> Schigolch: Geduld, Mädchen! Dich setzen deine Verehrer auch nicht in Weingeist. Das heißt schöne Melusine, solang es seine Schwungkraft behält. Nachher? Man nimmt's im zoologischen Garten nicht. *Sich erhe-bend* Die holden Bestien bekämen Magenkrämpfe.

(What are you now? Lulu: An animal. Schigolch: The devil you say!—What sort of animal!—A magnificent animal!— —Then I'll let them lay me away.—No more prejudices. Even against the washers of corpses. Lulu: You don't have to be afraid of getting washed any more! Schigolch: No matter. You just get dirty again. Lulu *sprinkling water on him:* It would bring you to life again. Schigolch:

We are mold. Lulu: If you please! I lubricate my skin every day with horse grease and then put powder on. Schigolch: Must be worth the trouble, to please the dandies. Lulu: That makes my skin like satin. Schigolch: As if even with that it were anything but filth. Lulu: Thanks. I want to be good enough to eat. Schigolch: That we are. We'll provide a great dinner soon, down below. We'll be a free meal. Lulu: Your guests are unlikely to overeat. Schigolch: Patience, girl! Your admirers aren't exactly going to pickle you in alcohol. They call you "schöne Melusine" as long as you're still vibrant.[79] After that? They won't take you at the zoo. *Getting up* The pretty beasts would get stomach cramps. I, 410).

In Schigolch, Wedekind has created an enigma on the order of the masked gentleman who appears like a *deus ex machina* at the end of *Frühlings Erwachen*. Schigolch is an intruder, even in the phantastic world of the Lulu Tragedy, functioning rather in the fashion of the seer Tiresias in classical myth, the only shade in the underworld, according to Homer, whose wits are intact. By human standards he is an amoral, murderous coward, and yet he seems ageless and a perspicacious satiric spokesman. His unbiased, nihilistic eye sees only morbidity, folly, and betrayal.

One additional device for assessing Wedekind's accomplishment is to compare it thematically with the work of other dramatists of the same two decades, 1890-1910, who chose to treat sex and the battle of the sexes in their plays. The first one that is likely to come to mind is Oscar Wilde's *Salomé* (1892). It was so apt and popular a representation of *fin de siècle* ideas about women that Wedekind had to note with dismay how directors and audiences identified his Lulu with Wilde's heroine. "Die Mode von 1904: Lulu war Salomé. Dr. Schön war Pastor Rosmer auf Rosmersholm," he complains in criticism of a Berlin *Erdgeist* production of 1903-1904.[80] There is an undeniable kinship with Salomé, but Lulu is a far more complex and contradictory character. Similarly, Wilde's exotic lyric playlet dealing with hysterical and perverted sexuality is quite unsatiric and far less ambitious than the Lulu plays.

Nor does Strindberg's *Dance of Death* (1901), for all its bitterness, have the aggressive quality of satire. To be sure, the state of marriage and indeed pretty much all of life are for Strindberg malignant. The battle between the sexes has become a stand-off and an end in itself, nurtured and maintained because that's all there is. The maneuvers and deceptions of husband and wife are fictions they construct in order to give their lives content. The only threatening force, if it is one at all, in *Dance of Death* is death itself, but he is a welcome guest, promising release from the hell of this marriage with its endless and fruitless bickering.

George Bernard Shaw locates the cast of *Man and Superman* (completed in 1901, first performed in 1903), also in hell, but only in the dream interlude "Don Juan in Hell," which he removed even further from immediate reality by assigning to each character a new name and identity from the Don Juan legend. Whereas

Wedekind's aggressive satire likes to make its point by saying that this life of ours is in fact hell—we will see that Brecht and Dürrenmatt are quite explicit about this—Shaw's devil is undemonic and urbane; his hell is a rather civilized place. In the end, Shaw's Don Juan/Tanner moves on to heaven because, like Goethe's Faust, he is a striver and essentially good. He is an agent of human social progress, however unwittingly; just as Dona Elvira/Ann by natural instinct carries out the bidding of the "life force" as she entraps him into marriage.

Shaw's Fabian Darwinism is benign. The struggle for existence appears, if at all, not in the battle for power or personal domination, but in intellectual debate and the antiseptic play of ideas in wit, aperçu, and paradox. The urbane and sparkling tone of *Man and Superman* is the opposite of Wedekind's medley of pathos, Grand Guignol, and bad jokes. In fact, Shaw's play, though its title may suggest a likeness of themes—the female triumphant—is in all ways the opposite of the Lulu plays. Wedekind accentuates the negative, Shaw the positive. *Man and Superman* rests on a traditional comic view of how men and women get along. It ends with a wedding and demonstrates the invincibility and goodness of the life force. Bergson's élan vital and the biological theories of comedy are confirmed and exemplified here.

Wedekind's social Darwinism, on the other hand, is evil. One can speak not of a force for life but for death at work in Lulu and her suitors. Human relations are governed by self-interest and aggression. Sex does not create life, it kills. Both leading men, Tanner and Dr. Schön, are self-confident, eloquent, powerful persons who are naturally and properly defeated by women. In Shaw's case, this means a marriage ceremony and the founding of a family. Wedekind's aftermath includes adultery, paranoia, and murder.

The inverse correspondence between the two plays extends to style as well as characterization. Shaw's diction is smooth and consistent, Wedekind's jumbled and forced. In general, the comparison with Shaw's *Man and Superman* indicates the distinction between comedy and satire. And in particular, it limns the peculiar morbid and overwrought quality of Wedekind's satire.

The differences between the two plays are also paradigmatic for the distinction between German and English attitudes toward the stage. Since the middle of the eighteenth century, Germans have thought of the theater as a moral and educational institution more than as a place of entertainment. German writers tend to publish didactic, activist plays of a radical sort. Because theaters on the Continent are state-supported, producers there are far less concerned than are their English colleagues with commercial success. Also, Wedekind's theater is a product of the ultramodern, hothouse atmosphere of Central Europe, particularly Berlin, in a time of incredibly rapid industrialization and urbanization. The resultant psychic strains fostered discontent and criticism, as we have seen, some of it quite rabid.

Wedekind is himself a broken figure, not to be dissociated from this milieu. Consequently he is well equipped to portray it accurately by letting it show itself and speak its own language. The art of quotation is the figural satirist's strongest weapon. He has no ideal to set against a dehumanized world. The positive counter to this picture is something he cannot formulate except to draw attention to its absence: a world of harmony, integrity, and charity.

2

Carl Sternheim's **1913**: Obsessed by Prestige

CARL STERNHEIM (1878-1942) PROTESTED, in response to theater reviews, that he was no satirist: "Not irony and satire, which the reporter had identified as my intent and the crowd parroted, but before general action from my writings the doctrine: Power is not lost, mankind need not listen to the litany of tradition but to its own fresh individual tone, quite unconcerned about the name bourgeois sensibility assigns his sometimes brutal nuance."[2]

Notwithstanding these protestations and some recent critical opinions that support them, Sternheim must be judged a satirist by generally accepted standards. One could argue that the internal contradiction in the phrase "brutal nuance" is a signal to readers of the above demurrer that he is playing ironic games. For further clues one can examine Sternheim's occasional writings, essays, and autobiography and find evidence of the same aggressive impulse that aroused Juvenal ("Difficile est saturam non scribere") and Jonathan Swift to anger and attack. Among these writings there are also some helpful self-interpretations that provide a glimpse into his workshop as well as a starting point for demonstrating that his play *1913* (published 1915, completed in February, 1914) is not satiric comedy like *Die Hose* (The Underpants, 1911) and *Der Snob* (1914) but thoroughgoing satire castigating political, social, and cultural evils peculiar to the time as well as to the human animal. It will be shown that Sternheim employs devices characteristic of the kind of writing that is, by consensus in the Anglo-American literary world and increasingly in Germany, called satiric.

One reason Sternheim fends off that the designation is his and his countrymen's inclination to think of satire and the satirist in the light of the moralistic and idealistic definition formulated by Friedrich Schiller in *Über naive und sentimentalische Dichtung* [On Naive and Sentimental Poetry, 1795].[3] According to Schiller the writer of aggressive, or punitive satire points to flaws in reality by juxtaposing it with ideals. In addition, if a satire is to have poetic merit, it must arouse revulsion by making readers aware, directly or indirectly, of the ideals and must partake of the artistic quality Schiller calls the sublime. Sternheim was not moved to express an ideal, nor did he, as a member of the early Expressionist school, want to make his plays poetic in Schiller's sense and so inappropriate to the time. And it is characteristic of satiric drama of the past one hundred years that the ideal of order and the inherent rightness of things, if it can be expressed at all, is made evident through the concrete, mimetic representation of its opposites: chaos, futility, folly, villainy.[4] The implication, of course, is that if things are so bad, there must be room for improvement.

Sternheim was writing figural satire, which is not anchored in any ideal or explicit authorial statement.[5] He notes that he has no firm standard by which to make judgments: "I had no point of view, except that I put my finger on the peculiar quality in each person; judged him fairly in respect to his incomparable qualities, with no value bias. I had to apprehend, not 'unmask,' not make fun of them as a satirist; show how fundamentally sad, comical, heroic, superior each was in himself" (X/1 268).[6]

Burghard Dedner has an interesting, if intricate and perverse, theory about Sternheim's reluctance to enunciate his message and instruct his audience. Sternheim, he believes, held the theater public in low esteem. It would, he may have thought, misinterpret his plays as merely more of the routine burlesques on the bourgeois philistine, that is, on someone other than themselves. And so he withheld the idealistic implications an audience might expect from a satirist and rejoiced in the antagonistic response of spectators, taking it as clear evidence of his success.[7] Dedner's theory fits neatly, moreover, with Brummack's idea that satire is a form of aggression and excites aggressive response in its audiences. And it is a documented fact, as will be seen, that Sternheim seemed to relish angry audience reaction to his plays and even encourage it by his presence in the theater.

Satire deals with reality—real people, situations, places, and ways of thinking. *1913* has this historical authenticity, as I will show in some detail. It presents and analyses the laws that Sternheim saw governing human relationships around him. The following paradox from the essay "Berlin oder Juste Milieu" (Berlin or Juste Milieu, 1920) gives us one side of the problem: "The modern feeling: I can distinguish myself in no way other than by being especially well adapted as a social being, destroyed all need for isolation in that, on the contrary, the conception of those with whom I live and struggle is indistinguishable from the struggle for existence, indeed it is its presupposition" (VI, 116).[8] In other words, I will adapt and go along with everyone else by fighting, like and against everyone else, for my place in the sun.

Sternheim saw to his dismay that men's actions were dictated by unconscious attitudes, unexamined doctrines, and group phantasies, and that these actions were leading to a catastrophic end. The attitudes he had in mind have to do with social Darwinism. The phrases "struggle for existence" and "well adapted" make this obvious. Sternheim's observation was that the desire to adapt and conform did not mitigate but reinforced the tendency toward aggression. Forming the psychic impetus behind the mechanisms of vitality and order, struggle and adaptation is another paradoxically linked pair: impotence and aggression. Sternheim describes his modern man of the *juste milieu:* "Man, chained to a mighty, ineluctable, natural mechanism, with no remnant of his own action in decisive matters, drugs himself inside its stiff hinges with unexampled license" (VI, 118).[9] Sternheim's characters fight their battles not for material gain but for prestige.[10] To win it they must conform to the accepted standard of behavior in the struggle for existence, or *bellum omnium contra omnes.* Success is nothing more than an enhanced public image; and what sets the prominent citizen apart from his fellows is his "brutal nuance," that is, his peculiar sort of ruthlessness, astuteness, and capacity for chicanery. He recognizes no ethical limits to his predatory acts, but these acts cannot be decisive because they are confined to the paper realm of journals, public relations, and mere appearance. Like Tantalus and Sisyphus, he is condemned to repeated failure.

The satirist Sternheim, having recognized the frenetic yet rigidly constrained villainy and folly of those around him, needed merely to record what he saw: "Behind ever so dynamic gestures and bold words there towered up an iron reality as a derisive shadow and knocked them down to the level of jokes, of metaphors. A person had nothing more to create, he had only to pay attention and stamp the actual happenings with a label" (VI, 118).[11] In 1913 that mocking shadow was the reality of war, an awesome cataclysm that made the most grandiose, pretentious undertakings look puny by comparison and which made the speculations of the entrepreneurs seem trivial exercises. Sternheim thought nothing needed to be added; the truth should be obvious without overt pronouncements.

In his essay on Molière (1917), Sternheim reveals some aspects of his satiric methods and goals in terms that come close to satisfying Schiller's full definition:

> A poet like Molière is doctor to the body of his age. To preserve man's qualities bright and gleaming in their totality and as his Creator made them is his urgent duty. To achieve his high aim, he, like the medical helper, avails himself of the allopathic or the homeopathic method. He can put his finger on humanity's critical spot and have his hero take up an impassioned battle position and risk his life (the nature of tragedy) but can also inject the characteristic to be revealed into his hero and let him be absurdly obsessed by it with fanatic delight (nature of comedy). The impression on the audience is the same in both cases: in the end it is overcome by yearning for a sweet moderation the stage hero lacked, which it is now passionately determined to restore, thanks to enlightenment by the poet (VI, 31).[12]

This is a Schillerian statement to the extent that it speaks of the uplifting effect satire should have on its audience, awakening a desire for harmony by negative example. Sternheim has Molière in mind here more than himself. His own plays are designed to elicit angry, even violent response sooner than the longing for sweet moderation.

Of course by "comedy" Sternheim means something other than the kind of play in which boy loves, loses, and gets girl—once, by happy chance, certain blocking figures have been removed; he means undirected, homeopathic satire. The heroes of the seven plays he wrote between 1907 and 1914 are infected with the vices and prejudices of the bourgeois *juste milieu*. The plays, in their ironic objectivity, employ the conventional satiric praise-blame inversion.

The satirist has always felt duty-bound to speak out, and his pose is that of plain speaker. If one did not keep in mind the idea of homeopathy, one could misread the first part of the statement Sternheim makes on his dramatic intent:

> I wasn't trying to kindle an urge for education or good breeding; on the contrary, I was warning the bourgeois not to criticize God's world and was giving him courage to stand up for his so-called vices, with which he achieved his successes, to remove concepts that measure with a bias toward ethical merit finally from his vocabulary as inconsequential and enervating. At bottom I hoped that the worker would finally recognize, instead of the prettified man of the *juste milieu* as he is represented, the true and genuine article ("der wahre und echte Jakob"); recognize behind the latter's literary accommodation and little cosmetic tricks his real, overwhelmingly vital, brutal vigor and measure by that as formidable reality and not by windy theories the impact of imminent decisions, a vigor that I faced up to with the sole desire that out of it, no matter on which side, the truth of the age might be revealed. (VI, 140)[13]

In other words, Sternheim gives his bourgeois "hero" the courage of his convictions and lets him drop the façade of "metaphor," that is, of stereotyped ideas and clichés provided by the press and the literati. He is then free, in a very small arena to be sure, to realize his true, "brutal nuance," i.e., his perfect, conscienceless self-interest, according to which he acts and which, he assumes, guides all his fellows. The true Jacob emerges, and the spectator must draw his own ethical conclusions. According to the rules of this game, however, no matter how cynical and ruthless one may be, in the end he is shown to be ineffectual. Sternheim's knaves are fools because they have no grasp of reality.

Sternheim's homeopathic method, his straight-faced ironic praise of his chief characters published in essays and letters to the press as well as the idiosyncratic, tortured style of his communications place a heavy burden on critic and spectator. Add to this his brilliant rendering of current jargon and received ideas, then it comes as no surprise that many scholars and reviewers have concluded that he is no satirist; they assume that he intends his heroes as models to be emulated.[14] A few go so far as to charge him with immorality and insanity. The most violent accusations come from W. G. Sebald who rightly detected the destructive madness in the stage figures and their ideas but, failing to grasp Sternheim's irony in such plays as *1913*, pilloried Sternheim as a traitor to literature and humanity.[15]

Every *ad hominem* argument Sebald adduces against Sternheim's ideas and style can better be used to demonstrate that his best plays, those from the years 1907-1914, are good satirical comedies *(Die Hose, Der Snob, Bürger Schippel)* or straight satiric drama *(Die Kassette, 1913)*.

The foregoing passages from Sternheim's prose were published after 1914. Yet I believe they refute Sebald's contention that the playwright was unaware of what his dramas "said" and was guilty of unwitting self-contradiction. The negative implications of the concept of "die eigene Nuance," the wedding of conformity and battle, the antinomies within each work, the absence of dialectic and resolution, the destructively aggressive character of the plays, the absence of a fixed standpoint for value judgment, the apparent diffuseness, and the mixing of banal and exalted elements can all be reckoned as virtues if one reads the dramas as satires.[16] *1913* in particular mirrors faithfully the madness, waste, and futility Sternheim saw about him in that "dreadful decade from 1897-1907" when Kaiser Wilhelm II ruled over a materially flourishing German Reich (VI, 217).

Like Wedekind, Sternheim consciously ran the risk of being misunderstood and yet complained bitterly when he was. Both attacked the same dangers, be they called egoistic *Realpsychologie* or *die brutale Nuance,* the *Gewaltmensch* (Wedekind) or the *Viechskerl* or tough customer (Sternheim), with the same means: undirected satire.

A first exposure to *1913* might lead one to classify it as a bona fide melodrama about a family circus. Sternheim demands a discerning audience, for his clues to his intentions are sparse. The events of *1913* are far closer to our experience than, say, the outlandish mixes and exaggerations of Wedekind's Lulu Tragedy. The travesty, or "fantastic vision of the world transformed," is there, but it is not immediately apparent in what could seem an Ibsenesque family drama played in the ornate interior of an upper-class household.[17] That fantastic vision, or satiric fiction, lies in the excitement about haberdashery, which looks at first like incidental comic embroidery on the main action.

Not that Sternheim ever tired in his essays of making explicit statements about his aims, namely: to represent the anarchy of the times, in which every man claims to be his own microcosm, and to do this by showing the bourgeois completely possessed by himself and running amok within his narrow confines (X/1,271). In "Das gerettete Bürgertum" (The Bourgeoisie Rescued, 1918) he states: "I wrote seven comedies between 1908 and 1913. The last one, which bears the name of the prewar year, showed as far as possible in all simplicity how far the bourgeois had progressed in his dealings. The poet had to add nothing to that reality. Despite various public presentations and propagation through the press, no one had noticed what I intended in my work" (VI, 46).[18] In this enterprise Sternheim knew but one ally, Frank Wedekind. In his "Lebenslauf" (Curriculum Vitae, 1921) he writes: "Wedekind, whom I met in my house in

Höllkriegelskreuth near Munich and elsewhere, has always seemed to me, even in personal matters, the only person dedicated to the same artistic aims [as I am]" (VI, 222).[19]

1913 is Sternheim's most ambitious and successful satire. It is one of the three plays he was proudest of. It remains to demonstrate how he realized his intentions and why it is a well made satiric drama.

Like the Lulu Tragedy, the play is anchored in its time and yet has timeless implications. The title tells us that this is Germany on the eve of a calamitous war. But other events were in the air as well: In 1913 all Germany celebrated the centennial of the defeat of Napoleon at the Battle of Leipzig, and Gerhart Hauptmann, whose fiftieth year it happened to be, was commissioned to write a festival play for the occasion. It was also the Silver anniversary of Wilhelm II's accession to the throne. It is the year in which Henry Ford started his assembly line and the Haber-Bosch process for synthesizing ammonia was perfected. The arrogance and influence of the officer corps revealed itself—not for the first time—in the incident at Zabern (now Saverne), Alsace, where a young officer so aroused the civilian population with his insults that the commander of the post felt obliged to protect the army's prestige by declaring martial law and arresting 28 citizens. Despite strong public condemnation in Germany and censure in the Reichstag, the commander was acquitted at his court martial, and Chancellor Bethmann-Hollweg remained in power. In October, on Der Hohe Meißner near Kassel, the German youth movement held its largest congress, which was to weld it into a unified, powerful cultural force. It failed its purpose, not because the imperial establishment succeeded in its aim to coöpt it through appeals to its nationalistic enthusiasm; rather, the war brought them into the fold. 1913 was a time when most believed that the nation was prospering as never before and that the best was yet to come. D. Sarason, editor of *Das Jahr 1913: Ein Gesamtbild der Kulturentwicklung* [The Year 1913: An Overall Picture of Cultural Development], fully expected to register further gains in the ensuing editions of his annual, which in fact never appeared.[20]

The scene of *1913* is Schloß Buchow, somewhere in Prussia. The details of the milieu are contemporary, and the characters are not pale caricatures but recognizable figures patterned after living persons. The play is dedicated to Ernst Stadler (1883-1914), and one secondary figure bears that family name, though he has little in common with the poet and scholar. Yet these characters are also types; King Lear, Lady Macbeth, and Oscar Wilde provided some models. And their vices are common to all humanity.

The satire has both political and moral dimensions. The incidents which take place in Baron Christian Maske's household anticipate and rehearse in miniature the downfall of a nation and of western civilization. ("Maske," by the way, is German for mask, but the Sternheim family had a much admired friend, a newspaper publisher, who actually bore the name.) Through telephone lines, the mails, and the daily press, petty intrigues within the family are linked with the machinery of world history. The question of who is to be the first dandy to astound the social world by wearing a piece of string in lieu of a watch chain can, under these conditions, have apocalyptic implications. This is Sternheim's great travesty, his phantastic yet logical linking of superficial banality with the chaos that looms in the near future and that is already there for those with eyes to see.

Through their skill at manipulation and conformity, the Maskes have risen to power and prominence in two generations. First, Theobald found financial security and limited freedom by aping the respectable bourgeois *(Die Hose)*. Then his son, Christian, succeeded in business and rose into the aristocracy by adopting its costume and mannerisms *(Der Snob)*. Now Christian Maske has assumed a new guise, that of the astute captain of industry and unscrupulous arms magnate. He has built an empire on the courage of his convictions and has acquired great prestige (I, 225). Yet in a single day his daughter Sofie is about to rob him of it all. "Ein Tag Abwesenheit kostet mich Prestige, Macht, Vermögen" (One day's absence costs me prestige, power, wealth, I, 226), he complains in admiration of her calculating ruthlessness. A simple public relations trick threatens to make him a nobody. His battle to regain his prestige by turning her weapons against her supplies the play's main action. Sofie says of him: "Diese von sich besessene Natur verträgt nichts Bedeutendes neben sich und wird uns, coûte qui coûte, niederwerfen" (This creature is so obsessed by himself that he can endure nothing important near him and will crush us, *coûte qui coûte,* I, 257). Sternheim's point is that Christian Maske has brought on his own demise. Or better, like Wedekind's Dr. Schön, he is done in by an opponent and methods for which he is responsible. He has created this jungle of business and human relations, and he dictates the selfish, materialistic rules by which it operates. He has realized his own "brutal nuance" and is sufficiently powerful to boast of his unscrupulous greed. And greed is a virtue in a world where only two things count: "Magenhunger des Pöbels. Machthunger der Reichen. Sonst nichts" (Stomach hunger of the rabble. Power hunger of the rich. Nothing more. I, 230). This is the sum of Maske's wisdom. He orders his affairs and acts on the assumption that all others think as he. That is, he is conforming by dominating. His talk of self-realization is merely a fraudulent euphemism for his self-interest and brutality. By reducing human relationships to the formula of hunger for food or power, he is able to devote his considerable energy to the exploitation of others and the enhancement of his prestige. Therein resides his power, that intangible fluid that owes its force to the fear and respect of others.

All the aggressive characters in this play are possessed and obsessed by their nuance as magnified into a prestigious public image. It is at the same time their only strength and their fatal weakness. They fight for it tooth and nail, for it has supplanted all other values. The superficial mask is their being. Without it they are nothing. Beneath the costume lies no substance. Through his rhetoric and public relations skill, Maske has made his fantasies of order and dynamism into a governing ideology. He has reduced human beings to stereotypes and made aggressive vitality the highest virtue. And his society has accepted these phantasies as truths, unaware they are part of a charade and that these dreams must soon become nightmares.

Because of his hunger for power, he has reified and impoverished human relationships in his private and public life. By making others impotent he has aroused their destructive instincts and defeated his own ends. His daughter Sofie has taken him at his word and is working to put him in the shade; and other, even more pernicious persons are scheming to take over the limelight. He now finds himself locked with everyone else in a mechanism created by his own estimate of his fellows (VI, 118). Within the narrow limits imposed on him by what Sternheim calls reality, he is battling to assert himself. But if he wins, he gains or maintains his prestige, usually by overshadowing someone else.

Through astute negotiations and by persuading the public she is a pious protestant, Maske's daughter Sofie has all but concluded, against her father's will, an arms deal with the Dutch government. Though near death from an unspecified ailment, Maske is unwilling to be pushed aside, and with weapons like Sofie's he conducts a campaign to regain his position at all costs. His grandiose coup is a simple trick: He becomes a convert to Catholicism and announces this in a press release to all important newspapers. Holland drops negotiations and the deal is off. Maske, however, never enjoys the fruits of this victory, which is as unsubstantial as his view of the world. It is all theater, as the words of his penultimate speech indicate. Rushing on stage in search of Sofie, he speaks: "Sie läßt sich nicht finden, will mich um letzte Wollust betrügen. Wo ist sie? Wer ist das? Hört mich, alle herbei! Beleuchtung, Rampe! *Er schreit:* Aus ist's mit dem Karfreitagszauber!" (She's hiding, wants to cheat me of my last satisfaction. Where is she? Who's that? Lights, stage front! *He shouts:* It's all over with that Good Friday magic! I, 292). In satire, a rhetorical kind of literature as I have mentioned, each fool and knave convicts himself through his own choice of words. Here it is theater talk. Elsewhere in this play the languages of the battlefield, of chauvinism, of finance, and of fashion serve a similar function.

Maske is in fact cheated out of his ultimate ecstasy. He mistakes his favorite daughter, Ottilie, for Sofie, curses and ridicules her instead, and then falls dead. True, he has foiled his enemy, but the strain has cost him his life. He leaves behind a family and a world in helpless confusion. His final performance follows the typically satiric course from purpose to passion to anticlimax, and the punishment reveals Sternheim's central meaning.[21] Sternheim has adjusted false appearance to correspond with the true state of things. He has collapsed mask and essence into one; and one sees that they are both empty and dead. He also shows that the struggle to gain and preserve prestige is not merely self-defeating but also indiscriminately destructive.

On the other hand, Sternheim also shows us the humanity of his protagonist. He lets him suffer defeat, degradation, and, in a strangely impersonal way, pangs of conscience. Maske loves his children and wants them to reap the benefits of his work. In the most mordantly ironic line of the play, he says to them: "Gesät habe ich. Die himmlischsten Ernten könnt ihr sammeln" (I have planted the seed. You can now gather the most divine harvests. I, 241). He means his fourteen factories, but the crop from his seed is and will be anything but divine. Shortly before his end he describes an odd moment of uncharacteristic insight into the social and economic calamity he has created: "Es geht mir schlecht. Ich mache Bilanz and fühle, von menschlichen Gefühlen mehr als von eigenen besessen: möchte es diesem oder einem anderen gelingen, von Grund auf Zustände zu erschüttern, die wir geschaffen" (I'm not well. I'm summing up and, in the thrall of human feelings more than of my own, I feel: it would be good if someone or other succeeded in shaking to their foundations the conditions we have created. I, 286). Sofie points out that he has created these conditions and bequeathed them to her generation; "Jedes Rezept habt ihr uns und das Hauptbestandteil aller Rezepte übermacht. Skrupellosigkeit. Wir gründen wie ihr, weit vorsichtiger und geschäftskundiger sogar, ohne freilich irgendwie sehen zu können, wohin das alles geht" *(Sophie:* You have passed on to us every formula as well as the chief ingredient of all formulas. Unscrupulousness. We are founders like you, far more cautious and with even more business acumen than you, granted: without being able to see at all where it's all heading. I, 285). The machine is running ever more efficiently but is out of control and headed for war. "Nach uns Zusammenbruch!" (After us the collapse!) cries Maske as if confirming a long held belief. His concern for the fate of mankind is an alien sentiment; he himself is incapable of emotion. And before the scene is over, he is once more totally possessed by the question of his prestige and hurls a bitter curse at Sofie (I, 289).

Maske is a self-obsessed monomaniac; yet he is far from a seamless figure. He is full of inconsistencies. He is moribund, calls himself "der gepflegte Kadaver" (the well groomed corpse, I, 229), and yet he preaches ruthless vitalism, "Lebendiges, ungezügeltes Lebensbewußtsein!" (Vital, unbridled sense of life! I, 228). He is a sentimental idealist and a hardboiled exploiter. He loves Ottilie and curses her. He works ostensibly to strengthen his fatherland, his firm, and his family but only hastens the debacle.

From Archilochus's time to the present day, the fictional satirist (Swift's Gulliver or Grimmelshausen's Simplizius) has been "a wonderfully ambiguous figure—part hero, part villain, part public censor, part private man."[22] Christian Maske is all these things. He rails in public against the evils of the system he helped institute, and yet he works to maintain it. He loves his children, yet battles and ridicules them. Like Lemuel Gulliver and other great misanthropes, he belongs with the creatures he scorns. He is also, along with Wedekind's Dr. Schön, Georg Kaiser's bank cashier, and the other satiric protagonists we will meet, a kind of redeemer, the herald of the new dispensation, who must die as a scapegoat when that new order proves to be not an idyllic community of saints but an intolerable hell. Maske's martyrdom and that of a long line of suffering satiric heroes that includes Petronius's Trimalchio is the skilled satirist's way of diffusing guilt, showing it to be reciprocal, and of frustrating the audiences' natural desire to lay the blame on someone else, on an obvious and hateful scoundrel. Swift's fictional spokesman in *A Modest Proposal,* for instance, has undeniably good intentions, however unthinkable the means.

Maske has grown strong through his transgressions and because of the vices of his victims.[23] That is, he pronounces openly, and acts upon the tacit moral, or amoral, assumptions of his society. Weaker fools may assume pious attitudes. Maske is unencumbered by any need to feign Christian virtue, though Christian is his first name. But now the forces and qualities that were embodied in him and which were his strength are breaking apart. They reappear singly in his progeny: his ruthlessness in Sofie, his snobbery in Philipp Ernst, his vital sensuality in Ottilie. Like other seed he has sown, each quality goes out of control, becomes hypertrophied, obsessive, self-destructive.

Yet each subsidiary character has his own inconsistencies. Ottilie promises to suppress none of her secret desires and whispers to her father of "Machttaumel! Menschen bewältigen—fressen" (Intoxicated with power! Overpowering—devouring people. I, 225). But she devotes all this energy to the seduction of her father's secretary, Wilhelm Krey. Sofie is a canny, heartless businesswoman and does not shrink from cheating her father or brother. Yet she acts in the interests of her husband, whom she loves with abject devotion. He is a weak man, incapable of getting children, and she wants to transform him into a powerful figure, at least in the eyes of the world. She explains her motives: "Es geht für dich, Otto, für dein Ansehen, deine Größe nach seinem [Christian Maskes] Tod. Dein schlagender Erfolg und sein platter Abgang müssen vor der Welt zusammenfallen. Läßt er über deiner Katastrophe eine Gloriole von sich in der Welt zurück, wandelst du für den Rest deiner Tage ein Schemen in seinem Licht. Das will ich nicht" (I'm doing it for you, Otto, for your reputation, your greatness after his death. Your brilliant success and his unimpressive departure must coincide in the eyes of the world. If he leaves behind in the world a gloriole of his own shining over your catastrophe, then you will be walking the rest of your days as a shade in his light. I don't want that. I, 258). Her tricks misfire, however, and her fears are realized. Otto, and the rest, remain at the end no more than shades in hell.

And in the end the remarkable figure of Maske's secretary, an eloquent anti-capitalist and propagandist for Teutonic virtue and the "neue deutsche Idee" (new German idea, I, 220) proves to be more concerned for the impression his clothes make on Ottilie than for the cause of nationalistic revolution.

Sternheim provides further inconsistencies that give pause. The opening scene of the third and final act begins with a rendering of Schumann's "Mondnacht," that jewel of Romantic and Roman Catholic piety, sung here by Ottilie with a priest—newly arrived—at the piano. It is applauded with cries of "Himmlischer Schumann" (Heavenly Schumann) and "Großer Eichendorff" (Great Eichendorff, I, 276). This song of death, peace, and harmony is Maske's private bad joke and utterly inappropriate to the situation. Maske has just completed his cynical conversion to the Catholic faith; and the remainder of the scene reveals the vicious battle going on within the family. Sofie defrauds her brother, Philipp, of his inheritance (I, 278-80); Wilhelm Krey, the secretary, promises to liquidate his capitalist enemies once he is in power (I, 281-82); and Christian Maske anticipates Holland's reaction to the news reports. In his inflated battlefield language he says, "[...] in diesen Minuten etwa platzt dort die Bombe" (At about this moment the bomb is exploding there, I, 278). Finally, at the center of the scene Sternheim devotes two pages (I, 279-80) to the incongruous, seemingly petty question of whether Philipp Ernst will have the sole right to wear a piece of string in place of a watch chain at the ball.

This strident incompatibility in a play dealing with the destinies of nations finds its counterpart in Sternheim's rhetorical devices. Through allusion and trope his characters work to exaggerate the trivial and belittle the sublime. Megalomaniacs allude repeatedly to heroic men of the past. Maske invokes Bismarck and Napoleon, and he speaks in words that make him a commanding general on the battlefield of business. Everything he plans and does is part of a life and death struggle and is expressed in metaphors of finance, violence, and warfare. "Breche ich ihr aber auch noch vor meinem Abmarsch den Hals, ist es dann Gewinn für euch," he says of Sofie to Philipp Ernst (If I break her neck too before I decamp, that will be to your profit, I, 242-43). Each of the main characters uses words, consciously or unconsciously, in an effort to transform impotence into power. The actions they take, on the other hand, expose their essential weakness. Also Christian Maske regularly deflates the pomposities of the others. He keeps reminding Otto, Sofie's husband, of his sexual impotence. As mentioned earlier, he reduces human motivation to two appetites: hunger for power and hunger for food, and he sees in human issues only the mechanical aspects of quantity and count. Germany is sixty-five million "Fresser" (mouths to feed) confined to 540,000 square kilometers (I, 223). This one fact is the brutal "formidable reality" Sternheim wanted his audience to see in his satiric protagonist (VI, 140).

This "reality" is in turn belittled and ridiculed by the ultimate backdrop of death and war (VI, 118).

The mixing of up and down movements, magnifying and belittling characterizes the movement of the play. On every rise follows a fall. The opening scene of Act I shows us Wilhelm Krey, the paper revolutionary, at his desk, writing as always with a "besessenen Feder" (obsessed pen, I, 252) and intoxicated by his own propaganda slogans. He is attacking the disease of international finance and the crass spirit of capitalism in the cause of "eine heilige, allgemeine, vaterländische Verbrüderung und allgemeine deutsche Ideen" (a sacred, common, patriotic brotherhood with common German ideas, I, 220). Krey is as hungry for power as the others. Through his writings he hopes to gain control of the revolutionary youth movement and then assert himself over the Maske family. Envy of their position and an obsession with his own prestige inform all his actions. In a monologue he says of Ottilie: "Mißbrauchen für eine Laune willst du mich, und von der anderen Seite bieten mir die prachtvoll begeisterten Jungen Gewalt über ihr Leben und Stoßkraft an. Es erhebt sich einer, da du ihn noch in abhängiger Stellung unter dir siehst, schon über den First deines Lebens; durch seine unbestochen freie Meinung macht er heldenhaft großen Eindruck auf die Zeit, die ihn dafür unsterblich nennt. Unsterblich—Ottilie! Du aber und dein Geld bleibst im Namenlosen. Es kommt der Tag, da mit der zwischen uns aufgehellten *wirklichen* Distanz ich die Frechheit deines bloßen Versuchs heimzahlen werde" (You want to misuse me to gratify a whim, and from the other direction the magnificently enthusiastic boys are offering me power over their lives and dynamism. Someone is elevating himself, while you see him in a subservient position, over the top of your life; through his uncorrupted free views he is heroically making a deep impression on the age, which in turn will call him immortal. Immortal—Ottilie! You and your money, on the other hand, will remain nameless and unrecognized. The day is coming when, with the real distance that has grown clear between us, I will pay you back for the liberty you took in the mere attempt. I, 251). Here, and particularly in the opening scene, Krey speaks and writes the language cultivated by patriotic organizations and especially the youth movement of the day. It tends to be elevated and sanctimonious in tone and is expressive of deep commitment to high goals. Krey's ideology is nothing exceptional: a moderate form of racism mixed with idealistic nationalism and anticipation, all tied together into one message about Germany's mission in world history. The modern reader, on the other hand, can easily hear these sentences from his letter as a proto-Nazi diatribe:

Wir wollen zwar menschliche Menschen, aber Deutsche wollen wir vor allem sein. Mit Bewußtsein forschen wir nach unserem Wesentlichen, heben die neue deutsche Idee, die jede Seele im Vaterland mit gleicher Sorge umfaßt, hoch über den verwaschenen Zeitgeist und, uns selbst mit Begeisterung ehrend, empfinden wir Achtung vor dem Fremden, Bedeutenden (I, 220).

(To be sure we all want to be human beings, but above all we want to be Germans. We are searching consciously for our essence and raise the new German idea—which embraces every soul in the fatherland with equal care—high above the dingy Zeitgeist, and, honoring ourselves with enthusiasm, we feel respect for things foreign and meaningful.)

The passage is vapid enough and is a parody on the rhetoric of the Wandervogel. Krey turns out to be a broken figure. His phrases are nothing more than that. He is in fact a weakling who asserts himself only through his obsessed pen or in monologues. Conforming has become his way of life, and he has no more substance than the faded phrases he devises. The first indication that this is so, if the clichés of the opening monologue were not sufficient evidence, is his insecure, obsequious behavior toward Ottilie Maske when she enters in scene two. His bow before her is an anticlimax and an overt denial of his fantasies of immortal heroism, power, and prestige.

Krey and Ottilie make a good match. She is the victim of her erotic and ideological susceptibility. In scene three, speaking of Otto Weininger's *Geschlecht und Charakter,* she tries the phrase "seelisches Neuland" (virgin land of the soul) on her father; and he promptly brings her back to earth with facts, figures, and his philosophy of hunger (I, 223-224). As he does this, he also exalts himself, through allusion to Napoleon, for instance; and it becomes clear that he is concerned solely with his public image: "[...] sie (Sofie) hat einen Saltomortale gesprungen, mich in den Schatten zu drängen" (She has performed a *salto mortale* to crowd me into the shadows. I, 231). He understands his daughter's intentions quite well. She is aiming to put him in the shadow and to rob him of his influence: "Diese genialen Instinkte sind gegen mich, mein persönliches Ansehen gerichtet" (These brilliant instincts are directed against me and my personal prestige. I,233).

His paranoid delusions emerge at the end of scene five. He is confident of regaining his earlier control over the nation, of once more "blinding the world with his flame" (I, 234). The anticlimax follows immediately upon the entrance of Philipp Ernst, his foppish son. The latter and Ottilie take up the final third of act one chatting about styles in fashion and hoped for sexual conquest.

It seems odd at first that this empty manikin, the narcissistic dandy Philipp Ernst, whose only battles are fought with sartorial weapons for the favors of a lady, assumes a central role in *1913.* In fact, the farcical clothes travesty occupies the very center of the play (II. ix-xiv), and costume becomes important again in the concluding three scenes. Sternheim wants of course to take a swipe at phenomena of decadence and conspicuous consumption among the rich, but has more in mind. The obsession with clothes is his central, satiric, synecdochic metaphor. Everyone in the play strives to build and maintain his "Ansehen" (appearance or prestige).

The pageant and costumes prescribed for the final scenes suggest a grotesquely inappropriate, rather chaotic dance of death in stylish, brightly colored costumes back and forth between the library and Maske's corpse in the next room: "Es entsteht durch die offene Tür ein lebhaftes Hin und Her [...]. Ein Diener erleuchtet die Szene. Man erkennt jetzt die modisch übertriebene Pracht der Nachtkostüme, insbesondere Philipp Ernsts und des Prinzen Oels, die wie Wilhelm eine Art Turban dazu tragen, und ihre Übereinstimmung in etwa mit dem Anzug Wilhelms" (People begin to move quickly back and forth through the open door. A servant lights up the scene. There now comes into view the exaggeratedly fashionable splendor of the nightclothes, especially Philipp's and Prince Oels's, who, like Wilhelm, are wearing a kind of turban on top of it all, and their approximate conformity with Wilhelm's outfit. I, 292-293).

They all look alike in their garish nightclothes. Krey has fully conformed and belongs with them now. He has merely exchanged his phrases for another kind of show. Sternheim inverts the fairy tale and shows that the new clothes are there but the emperor is missing. This is all that remains of their prestige. As they have feared all along, they are now shades, soulless creatures like the new dead in the dance of death, moving willy-nilly to the piper's tune toward the debacle suggested by the title *1913*. Maske's hour of flaming glory has turned out to be an hour of failure and confusion. The "divine harvest" of egoism stands briefly illuminated for the audience to observe. Then the servant turns off the light and the curtain falls on a darkened stage. The contest is over.

The idea of struggle ("Kampf") obsesses all Sternheim's characters and saturates the play. Maske and Sofie battle for prestige and power; Ottilie for erotic domination over Krey; and Philipp Ernst for the title of best dressed man and lady-killer. "Es gilt gegen ein Weib" (I'm off to the fray against a woman), he says to Easton the tailor, challenging him to produce his finest wares (I, 267). At bottom, each is competing for the limelight and to push others off into darkness. To glow or to be in the light is to enjoy prestige. Without it one is nothing. Prinzessin Oels, by the way, the woman against whom Philipp Ernst is going into battle, never does appear at Schloß Buchow. All his tricks and all Easton's sartorial arts are wasted.

The contest is over and all have lost. To tell us this, Sternheim gives his last and most striking signal. The final words of the play, the hackneyed phrase "Leuchte zum großen Ziel" ([I] light the way to the great goal) is the cue for extinguishing all light on stage. This incongruity, like the other dissonances, exaggerations, and ironies of the play, is one of Sternheim's devices to draw his audience into the other struggle, namely, his altercation with evil and folly. Sternheim's satiric fictions are, first, the improbably wealthy, decadent, and vicious Maske household and, second, the transposition of the basic issue—the elevation of ruthlessness to a Weltanschauung—to the realm of fashion. For satiric ends, egotism is reduced and mocked by transforming it into foppery. The blackout just before the curtain falls casts Krey, Philipp Ernst, and the others into total obscurity, the fitting punishment for those whose sole concern was to capture the spotlight.

II. *Die Kassette* [The Strongbox]

The earlier of Sternheim's two serious satiric plays, *Die Kassette* (1912), also dramatizes a battle for prestige fought within the family and develops the same themes: waste, futility, adaptation and the struggle for existence, impotence and violence. A resentful maiden aunt beats down a household revolution; through petty deceit and the power of her money she regains her position of dominance and respect in the house. And she makes fools of the two men who believe they are in charge.

Though there is talk of artillery and bombs here as well, the express sociopolitical significance of *1913* is lacking in *Die Kassette*. Yet, as Siegfried Jacobsohn noted in his review of the Berlin première in 1911, astonishing perspectives open up from the modest action. The three main characters become representatives of a whole social class of powerless people trying to advance themselves by conforming and bowing to authority while indulging in daydreams of omnipotence and ferocity. They confuse ends and means and go to war against one another over the possession of stocks and bonds.[24]

This helps to explain why it provoked audiences to antagonistic responses in 1912, 1946, and as late as 1961.[25] The picture of the average family as a bestiary in which the animals prey on one another in their mad scramble for dominion over money and their fellows is calculated to arouse the spectator. The appearance of Aunt Elsbeth's strongbox containing her fortune of 140,000 Marks in securities sets off the hostilities and turns the house into an inferno. It is her ultimate weapon, the "bomb" (I, 366) with which she intends to defeat the newly arrived threat to her dominance over the household, her niece Fanny Krull. Fanny has just married Krull, the forty-seven year old man of the house, and has plans to depose Elsbeth through him. Her sole weapon is her sexual attraction, which has served her well until now. But she learns that physical appetites are not as strong as the greed for prestige and the desire to rule and exploit others. That is, for these people power is an end in itself and pleasure no consideration.

As the play opens, Krull returns from his honeymoon to find himself the prize in a power struggle between his sensuous wife and his parsimonious, voyeuristic, and seemingly moribund aunt. During acts one and two he presents the pitiable, laughable figure of a pawn in the game between two aggressive women. His efforts to accommodate each consistently fail. To please one, he promises to assert himself against the other. But each confrontation ends with his humble submission. At the end of act two the tension has become so great that he suffers a physical collapse.

Two events in act three show Krull in a new light and give Sternheim's satire its acid bite. In the opening scene Krull reads a draft of Aunt Elsbeth's will, which she has intentionally left for him to discover. It confirms his—false—belief that his wife will inherit the fortune and that he will have control over it. With this trick, Elsbeth wins her battle against Fanny.

Krull is now not so much her victim as he is possessed by the idea of wealth. On reading the terms of the will, he concludes a monologue with the following triumphant words, which in fact announce his intention to toady to his aunt:

> Welch bedeutendes Bewußtsein muß der Besitzende haben, wirklich ins Blut Herr der Schätze zu sein. Das gibt Beschäftigung für lange Winterabende, und ich darf jetzt schon versichern, Tante: ich will ein rechter Besitzer für meine Familie sein. Allen Werten werde ich bis ins Mark ihrer Eigenschaften nachgehen; erkennen, vergleichen, beschließen. Da türmen sich Perspektiven: das Wesen des Wertpapiers, das von Rothschild stammt. Faust zweiten Teil Szene mit dem Kaiser wieder ansehen. Die Judenfrage. Wie reich ist der Besitzende, wie reich! [...] Was die Kurse verbürgen, soll untersucht werden—und mein Schulmeisterelend fällt in den Papierkasten. Ich möchte, Tantchen, dir in diesen Augenblicken sehr lieb tun, und kein Mensch dürfte lachen.[26]

(What a significant consciousness the propertied man must have of being master through and through of the treasures. That will keep me occupied for long winter evenings, and I can assure you, Aunt, I intend to be a proper owner for my family. I intend to pursue all the securities to the core of their qualities; study, compare, decide. The perspectives rise high: the essence of the note that stems from Rothschild. Better look at *Faust, Part Two,* the scene with the emperor. The Jewish question. How rich the propertied man is, how rich! What the rates guarantee shall be investigated— —and my schoolmaster misery falls into the wastebasket. At these moments, Auntie, I'd like to demonstrate my love for you, and no one would dare laugh. I, 409).

Then, in the final scene of act three Aunt Elsbeth secretly bequeaths everything to the church. Thanks to this bit of dramatic irony, the spectator knows from then on that Krull's talk and energies are wasted. His grandiose plans to assert himself are in fact the delusions of a man doomed to bankruptcy. A slip of paper suffices to bring forth the worst in him: his spinelessness and cruelty. By the end of the piece he has forfeited any pity one may have felt for him.

On the one hand, he has subjected himself to years of groveling and self-denial; and he cautiously plans to continue his chameleon-like existence until the coffer is really his. He accepts this as the way of the world, and, after all, conformity is the way to success. He tells his wife: "Rothschild, Donner und Doria, braucht auf niemand Rücksicht zu nehmen, das wissen wir. Unsereinem sind cäsarische Instinkte untersagt. Wir müssen uns strecken, anpassen; das ist Weltordnung. Den habe ich gern, der gegen sie murrt. Welches Kapital von Schmeicheleien und Erniedrigungen habe ich an die wracke Fregatte gewandt, und bin ich weniger als du, mein Stolz geringer?" (Rothschild, thunderation, has no need to be considerate, that we know. Caesarean instincts are forbidden to people like us. We have to comply, to conform; that's the universal rule. I like the man who grumbles against it. What a store ["Kapital"] of flatteries and degradations I have spent on that old wreck, and am I less than you, my pride at all inferior? I, 417).

On the other hand, the prospect of wealth has stiffened his spine. Though he continues to kowtow to Elsbeth with flattery and grotesque caresses, he shows his fangs to others. He becomes more rogue than fool. His habit of knuckling under is revealed to be his device for reaching the top of the heap. Once there, he will be as egoistic and ruthless as he expects others to be. To adapt is to attack, as Sternheim noted in 1902.[27] Krull's monologue in act four, scene seven leaves no doubt about this:

> Stark aber, voll Hochgefühls, strecke ich aus dem Schein des Ansehens, das der Besitz verleiht, vorwärts in die Welt meine Fänge gegen die Menschen und lasse sie aus ihrer Demut vor der Chimäre tanzen.
> Mit den Veitstänzen der hablosen Habgierigen, dem Festgebrüll der Unwissenden und Hungerigen um mich, lasse ich die stündliche Angst um die Unsicherheit meines Besitzes mir betäuben. Denn ob Bayern, ob Elektrizitätsaktien—das Wesen deines Schatzes bin ich, und die Frage ist, amüsieren dich meine Kapriolen hinreichend zu vier Prozent? Doch ich schwöre mit der Kraft meiner Seele: nicht vergeblich erkannte ich das; bleibe nicht mäßig, sondern folge dir; und mein Stolz soll sein, wo du mäßig genießt, muß mein Genuß an meinen Objekten über Grenzen unmäßig werden. Aus einer Vergangenheit von dreißig Jahren in künstlicher Demut wuchs Wille, Menschen zu meiner Wollust auszubeuten.

(Strong, however, full of exaltation, I will stretch my claws out from the gleam of prestige bestowed by ownership forward into the world toward people and make them dance in submission before the chimaera. With the St. Vitus dances of the covetous beggars, with the festive roars of the ignorant and hungry about me, I'll anaesthetize my hourly fears about the insecurity of my ownership. For whether Bavaria or Electricity stocks—the essence of your treasure is me, and the question is: do my capers amuse you sufficiently for four percent? But I swear with the force of my soul: I didn't learn that in vain; will not remain idle but will follow you; and it will be my pride that where you enjoy in moderation, my pleasure in my objects will be immoderate beyond all limits. Out of a past of thirty years of feigned humility has grown the will to exploit others to my own sensual gratification. I, 441-42).

Here again Sternheim's bourgeois bares his breast and reveals his unvarnished self realizing his "sometimes brutal nuance," prostituting himself in order one day to prostitute the world. Whether he is accommodating or exploiting, his power derives from the semblance of prestige, the chimaera before which he, like his intended victims, dances.

The brief farcical scene that follows the monologue and closes act four reminds us that Krull has been delivering his tirade outside the bedroom where his wife lies with the photographer Seidenschnur. By the time the play is done, Krull has sacrificed not only his own manhood but also his wife and daughter to the strongbox, that fetish which he now takes to bed with him.

The events of act five demonstrate the effectiveness of the "Schein" (a pun: glow or appearance) of prestige. Krull, speaking in tones his aunt used in act one, uses the power contained in the strongbox to turn his new son-in-law, Seidenschnur, into his court jester: "Aus Ihrer romantischen Veranlagung lassen sich hübsche Überraschungen hoffen. Bisher war unsere Ausbeute mager. Hoffentlich haben Sie heute einen tüchtigen Schuß auf der Pfanne" (We can look forward to some nice surprises from your romantic talents. Our yield has been meager so far. I hope you've got a good shot ready to fire. I, 448). This is Seidenschnur's position in the microcosm of the household. His indignation at this degradation sends him raging after Krull. But like every other attempt at independent, liberating action in this play, this ends with a pratfall. And by the play's end he has joined the dance around the casket.

At first glance, the figure of Seidenschnur seems designed to provide comic relief. He appears to stand on the outskirts of the main action, preening himself and playing Don Juan. His vanity and foppery remind one of Philipp Ernst in *1913*. And like Philipp Ernst, he is a walking symbol, complementing the coffer, of the dangerous, glittering superficiality that the play attacks. This mediocre photographer thinks of himself as a "gottbegnadeter Künstler" (divinely favored artist, I, 367), Michelangelo, Phidias. He seduces Krull's daughter with literary quotations, allusions to *Romeo and Juliet,* and talk of Nirvana. On their honeymoon he dallies with chambermaids. He is alone on the stage at the end; and as the final curtain falls, he is walking off in a state of trance, dreaming of certain affluence. The action of act five, Seidenschnur's return from his honeymoon and eventual surrender to the spell of the strongbox, works like an accelerated travesty of Krull's earlier struggle and defeat. The course of events is much the same; but the tone is more vulgar. The pattern of the vicious circle once more suggests that we are witnessing a *danse macabre* into which the new dead are drawn willy-nilly and from which there is no escape.

Krull has refused to accept the reality of his miserable schoolmaster's existence and has constructed a new one based on a few pieces of paper that don't belong to him. Satire of all ages has shown the folly and consequences of the yearning for excitement and escape from boredom. Wedekind infected his figures—Lulu, Effie, Hetmann—with it. In this case, Krull's mania for diversion seems to be satisfied and his wishes fulfilled at the play's end. It appears that the fools have become kings, the poor rich, the weak strong. The drama's action has progressed through steps one and two of the satiric rhythm, from purpose to the height of passion. A deprived and humiliated Krull is transformed into a tiger through the catalytic action of the box and all the power with which his imagination has invested it.

This is the point at which, in these satiric plays, the dunces become vicious. They abuse their new found freedom and power. Krull is persuaded that his dream is realized. He feels the glow and semblance of prestige, and he uses it to dominate Seidenschnur, who in turn does not hesitate to bare his claws. The "true Jacob" emerges ever more clearly as the play progresses. To be sure, his rhetoric is bellicose, but there is no real force behind it. He is a citizen of Sternheim's bourgeois *juste milieu*, who, though locked into an inescapable natural mechanism and having only the minutest range of movement, is intoxicated by his own unexampled aggression (VI, 118).

The audience knows that both are deluded. They move like sleepwalkers toward the third step of the figure, the great disappointment that will come when Aunt Elsbeth's true will is read. Their present power and prosperity are borrowed; they reside in the credit they enjoy in the eyes of others. They will continue alternately to threaten and cower until they discover they have gained nothing. Unlike most satirists, Sternheim here withholds the final reckoning. But there is no doubt that it will come. The conclusion is nevertheless frustrating and anticlimactic. Some audiences kept their seats after the final curtain, expecting to enjoy the resolution in a final scene. But the satirist Sternheim purposely denied this satisfaction. That is why he merely laughed when Albert Bassermann, who played the role of Krull in the première, recommended adding a theatrically powerful scene in which Krull inherits the box after all. The effect of the play is frustrating, and frustration is its basic theme. That's why the final moments of the play are dominated by the figure of Fanny Krull. In eager anticipation she repeatedly opens her bedroom door, only to be ignored, first by her husband and then by her lover, Seidenschnur, whose minds and hearts are occupied solely by the strongbox.

Once again a secondary figure and a seemingly secondary issue crowd the primary ones aside. In *1913* it was Philipp Ernst and his clothes. Here it is Seidenschnur, a ridiculously foppish yet potentially evil character. Sternheim has given him some of his own weaknesses and vices: the obsession with dress and outward appearance as well as his erotomania. Seidenschnur is a professional photographer and deals in counterfeits of reality. His sole talent is mimicry. He is a bad painter. In all his activities he is concerned not with substance or style for its own sake but with what others will think of him, his image. Though he fears loss of face most of all, he is nevertheless so pliant that he quickly consents to play the role of court fool in Krull's household, a role which finds its counterpart in Krull's fawning attendance on his aunt. Because they have next to no freedom to act, they deal in semblances. Their speeches are built of clichés and quotations.

They take seriously the slogans of others as well as the paper contents of the strongbox. Sternheim's purpose is to show the audience the banality of these figures and, more important, the danger they represent because their cast of mind is shared by so many.

In his autobiography Sternheim tells of the loathing he felt for Berlin when he returned there around 1902:

> Everything false and unacceptable that had emerged meanwhile had asserted itself in Germany's capital city.
> In that world a mixture of petit bourgeois, proletarians had become the people [Volk], whose neck had been broken at the end of the last century by the double catastrophe: Darwin, Einstein, the machine; *on top of it all resided the upper classes, who were living in luxury.* But even in them there was no longer any intent to excel; they did their mimicry in a different way, which protective device Darwin had shown to operate in the raging struggle for existence (X/1,226. Sternheim's italics).[28]

1913, the more ambitious of the two plays in its choice of material, has from its publication in 1915 been admired by critics, dramaturges, and even the Berlin Police censor, who nevertheless recommended it not be performed publicly during wartime.

Siegfried Jacobsohn reviewed the printed version of the play in 1915, five years before the drama reached the stage. With high praise for its potential theatrical effectiveness, especially in the final scene, he argued that though it mocked some German types and for that reason had been censored, it had inherent therapeutic value. Sternheim is, he wrote, "an artist filled with repugnance toward foul air and with the unconquerable inclination to offend idols, show up the vacuity of the fakes [...]".[29]

In 1960, Friedrich Luft, dean of postwar Berlin reviewers, wrote a critique of Hans Lietzau's production in the Schiller Theater, in which he judged it to be at best a worthwhile effort. In his evaluation of the text, however, he waxes dithyrambic, praising Sternheim's explosive, metallic intensity and providing an insightful appreciation:

> They [Sternheim's figures] are like raving mad machines racing into one another and toward their destruction. The humor that produces clearly has a sadistic strain. Annihilation is ordained and loved.
> *1913* is surely not the best of his comic flings. In this one he pours out satiric acid with both hands. The corrosive force of his mockery sprays over the dullness of the materialists, over the matadors of the Economic Miracle before the First World War.[30]

Luft also values the objectivity and balance of Sternheim's vision and points to the other side of the medal: Wilhelm Krey's blue-eyed, antirational, Teutonic idealism. "Sternheim's prophetic disposition," he writes, "saw where things were headed. The play gives you the shivers even in places that make you laugh. A person shudders at this clear evil eye."[31]

The conflicts at the heart of *1913,* one between the generations and the other between visionary idealism and practicality, have by no means gone out of date. Yet *Die Kassette* has enjoyed the better productions and provoked noisier response from audiences. The play slipped through the meshes of censorship, probably because it reads superficially like a drawingroom or bedroom farce in the French boulevard tradition. From the start it was a stage success and the occasion for "Theaterskandale," especially when skilled actors, such as Albert Bassermann in the première of 1912 and Theo Lingen in 1960/61, had the lead role.

With some relish, Sternheim gives a vivid account of scenes in Munich's staid Residenztheater on the night of March 25, 1912:

> Under Albert Steinrück's direction with him in the lead role of Krull and with the actors in the remaining roles there broke out—after the audience had shown clearly as early as the opening moments that the play went beyond anything on the stage they had ever been subjected to—such stormy scenes during the last act that they threw hard objects at the actors on the stage as they whistled and howled; and the iron curtain had to be lowered. *Opponents and supporters came to blows in the Mozart Festival hall* (X/1, 278, Sternheim's italics).[32]

This audience had grasped the play's intent altogether correctly and answered aesthetic aggression with the real thing. As if to taunt the spectators and to keep tempers hot, Sternheim himself appeared repeatedly on stage to take curtain calls. To add to his malicious satisfaction, the presence in the theater of several members of the royal court of Bavaria made the riot a sensation all over Germany. It set off a "mortar barrage" in newspapers of all sympathies against the man they thought responsible, Baron von Speidel, general manager of the Munich State Theater (X/1, 278).

In 1920 the Vienna Burgtheater, an even more conservative and aristocratic institution, added *Die Kassette* to its repertoire and gave the premiere performance on June 2. This was the Burgtheater's first and last Sternheim evening. It provoked a "Skandal" unique in the history of the house. The spectators began making disruptive noises during the second act. Ignoring the growing tumult and cries of "Stop the play!" the performers carried on to the end. Then, as some members of the audience engaged in fisticuffs to settle disagreements, the director, Paulsen, stepped to the front of the stage holding a telegram from Sternheim. Paulsen announced, "I have the honor of thanking you in the name of Mr. Carl Sternheim." (Ich habe die Ehre, Ihnen im Namen von Herrn Carl Sternheim zu danken.) This brought unanimity out of division, and the theater was filled with an ear-splitting chorus of boos, catcalls, and whistles.[33] The production was moved to a less prestigious Viennese house and there experienced a successful run.

The response of the Burgtheater and Residenztheater audiences was by no means atypical. Early productions in smaller cities, specifically Mannheim and Magdeburg, were judged by audiences and critics to be indecent, wantonly and destructively negative, and in violation of all principles of art and culture.

The opening night in Munich of Rudolf Noelte's 1960 production on tour proved to be another high point in the stage history of this, Sternheim's coldest, most hate-filled attack on the Wilhelmine bourgeoisie and the human animal. He would have been pleased by the excitement. Forgetting the Vienna "Skandal" of 1920, Joachim Kaiser, theater critic for the *Süddeutsche Zeitung,* ends his account of that evening in Munich with the words: "What audiences have failed to do since 1912 a few Munichers made up for 39 years later."[34] As Kaiser describes it, some spectators were uttering loud expressions of displeasure early on. Then people in the balcony began to shout and curse at one another. Many others were then angered at this disruption. Kaiser notes that the protest was loudest at points where Sternheim criticized what were taken to be specifically German character traits most bitterly and that the troublemakers were not chauvinists or anti-Semites but rather young people who were wounded by the aggressive irony. They rejected the play, he opines, as morally and ideologically bad theater out of enlightened, German, Christian, sophisticated indignation.

The same noisy group that could follow in quiet reverence the sufferings of Grischa along with Brecht's irreverences in *The Caucasian Chalk Circle* here cried out at Sternheim's sting. They were angry not, as is usually the case, because the play seemed poorly made and played but because of its message and the character of Krull. Sternheim succeeded very well in insulting cultivated and morally concerned audiences like Burgtheater first-nighters and liberal or leftish Munich students.

The sociology and psychology of theater audiences would have to be reformulated with each new generation; but it seems clear at least that an audience's quarrel with a performance rarely arises from disappointed expectations with regard to the play's form or content. For most, the theater is a kind of haven where one can find release from the constraints of daily life, where one can identify with an idol or ideal on the stage, and where one can indulge the inclination to phantasize by projecting oneself into the events and characters on stage.[35] What wonder then that spectators vent their anger by booing, rioting, and whistling at plays like *Die Kassette,* Wedekind's *Schloß Wetterstein,* or Dürrenmatt's *Frank V.* Not only do they provide no acceptable role models or ideals, quite the contrary. But the expectation that one will be carried away by inspiration and the excitement of tense dramatic action and its resolution seems blatantly and intentionally frustrated. In fact, the very idea of indulging in daydreams and wish-fulfillment phantasies is made to seem consonant with sin and evil.

Sternheim's satiric bite comes in large part from his use of language. Satire, as I said before, is a profoundly rhetorical mode and often makes use of the insight that the corruption of language is symptomatic of deep cultural infections. The dialogue of *Die Kassette* and *1913* is an exaggerated, drastically condensed, but poetically accurate rendering of the way people spoke in the early years of this century: a mélange, as befits satire, of the stilted and snotty Prussian officers' club jargon that set the tone outside the military as well together with Rhine romanticism, fashionable literary allusions drawn from Nietzsche, Wagner, and Weininger, and conversational clichés, all of which cast contemporary patterns of thought and prejudice into high relief.[36] Sternheim had first-hand acquaintance with the military manner of speaking. In 1902 he served, like so many middle-class Germans, as a reserve officer and joined the prestigious first squadron of the Sixth Kürassierregiment Kaiser von Rußland. His constitution was too weak to stand up under army regimen, and his one-year training program was cut short by a medical discharge. He also associated with important people in the arts, journalism, and industry (Harry Graf Kessler, Hugo von Hofmannsthal, Walther Rathenau), and he consequently knew the latest gossip as well as the most up-to-date slang.

Sternheim's plays are, in their action and stylistically, redolent of political, industrial, and everyday life in Germany and Europe as it had developed since the 1860s and '70s. The historian Gerhard Ritter describes this European cultural and historical process that parallels the plot of *1913*.[37] He notes that Bismarck's quick victories in the 1860s and 1870s were an inspiration to the military throughout Europe and led to ever increasing arms competition. Bismarck's reasoned idea of *Realpolitik* gave way to aggressive passion. Military and patriotic ambition, the yearning for power obsessed both liberals and conservatives. The Second Moroccan Crisis of 1911 only excited a demand for faster armament.

Sternheim's Baron Christian Maske von Buchow is a man of the Bismarck era, of the "Gründerzeit." He is a builder, an industrialist, and a patriot. His daughter Countess Sofie von Beeskow is representative of the following generation. She admires the accomplishments of her father and other "founders" but is mistaken in her interpretation of their success. The newcomers, and this includes Kaiser Wilhelm II, began to confuse power with violence and threats of military action.

As slogans about world power, sea power, a place in the sun, and the rights of young and growing nations gained circulation so grew the prestige of the officer class. Carl Zuckmayer's play *Der Hauptmann von Köpenick* [The Captain from Köpenick, 1931] based on real events in Berlin in 1906 and earlier, gives a comic and rather harmless picture of the way Germans, and not only Germans, respected and mimicked the way of the army officer. A tour of duty as an officer, especially in an elite unit, was a requirement for status in civilian life. In the Wilhelmine era, when power and prestige were the most admired qualities, the uniform or other outward evidence of a military background commanded blind respect. The Zabern incident is one symptom of the degree to which members of the officer corps had been corrupted by unquestioning adulation. One could identify the reserve officer by the speech mannerisms he affected. His terse, near monosyllabic, impersonal, aggressive, arrogant tone—not unlike Sternheim's essayistic prose style—was unmistakable.

Friedrich Nietzsche attributed the rising popularity of "Offizier-Deutsch" among Germans of all stations to its aristocratic sound and understood well the process by which it affected ways of thinking and acting. In paragraph 104 of *Die fröhliche Wissenschaft* [*The Gay Science,* 1886] he writes:

> It is certain the Germans are now becoming militarized in the sound of their language, it is probable that, once they are habituated to speak militarily, they will ultimately write that way too. For becoming accustomed to certain sounds affects the character deeply:—first one has the words and phrases and finally also the thoughts that conform to this sound.[38]

The members of the political-military-industrial complex ruling Germany in the early 1900s were inclined to concur with social Darwinist and militaristic trends. These board chairmen, ministers of state, newspaper tycoons, and generals are the marks for Sternheim's satire in *1913*. At the level of gossip, he used the audience's certain awareness of scandal in high places. His foppish Philipp Ernst Maske is at least a fictional relative of Philipp (nicknamed Phili) Fürst zu Eulenburg und Hertefelt, fawning confidant of the Kaiser until 1906, when the publicist gadfly Maximilian Harden started a press campaign that exposed him as a homosexual.

Members of the power elite of 1913 were apparently still recognizable to audiences as late as 1960. Ernst Schröder, who acted the part of Christian Maske, affected the dress, manner, and coiffure of Alfred Hugenberg, the man who in 1913 was chairman of the board at Krupp, was later a minister in the imperial government, and in the 1920s became Germany's most influential media tycoon, controlling newspapers, press services, and UFA, the major film company. He was recognized by his sergeant's mustache and brush haircut.

From Harry Graf Kessler comes a suggestion concerning the real-life inspiration for the figure of Wilhelm Krey:

> In the evening Sternheim's *1913* at the Kammerspiele. With great comic and dramatic force Sternheim has exposed the decisive factors in the structure of the German nation before the war. Krai [*sic*] is [Gustav] Stresemann in his developing years, the "teutonic" youth with poetic ambitions who is "corrupted" by a rich industrialist's daughter, not by a wanton (*cocotte*) as conventionally happens. A strong and deep play.[39]

In the first manuscript version of his autobiography Sternheim lumped Stresemann together with Ebert and Hitler as lower-class opportunists and *arrivistes* on the model of Molière's Tartuffe. Sternheim's scorn was directed at the younger Stresemann, who, before the Kapp Putsch of 1920 persuaded him of the advantages of constitutional government, had been a man of the right: a monarchist, an uncritical supporter of Chancellor von Bülow—another object of Sternheim's loathing, as will be explained shortly—and of the military. Stresemann became Chancellor in 1923 at the height of Germany's disastrous inflation and in the six years of his career as cabinet member, up to his death in 1929, did more than any other political figure to stabilize the Mark and preserve democratic institutions in the Weimar Republic.

Mentioned nowhere in Sternheim's work but surely familiar to him is Walter Flex (1887-1917), whose *Der Wanderer zwischen beiden Welten* [The Wanderer Between Both Worlds, 1917], a book about a much admired comrade in arms, was long a best seller and was understood to convey the quintessence of German youth's sentiment and idealistic fervor. In all his writings—he had earlier been an unsuccessful playwright—Flex exhorted young people to remain pure and be prepared to sacrifice themselves for the higher cause: the German nation. He addressed his message to the youth because the older generation, the parties of both the Right and the Left were, in his eyes, indifferent to the national good. "I see only two great economic interests," he wrote, "agriculture and industry, which fight each other in the name of conservatism and liberalism and exploit the idealism of the masses with patriotic or democratic phrases."[40] Flex did much of his writing in the years 1910-1914 when he was a tutor in the Bismarck household in Varzin and Friedrichsruh. This fact, along with his ideological stance and "obsessed pen," makes it altogether probable that Sternheim endowed his Wilhelm Krey with the position and ideas of Walter Flex.

The figure of Krey, the outwardly idealistic yet power hungry chauvinist, is the one that for post-World War II audiences most chills the spine. For Sternheim too he is a dangerous fool. But Sternheim's sharpest attack is reserved for a different prey, people in power obsessed with prestige. He has his sights on Kaiser Wilhelm II, to be sure, but more specifically on the people under him who fostered his lust for glory and thereby enhanced their own (X/1, 222-223). Two in whom this obsession was strongest were Prince Bernhard von Bülow (1849-1929) and Alfred Hugenberg (1865-1951). Both were practiced manipulators of public opinion.

Von Bülow, Sternheim writes, was swollen with envy, malice, and fatuous arrogance (X/1, 231). Initially brought into prominence by the backing of his patron, Philipp Eulenburg, he was Chancellor of the Reich from 1900 until 1909, in those years Sternheim called the worst of his life. He was known to be a braggart and a bootlick; he never contradicted the Kaiser in public. He memorized his

Reichstag speeches in such a way that his quotes from classical authors would seem spontaneous and make him seem learned. He was always primarily concerned with his effect on others, and his public relations staff, charged with the official task of representing imperial policy, in fact devoted much of its energy to generating publicity for von Bülow himself, at his express direction.

This was not unadulterated vanity. Von Bülow was one of the first to study and develop the art of influencing public opinion systematically and on a grand scale. The press secretary of the foreign office, a contemporary, wrote: "History knows no statesman who occupied himself as indefatigably and urgently with public opinion as Prince von Bülow."[41] Others may have eclipsed his accomplishment since; yet he deserves recognition as a pioneer in the field.

The fall of the historical von Bülow reads like the plot of Sternheim's satire. He was brought low by the monster he helped create, namely, public opinion as aroused by a newspaper story. In 1908 the *London Daily Telegraph* published an interview with Kaiser Wilhelm II, in which with characteristic bluster he took credit for preventing a Russian attack against England and for having given the British advice on strategy that brought the Boer War to an end. The interview not only threatened to worsen Germany's relations with England and Russia; it was also sure to show the world that the Kaiser was an irresponsible fool. Wilhelm had been cautious enough to submit a copy of the interview to von Bülow before authorizing publication, but the Chancellor had ignored it. A mere three hours after the interview appeared in London,the *Berliner Zeitung am Mittag* (BZ) had published the text of the Kaiser's interview that so damaged his already tarnished image at home and abroad. This all happened so fast that von Bülow was unable to suppress the news and had to bear the blame for the disaster. The Kaiser came close to a nervous breakdown and considered abdication. He never forgave von Bülow for this sin of omission and dismissed his faithless chancellor at the first opportunity.[42]

Alfred Hugenberg, one of Wedekind's victims in *Erdgeist,* becomes important again for *1913.* And the reasons why Ernst Schröder chose to mimic him on the stage in 1960 become clear and persuasive when one considers his brilliant career. Hugenberg served here as representative of the new order and new generation of entrepreneurs, who, like Hugo Stinnes and August Thyssen, were "personally more ruthless and more familiar with the niceties of capital management than the older generation represented by Krupp, Stumm, Vögeler [...]."[43] He worked also to reinforce the close link in Germany between business and politics. Until 1933 he held positions of power in both, moving with apparent ease from one to the other. In his early years he served on government commissions and was co-founder of the Alldeutscher Verband (The Pan-German League, AV), a right-wing political-cultural organization with the motto "Remember that you are a German." The historian Winfried Baumgart provides a sketch of its ideological tenets which reads like a catalogue of the things Sternheim most abhorred:

> The Pan-German ideology is a mixture of social Darwinism as popularized by
> Haeckel, Paul de Lagarde's theories about the German race, and Friedrich Tatzel's
> on *Lebensraum,* but also Nietzsche's ideas about the "superman," about the "mas-
> ter race," about the "will to power," in general of all imaginable intellectual frag-
> ments of vitalist philosophy, voluntarism, irrationalism, and materialism. The line
> leading from here to the intellectual trash heap of National Socialism is
> unmistakable.[44]

Hugenberg had judged well the temper of the times. By 1905 the league had
130,000 members. Many of these belonged originally to academic youth groups
which chose to merge with the AV. Then he switched his allegiance from the
youth movement to the military-industrial complex; for after serving briefly in
the Ministry of Finance, Hugenberg became in 1907 director of a large Frankfurt
bank. From 1909 to 1918 he was chairman of the board at the Krupp
Corporation.

Yet it was in the realm of public relations, the communications media, and
what had become the "Bewußtseinsindustrie" (consciousness industry) that he
celebrated his greatest victories. The first came in April of 1913 when he was
asked by Alfred Krupp to quash the bribery scandal that Karl Liebknecht, a
Social-Democratic delegate, had revealed to the Reichstag. The head of Krupp's
Berlin office had purchased illegally the state's own price estimates for a sizable
contract so that Krupp could underbid the competition. Hugenberg saw to it that
the matter soon disappeared from the newspapers and was referred to a hand-
picked Reichstag investigative committee, where it could be quietly buried. The
committee saw no need for state control of the munitions industry. Krupp
received further support shortly thereafter when a much enlarged military
appropriation was passed for the forthcoming year. In response to this encouragement and doubtless out of patriotism, the firm continued to expand its munitions capacity so that it reached a point far beyond peacetime needs by
mid-1914.[45]

To follow the story to its end, Hugenberg, like von Bülow and Sternheim's fictional Maske family, recognized that newspapers, film, and the wire services
were the instruments of power and began in 1916 to build his conglomerate, later
known as the Hugenberg-Konzern. After World War I he got the financial support of Stinnes and other big industrialists in exchange for his offer to improve
their image at home and abroad. As his empire grew, Hugenberg used it in the
service of his right-wing Deutschnationale Volkspartei and in opposition to the
parliamentary institutions of the Weimar Republic. He was confident he could
absorb and exploit the Nazi party. The Nazis, however, had learned well from
Hugenberg and outdid him with cruder and totally unscrupulous methods. In

1933 they dissolved his party and decreed that his "Konzern" was now property of the state. This is poetic justice of a sort. Hugenberg continued his public career as a member of the puppet Reichstag until 1945. But the consequences of his manipulations were far worse than anything he could have imagined, once the coordination, or amalgamation of industry, party, and military became no longer tacit but official.

The rich topical allusiveness of *1913* was in all likelihood one of the reasons the army's high command and, at its suggestion, the Berlin Police censor withheld permission for public performance during the war years. Krupp and Maske, Phili Eulenburg and Philipp Ernst were identifiable as close kin, if not as perfect doubles. Sternheim's great accomplishment, however, is that he captured the chaos and vulgarity that prevailed in Germany's power elite, along with the unexamined habits of mind that made them so alarming, in his family drama and reduced the whole complex to a masquerade in modish costume.

1913 marked a turning point in the development of German industry. Newspaper firms had been expanding just as rapidly as the munitions companies, the German economy as a whole, and the country's population. Between 1871 and 1914 the number of inhabitants rose by 61%, and the national wealth grew to be greater than that of England or France. Berlin, with 3.7 million people, became larger than Paris. These hard data are cited by Sternheim's Maske. The trouble in 1913 was that a recession was in progress, the Kaiser's foreign policy had made more enemies than friends, making a two-front war inevitable, and the opposition's activity, of which the Krupp scandal was symptomatic, was growing more effective. Industry and government leaders devoted themselves more and more to mobilization and radicalization of public opinion in support of the nation's and the Kaiser's prestige. Trapped by circumstances of their own making, without power to take decisive action, these leaders together with the mobilized right—not merely of Germany—were therefore able to vent their frustration only within very narrow limits.

Similarly, Oberlehrer Krull's and Seidenschnur's aggressions are confined to family power struggles and daydreams. For the Maskes, as for Hugenberg and the imperial government, the prize was favorable public opinion, and the weapons were press releases and interviews. In the play, Maske's conversion to Catholicism or in real life, rumors of homosexuality in court circles and the Krupp family: these were bombshells in the struggles to enhance and destroy images.

In 1866, Berlin had 700,000 inhabitants and ten newspapers. In 1914, for 3.7 million there were thirty daily morning papers; an additional ten appeared as evening editions; and there were some fifty smaller local dailies.[46] The newspaper was the mass medium for the "Bewußtseinsindustrie" that developed during the Wilhelmine era. The keen competition for readers and profits encouraged investment in linotype machines, rotation presses, and techniques for making plates from photographs. To use the plant to full capacity and to make it pay, more newspaper editions had to appear at different times of day—evening and noon—and bring not merely the latest reports but enough sensation to establish a market.

The *Berliner Zeitung am Mittag,* for instance, was founded to keep presses from lying idle. It was an immediate success because it was designed to sell itself on the street with short, spicy items. Editorial policy was merely to provide enough sensational material so that buying it would become a habit.[47] It was the *B. Z. am Mittag,* "the fastest newspaper in the world," that scooped all the other German journals in 1908 with the publication of the full text of the Kaiser's unfortunate *Daily Telegraph* interview, before von Bülow could take measures to hush things up. Journals like the *B. Z. am Mittag,* together with the wire services, were glad enough to serve the Maskes, daughter and father, in their tooth and nail battle for prestige.

Sternheim notes in his essay "Berlin oder Juste Milieu" that for the average Berliner reality was determined by the daily press. It existed only in newspapers and the minds of their readers. Reporters were viewed, and acted, as seers and ultimate authorities. In the words of the essay: "If something improbable, irrational, happened to take place, it remained unmentioned in the press and consequently didn't exist at all. Journalists had long since learned that things they didn't speak about were not to be found in the brains of Berliners either. That doesn't exist! [in Berlin dialect]" (VI, 133).[48]

With good reason then Wedekind makes his Dr. Schön a newspaper publisher. By manipulating public opinion, Schön creates a market for the mediocre paintings of Lulu's second husband and promotes Lulu's undeserved reputation as a dancer. His primary concern on the occasion of the painter's gory suicide is to keep the scandal out of the newspapers (II. vi).

As early as the 1890s the press had created an appetite for sensation and a cast of mind that was satisfied only by shocking and provocative news. The weekly illustrateds—the first one, the *Berliner Illustrirte Zeitung,* was founded in 1890 and had by 1900 a circulation of over 100,000 and by 1906 six times that—fed readers' daydreams and whetted their appetites for excitement. Lulu's exploits, like Jack the Ripper's, would have been ideal material for them. The proven combination of folksy hometown sentiment, movie-star love life, and limitless financial and political power that makes up the existence of Claire Zachanassian in Dürrenmatt's *Besuch der alten Dame* is a kind of collage drawn from these organs and represents a phantasy of the exotic life with general appeal.

The newspapers of course are merely the weapons with which Maske and his daughter Sofie wage war against one another. Clues to the intellectual maladies that so disturbed Sternheim must be sought elsewhere. A remarkably fine source is the collection of reports and essays edited by D. Sarason and entitled *Das Jahr 1913: Ein Gesamtbild der Kulturentwicklung* [The Year 1913: An Overview of Cultural Developments, 1913].[49] The report on political events mentions the Krupp bribery scandal, to be sure, but makes much more of the public-opinion victory of the conservative ideology as reflected in a larger military budget. General Bernhardi in his report on the army says that as a result of the Moroccan crisis public opinion backs the proposal to increase the military budget. Events in Morocco and the Balkans, he says, make war seem imminent. Interest in the psychology and personality of the capitalistic entrepreneur was strong in these years. Specifically, Werner Sombart and Lujo Brentano were still taking issue with Max Weber's *Protestant Ethic and the Spirit of Capitalism* (1905).[50] And the article on psychology by W. Stern in Sarason's omnibus volume views with alarm the growth of the Freudian "sect" and calls it a threat to the common welfare.

Aside from sociology, two new social sciences are mentioned repeatedly in Sarason's text: eugenics and the economics of people ("Menschenökonomie"). The latter treats humans as an economic resource and aims to solve the population problem Maske sums up as that caused by sixty million "Fresser." Taylorism as presented in Frederick Winslow Taylor's *Scientific Management* (German version, 1913), the rationalizing of work in factories with the help of time and work studies, was viewed as a practical application of "Menschenökonomie."

The science of eugenics is also a way of dealing with human problems in an abstract and potentially inhuman way. The ideas described in Sarason's book are the ones abused later in the Nazi period to justify euthanasia and genocide. Improvements in medicine and health care, so these racial hygienists argue, have a contra-selective effect and work to undermine the national health in the long run.

In its survey of sociological studies, Sarason's book registers yet another variant of Darwinism prevalent in the scientific literature of the time, namely the idea that the principle of struggle ("das Kampfprinzip") is essential to cultural growth and that we should refrain from sentimental interference with the mechanism of natural selection wherever it may operate. Sternheim shows how it operates within the family.

This composite of Darwinian and Nietzschean ideas was, for Sternheim and his Maske, quickened by the work of the philosopher Max Stirner (1806-1856). Stirner's work went for many years unheeded until John Henry McKay reawakened interest in him with his biography of Stirner around the turn of the century. The third edition of McKay's book appeared in 1913. Stirner's *Der Einzige und sein Eigentum* [The Individual and his Ownership], published originally in 1844 and then in Leipzig by Reclam in 1892, could have served as Christian Maske's Bible. It can be likened to Macchiavelli's *Prince* recast for those who would rule in industry and commerce. It is a philosophy of pure, solipsistic self-possession and egotism based on the assumption that because each is concerned solely with his own welfare, he will collide with others and have to fight ("kämpfen") to assert himself.[51] In forceful language Stirner exhorts his readers to adopt "laws of egoism," to act according to the dictum "might is right," and to subscribe to the ethics of power and self-serving. Stirner's prose style and his antialtruistic ideas are Christian Maske's as well, down to the observation on prestige: "Sieh Dich als mächtiger an, als wofür man Dich ausgibt, so hast Du mehr Macht; sieh Dich als mehr an, so hast Du mehr" (Look on yourself as more powerful than you are reputed to be, then you will have more power; look on yourself as more, then you will have more).

These are some of the sources of Maske's self-image and of his saber-rattling metaphors. His speech and manner are constant assertions of dominance and ownership. On the other hand, Sternheim shows us he is inwardly weak. Maske, and Germany, have reached the point where, to cite Hannah Arendt, "[...] loss of power becomes a temptation to substitute violence for power [...] and [...] violence itself results in impotence."[52]

The second ideological complex, the one behind Wilhelm Krey's propaganda slogans, is also at bottom a form of Darwinism and in the end, as Sternheim shows, a weapon in this world where, according to Max Stirner, there exist only two sorts of people: victors and victims. On the one hand, Krey seeks to overturn the existing power structure, place himself in charge, and avenge himself on those who thwarted him. In this he is a classical embodiment of Nietzsche's "Ressentiment." In his revulsion at the brutality of commercial competition and his advocation of "vaterländische Verbrüderung," however, he represents not Maske's "tooth and claw version of natural selection" but the new wave of "Darwinian collectivism of the nationalist or racist variety."[53] He uses the Darwinist perception that group cohesion and solidarity are aids to survival to support aggressive policies of foreign expansion and the idea of racial superiority.

Dr. Alfred Hugenberg's *Alldeutscher Verband* and the *Wandervogel,* both founded in the 1890s were two of the primary organs of this countercultural movement. Their manner was revolutionary, but the ideas were reactionary. These and comparable confederations organized bonfires, torchlight parades, and mass meetings in the cause of nationalism and racial consciousness. The *Zupfgeigenhansl,* official *Wandervogel* songbook, says in the introduction to its 1915 edition: "The war has proved the *Wandervogel* right, has placed its profound national basic idea free of all non-essentials, strong and bright, in our midst. We must grow increasingly German. Hiking is the most German of all instincts, is our basic essence, is the mirror of our whole national character."[54] Even abstinence from liquor and tobacco, so important in the statement emerging from the great convocation on the Hohe Meißner in 1913, is presented as a national or Nordic trait. Capitalists in the urban world, non-Germans, that is, used alcohol and nicotine. Pure-blooded Germans did not. The admonition to shun stimulants is about the only concrete statement the youth organizations agreed on. The grandiose convention ended with an anticlimax.

Ernst Troeltsch's report on "Religion" in Sarason's *1913* recognizes these two strands, anarchistic and communal, of Darwinism in all civilized lands, except perhaps for America. He brings them both under the heading of what he calls "The New Romanticism" and writes: "In this Romanticism, as in the old one, there appear to some extent anarchistic-subjectivistic features which were brought to greatest power by Nietzsche and have, in modern times, been bolstered Darwinistically, and for the remainder the yearning for community and mystic unity of the will."[55] Troeltsch remarks that Alfred Weber and Walther Rathenau have also sensed a revival of religiosity, a new spirit of mysticism and prophecy that "unites Christian depth of feeling, Nietzschean worldliness, and social innovation and has the flame and the Cross as its dual symbol." Germans and Europeans yearn, they believe, to find an antidote to the arid materialism of their lives.

The *Alldeutsche Blätter,* the organ of the Alldeutscher Verband, published in its 1914 issue an exhortation, clearly in anticipation of the outbreak of war, in religious tones calling on Germans to renounce commercial profit and to prepare themselves spiritually *and* militarily for the great battle soon to come:

> Whoever tries intentionally to veil the high seriousness of a not distant future because he fears it will weaken us economically is sinning unspeakably grievously against the German nation ("Volk"), he is to be charged with high treason against the German nation. We will hold our own in the great decisive struggle ("Kampf") only if we enter into it in fullest military but also in loftiest spiritual preparedness.
> . . . .
> Our hand on the plow to the last moment, but our sword loose and sharp at our side, thus we Germans intend to stride toward the future, only this is the true German way.[56]

Adolf Hitler, who studied and learned from the Alldeutscher Verband, and the National Socialist propagandists melded the mystical and aggressive strands to overwhelming effect. In his review article, "A Farewell to Hitler," Geoffrey Barraclough perceives tooth-and-claw social Darwinism—an ethical system quite unlike any Darwin would have endorsed—as the central tenet of Hitler's thought. "When and by what stages he had acquired it is not clear," writes Barraclough, "[...] but once he had acquired it, it shaped his whole outlook. War was inevitable, [...] nothing would be obtained without fighting, only those ready to fight would survive [...]. It accounts for his hardness and ruthlessness [...]. Like all his other ideas it is derivative, but he developed it with a logical rigor which is all his own."[57] It was in the air, in the phrases of everyday speech, and in people's minds, whether they were aware of it or not.

Barraclough leaves out the mystical or adaptive half of the formula, without which Hitler would have had less success: namely, what Hofstadter calls Darwinian collectivism, or what Troeltsch calls a mystic unity of will that binds *Volk* to *Führer*. Sternheim's *1913* carries the satiric attack against both aspects as represented by Christian Maske and Wilhelm Krey.

*...recent comedies tend more and more
to take on the static irresolute quality of
thoroughgoing satire. It may not be
long before one must say that comedy is
satire.*

Peter Thorpe

3
Civilization's Discontents: Kaiser, Brecht, Dürrenmatt, and the Satiric Tradition

THE REVOLUTION IN DRAMATURGY and staging techniques that began shortly after World War I, much of which Wedekind had anticipated, gave new impetus to the development of dramatic satire. More abstract styles in stage design, the exaggerated pathos of Expressionist acting, and the increasing sophistication of audiences led away from verisimilitude and made possible the presentation of outrageous fictions, while improvements in theater machinery and stage design enabled directors like Leopold Jessner to choreograph big crowd scenes. The three- and five-act drama all but disappeared and was replaced by a loosely constructed, often filmic series of episodes, giving playwrights and directors the means to represent the free play of imagination in both verbal and visual ways.

Three of the best known dramas from the period beginning with the Great War and ending with the Cold War contributed significantly to the strengthening of the modernist trend while at the same time remaining conservative in regard to satiric themes and conventions. That is, none departed very far from the sub-genre as Wedekind had initiated it. Each of the three is representative of a different literary movement and originated in a distinctly different historical epoch.

Georg Kaiser's *Von morgens bis mitternachts* (completed ca. 1912, published 1916) is Expressionist drama. Bertolt Brecht's opera *Aufstieg und Fall der Stadt Mahagonny* with music by Kurt Weill, was completed in 1929 and belongs to a movement called "die neue Sachlichkeit" (the new objectivity or new functionalism). And Dürrenmatt's *Der Besuch der alten Dame* (1956) appeared in the heyday of the theater of the absurd, though it cannot fairly be reckoned to that school. Kaiser, like Sternheim, is a satirist of the late Wilhelmine era, Brecht of the Weimar period, and Dürrenmatt of the Cold War, Economic Miracle, and affluent society. All three plays were composed in boom times and are set in worlds where money is plentiful.

In each, Wedekind's principle of *Realpsychologie* or its twin, Sternheim's "eigene brutale Nuance," is understood as the basis of human relationships. Kaiser's world is governed by the idea of *quid pro quo;* his hero expects proper return for cash paid. Brecht's refrain "Wie man sich bettet, so liegt man" (You must lie in your bed as you made it) has the force of law in Mahagonny.[1] And Dürrenmatt's old lady says phlegmatically, "Wer nicht blechen kann, muß hinhalten, will er mittanzen" (Those who can't pay up, have to prostitute themselves, if they want to join the dance).[2] As in Wedekind's and Sternheim's works, money is a fuel that fires the action. In these and other respects the plays resemble one another closely. They carry on the tradition of satiric drama that began with Wedekind and reaches its artistic high point in *Der Besuch der alten Dame.*

Von morgens bis mitternachts tells the story of a day in the life of a small-town bank clerk. It begins when, in hopes of finding an erotically exciting new life, he absconds with 60,000 marks in cash. In five episodes he then seeks the fulfillment the money promises: in a hotel room with an Italian woman; at home with his family; and then, suddenly in Berlin, at the six-day bicycle races, in a night club chambre separée; and finally as a penitent in the Salvation Army hall. In each instance he is frustrated and cheated of the anticipated ecstatic transport. At midnight he shoots himself.

The plot of *Mahogonny* follows roughly similar lines but is more complicated and deliberately unrealistic. The city of Mahagonny is founded as a place of recreation and entertainment for men tired of work and city life. Four Alaskan lumberjacks, led by Paul Ackermann, find the place dull and are about to leave with most of the remaining customers when Paul hits on the idea of abolishing the old house rules in favor of his new one: You can do anything you like as long as you pay. The management is pleased to accept, and the second half of the opera demonstrates in a series of scenes what happens when everything is permitted. People kill themselves and others. Lover betrays lover, and just before the city burns down, Paul Ackermann is electrocuted for not having paid for a round of drinks.

In *Der Besuch der alten Dame,* Alfred Ill is killed by his fellow townsmen ostensibly for having bribed witnesses in a paternity suit brought against him 45 years earlier. The mother of his child, Claire Zachanassian, now the wealthiest woman in the world, has returned to Güllen with the intention of buying justice. She offers two billion to the town in exchange for Ill's corpse. The greater part of the play shows how an altogether decent citizenry is corrupted by the offer and the yearning for the delights of affluence and how the Gülleners go about rationalizing the communal murder.

It is true that none of the three is explicitly labelled as satire. Kaiser calls his piece a play in two parts; *Mahagonny* is called simply an opera; and *Der Besuch der alten Dame* is a "tragische Komödie." Yet they are sisters under the skin with so much in common that one can speak not only of a tradition but also of shared conventions. That is, we can discern certain themes, motifs, kinds of characters and scenes, and structural and linguistic traits that belong to this type of literature both in this century and in the more distant past. All three draw material and devices from the stock used by satirists since ancient times.

I believe we are justified in calling the plays satiric. Though their authors avoid that term, they also avoid, or qualify, the designation comedy. For these dramas are mixtures, in another sense, of deadly, near tragic earnest and wild farce. No audience can look as disinterestedly on the destinies of Kaiser's cashier, Brecht's Paul Ackermann, or Dürrenmatt's Alfred Ill as he might on those of a comic antagonist like Tartuffe or Kleist's village judge Adam. The latter two play the conventional comic role of alazon or obstacle to the marriage of well matched lovers. On the other hand, our three satiric protagonists play variegated roles as fool, rogue, satirist, scapegoat, and tragic hero. They excite empathy, and their downfall arouses feelings akin to pity and fear. Bitter irony, ridicule, and despair far outweigh the comic elements. Boy does not get girl. In fact, girl betrays boy by delivering him to the lethal forces of the old society he tried to change.

Near the end of each play there stands a speech that seems to pronounce the moral lesson. Just before he throws away the money he embezzled, Kaiser's cashier speaks, or rather preaches, to the assembly in the Salvation Army hall: "Mit keinem Geld aus allen Bankkassen der Welt kann man sich irgendwas von Wert kaufen. Man kauft immer weniger, als man bezahlt. Und je mehr man bezahlt, um so geringer wird die Ware. Das Geld verhüllt das Echte—das Geld ist der armseligste Schwindel unter allem Betrug" (With all the money from all the banks in the world you can't buy anything of value. You always get less than you pay for. The more you pay, the cheaper the goods. Money obscures everything genuine—money is the most miserable swindle of all the frauds).[3]

Bertolt Brecht's Paul Ackermann says much the same thing, but with more subdued rhetoric, in his final speech, delivered from the electric chair to the staff and customers of Mahagonny: "Jetzt erkenne ich: als ich diese Stadt betrat, um mir mit Geld Freude zu machen, war mein Untergang besiegelt. Jetzt sitze ich hier und habe doch nichts gehabt [...]. Die Freude, die ich kaufte, war keine Freude, und die Freiheit für Geld war keine Freiheit" (Now I know: When I entered this city to enjoy myself with money, my doom was sealed. Here I sit and have gotten nothing. The joy I bought was no joy, and the freedom for money was no freedom. 253-254).

Dürrenmatt refuses to blemish the dignity of the doomed Alfred Ill by giving him clichés to pronounce. Instead, as if reluctant to give it weight, he puts the banal statement "Geld allein macht nicht glücklich" (Money alone doesn't bring happiness) in the mouth of Ill's wife as she provides the reporters with the sentiment they expect and so distracts them from the true situation in Güllen (329).[4] For all their irony, these words convey the play's most obvious message, another version of the. cashier's perception, cooler still than Paul Ackermann's flat phrases.

One thinks of adages from our own stock. "The best things in life are free" or "money isn't everything" seem too tame to render the idea. "Money is the root of all evil" comes closer to the mark. But neither satisfies completely, for money and capitalism are only secondary issues. Financial power and, to some extent, sex may be an end for some characters, but money is the readiest means by which the cashier, Paul Ackermann, Ill, and even Claire Zachanassian, who is looking to restore justice, hope to change the world for the better. For they believe they alone hold the key to human happiness.

The most crass, overdrawn example of this messianic complex is the six-day bike race scene in *Von morgens bis mitternachts*. Georg Kaiser's nameless cashier-embezzler offers an unheard of amount in prizes to the racers taking first, second, and third place in the next sprint. He knows that some of the frenzied spectators will be injured and that the exhausted racers are endangered as well. These are incidental matters, however, when one is striving for the absolute: a totally free and united humanity. The cashier raves in the breathless rhetoric of aniticipated ecstasy:

> Das sind Erfüllungen. Heulendes Wehen vom Frühlingsorkan. Wogender Menschheitsstrom. Entkettet—frei. Vorhänge hoch—Vorwände nieder. Menschheit. Freie Menschheit. Hoch und tief—Mensch. Keine Ringe—keine Schichten—keine Klassen. Ins Unendliche schweifende Entlassenheit aus Fron und Lohn in Leidenschaft. Rein nicht—doch frei!—Das wird der Erlös für meine Keckheit. *Er zieht das Bündel Scheine hervor.* (I, 498)

(These are fulfillments. Howling winds of a spring hurricane. Surging stream of humanity. Unchained—free. Curtains up—pretenses down. Humanity. Free humanity. High and low—mankind. No balconies—no levels—no classes. Infinite release from slavery and wages into passion. Not pure, to be sure, but free!—That will be the proceeds from my boldness. *He pulls out a bundle of banknotes.*)

Money, however, is the tool each protagonist uses to dominate and even kill others. It turns groups into mobs. They speak of ideals, but in fact they are out to satisfy their greed and aggressive urges. The satirist's eye sees the negative results—death and chaos—of deeds performed in the name of humanity, justice, and happiness. The satiric protagonist compounds rather than cures the evils of society.

The cashier, Paul Ackermann, and, up to a point, Alfred Ill act on the assumption that everything and everyone has a price. But then they too discover that they are for sale, no less commodities than the rest. The world takes them at their word. They are sooner sold than sacrificed. They lose their lives to satisfy cravings they have aroused in others.

The primary, overall action of each play begins with a condition of severe repression, deprivation, boredom, and stagnation. The purpose is to escape from these severe limitations of what we may call the old order or, with Freud, the reality principle. The simple lust for distraction through something like Brecht's quartet of pleasures: gluttony, the sex act, sport, and alcohol, impels the fools to desperate measures. Then, suddenly and by lucky chance, they acquire the means to realize their dreams. The wish fulfillment, which normally occurs at the end of a comedy, takes place here at a central turning point when with new power in the form of cash in hand or credit they set about to enjoy themselves. The pleasure principle now rules unencumbered.

At this breaking point the Saturnalia begin; and with this release and reversal, the plays take on a new atmosphere of carnival festivity after the famine of winter. Now comedy generally stops with this sort of happy ending and leaves us to surmise that everyone will live happily ever after. Satire, on the other hand, leads us to the realization that this supposedly new and better world is not merely a fool's paradise but a hell on earth.

This perception breaks in on the satiric protagonist at the point where his world collapses morally. The pressure toward collapse and chaos builds up in a series of essentially similar episodes. The mob's and the protagonist's tastes grow ever more jaded as they discover that there is no cure for boredom and no food that will satisfy their hunger for excitement. The new freedom proves worse than the earlier bondage and ends in riot, murder, suicide, and a despairing cry for help.

The final calamity takes place in a ritualized crowd scene when the protagonist meets a violent end; two are publicly executed, and two die on a stage within a stage. The conclusion climaxes a series of episodes which follow a common course. A clearly discernible rhythm governs the action, and it is analogous to Francis Fergusson's tragic rhythm of Purpose, Passion, and Perception. But in satire the purposes of fools and knaves are self-defeating. Step three is rather frustration and anticlimax.[5] This is the story of the biggest day in the life of Georg Kaiser's bank cashier.

> *...the stage is not a moral institution–it's a battleground.*
>
> Georg Kaiser

Von morgens bis mitternachts, if we are to trust Kaiser's memory, was completed in 1912, while Wedekind and Sternheim were still active. Though he was born in the same year as Sternheim, 1878, he belongs to a newer generation of playwrights far more venturesome and innovative in their dramaturgical ideas. Sternheim's *Die Kassette* is a five-act play divided in Shakespearean fashion into numbered scenes, one for each entrance and exit. *1913* has three acts but is otherwise structured in the same manner. Both observe strict unity of time and place and confine their action to the living room or library of a home. Kaiser, on the other hand, gives us no plush salon interiors. He moves his protagonist out of the provincial bank and modest parlor into the great world. He lets him move alone across a snow covered field and later puts him into noisy crowd scenes in the city. *Von morgens bis mitternachts* is a "station" drama consisting of seven independent scenes, each with its own action and milieu. The play later served Bertolt Brecht as a model in his development of the idea of epic theater. It has been canonized and is nowadays read in the classroom as the classic example of what is sometimes called chaotic Expressionism and as a statement on the theme of the New Man that was so often invoked in the time right after World War I.

Read in this way the play nevertheless causes uneasiness today, as it always has. The message is not utopian. It is antiutopian. Kaiser himself resorted to murky and mannered phrases when asked for an explanatory note to appear in a theater program. In 1921 he wrote, "Aufbruch des einzelnen in die Menschheit—Irrtum als einzelner Mensch zu sein—ein Nein—gegen Betonmauer geführte Straßenkurve: das ist *Von morgens bis mitternachts*" (Going forth of the individual into humanity—erroneous belief that individual is human—a No—the curve in the highway leads into a concrete wall: this is *Von morgens bis mitternachts*. IV, 563). This might be the Expressionist abbreviation of the career of Freud's rebel against civilization.

Kaiser's perverse, fatalistic plot summary may not elucidate much on the face of it; yet it is telling and suggestive. Official German police censors, undeniably illiberal but keen detectors of disruptive and malevolent tendencies, didn't release the play for production until 1917, and then only to be performed in Munich and after the deletion of several passages thought to be blasphemous or morally objectionable. In the months before Gerhart Hauptmann's successful intercession with the Munich censor, Kaiser feared for his artistic and material existence. "*Von morgens bis mitternachts,* was refused permission for performance in the Deutsches Theater in Berlin, the Schaupielhaus in Düsseldorf, the Neues Theater in Frankfurt, in Munich the Kammerspiele are still fighting for its release, Vienna has no word yet" (IV, 543).[6]

A nation at war will naturally censor, officially or unofficially, topical and misanthropic satire because, as the Berlin Chief of Police, with the backing of the military high command in Prussia, said of Sternheim's *1913*, it will disturb the peace on the home front. And it is as satire, as aggressive irony, that *Von morgens bis mitternachts* is best read. In his early stage works, bloody and farcical tragicomedies, as Kaiser said in 1921, he vented his savage indignation at Wilhelmine Germany and then moved on to more important matters: "When I had cleansed an intolerable, rotten, poisoned atmosphere with my comedies, I wrote *Die Bürger von Calais* [The Citizens of Calais, 1912/13]" (IV, 565).[7] According to the chronology of Kaiser's work then, *Von morgens bis mitternachts* falls into the earlier category of antiseptic, angry pieces. And it is, like much satire in the theater, a primitive sort of comedy. Instead of ending with the conventional marriage and happy resolution of comedy, it concludes with betrayal, frustration, anticlimax, and, ultimately, darkness and doom. The conventional comic action of Kaiser's play ends before midpoint when to our glee the fatuous bank officer is robbed by the cashier he exploited and when the liberated cashier embarks on his new life. The remainder, the larger portion, is a mixture of pathos, slapstick, and nightmare.

In later years no less than before World War I Kaiser still speaks in his occasional writings like an irascible battler for whom Europe is hell, the human race unbearable. He wants to express his horror and rage in the most striking way possible: in hard, cold, cerebral words and forms (IV, 549). The stage remains for him not a moral institution but an arena of battle (IV, 545). He is, as he says of Iwan Goll, a "conscious attacker of the prevailing conditions using the material and form of those conditions," fighting the enemy with its own weapons (IV, 575).[8] Like all satire, Kaiser's play is the aesthetically socialized expression of this aggression. As with Wedekind and Sternheim, the method is homeopathic, attacking the malady with its own serum, and is characteristic of what is called undirected or hermetic satire. Kaiser lets dullness and villainy act themselves out and speak their own language but supplies sufficient grotesque incongruences and distortions to encourage the audience to look beneath the surface and piece together a satiric interpretation.

Situated on the watershed between his juvenile, erotic, destructive "comedies" and the visionary pieces like *Die Bürger von Calais, Von morgens bis mitternachts* works a cutting irony. It uses vitalist clichés and the chiliastic Expressionist "O Mensch" pathos of the day—calling for a return to the innocence and essence of original man—the language of the opposition, that is, to expose society as a charnel house and man as a foolish, thrill seeking, predatory, and ultimately suicidal creature.

The play is about death, the death principle in society and the individual. Kaiser shows two kinds. First is the suffocatingly repressive, lifeless atmosphere of the bank with its mechanical obscenity and of the cashier's insufferably petty family existence. There's a lot of crude comic material here; one need only think of the caricatured types among the bank customers and of how grandma keels over dead when her son leaves the house without eating his noon meal. The second face of death, revealed in part two, is more terrifying by far as it emerges after the cashier's embezzlement and escape from bondage. Given the opportunity and wherewithal to realize his long repressed wishes, to live out his phantasies, to break out and come alive, the cashier fails to become, or bring into being, the "New Man." He may speak of a perfectly harmonious humanity where all barriers are removed; he may preach renunciation of private property and the perfect union of woman and man; but Kaiser demonstrates with powerful theatrical effect that deeds performed in the name of togetherness, happiness, Eros, the life principle, and humanity in fact issue in chaos and death. Kaiser is not subtle about this. There is a lot of thoughtless, cruel talk in the play; the cashier is totally self-centered and indifferent to the lethal consequences of his actions. He compounds, rather than cures, the evils of society; and appropriately, in the end he destroys himself. Yet the play is not as gloomy as this suggests. It is leavened by slapstick—e.g., the cashier pulls a dignified official's top hat down over his ears at the bike race—and bad adolescent jokes. To put it another way: First, family and job exert a dehumanizing influence on the cashier. Then the tables are turned, and he, a sorcerer's apprentice with his 60,000 marks, transforms the world into a hell of unsatisfied and insatiable lusts. The voltage of expectations, in him and in others, rises until finally the fuse blows and all grows dark.

After seeing the Berlin première in 1919, the reviewer Alfred Kerr surprised no one when he panned Kaiser and his play. In the course of his review, he pointed to the contradictions between rhetoric and deed, taking them to be blameworthy artistic lapses. More serious in Kerr's eyes was the moral obtuseness of protagonist and author. He wrote with some indignation, addressing the cashier, "People are all bad because of their greed for pleasure, so the bank employee feels. And you, Mr. Hero? Who was it that made his two daughters and his wife unhappy, who brought on his mother's death, eh?"[9]

Harry Graf Kessler, after attending the same première, recorded in a journal entry his disappointment at the drama's tastelessness; but he did catch the crucial importance of phantasy and imagination, calling the piece "the tragedy of a man with an adolescent imagination."[10]

Respected theater critics other than Kerr have had only praise for the play's theatrical excitement: its tempo, color, bold mixing of laughter and melodramatic pathos. On the other hand, academic interpreters are generally content to note that the cashier's hoped for regeneration fails to take place because he uses money and because he remains caught in the old bourgeois-capitalist modes of thought and action. Wilhelm Steffens is particularly put off by his impression that Kaiser's work wants moral and ideological conviction; the plays take no consistent ethical stand; they are, he complains, "wertneutral."[11]

The reason for the dissatisfaction and uncertainty in the various readings of Von morgens bis mitternachts is first of all Kaiser's mixing of opposites, largely vitalist and antivitalist motifs. For example: the dance of life is executed on a wooden leg, innocent love proves a disguise for venal betrayal, and spring winds reveal the figure of death. Second, Kaiser employs irony. His ironies of the stable sort are obvious enough: the repentant sinners scramble for the coins and bills the cashier has thrown away in disgust; the seemingly dedicated Salvation Army lass betrays the cashier to earn the reward for his capture. But there are also unstable ironies in the play's language, in gestures, and in the structure which suggest that we must assume the vitalist New-Man message to be false, that we should reject it as the surface meaning and look for the true object of Kaiser's covert attack. Take for instance the Cranach painting of Adam and Eve in the Garden which figures prominently in the first half of the play. It would seem to support a utopian reading, particularly after it is viewed as "selige Menschheits-verkündung" (joyful proclamation of humanity. I, 475). Yet if this phrase were not suspicious enough, there are several other disturbing things about the picture and the way it's treated.

First, the scene—Adam and Eve in erotic congress, apple half eaten on the ground, snake looking on—promises not paradisal bliss but certain expulsion, suffering, and death. In addition, the painting serves as a touchstone to reveal the ignorance and lasciviousness of characters in its presence. The art historian, who discovers it turned against a barroom wall and serving as backing for a photo of the proprietor, treats it first as a financial windfall, then as means to get ahead in the profession, and in the end as an aphrodisiac to keep on hand indefinitely for his private purposes. In the eyes of the cashier the picture is sheer pornography. And ultimately, for Kaiser, it serves as the occasion for a bad joke as the cashier, with his adolescent dirty mind, asks the matron if she posed for it. One concludes that the painting might better have stayed out of sight.

The play's final episode gives this motif its sharp bite. Alone in the hall with the Salvation Army lass, the cashier seeks, with all the lyric force of his being, to invoke and live a mythic primal existence: "Mädchen und Mann. Uralte Gärten aufge-schlossen. Entwölkter Himmel" (Maiden and man. Primeval gardens unlocked. Cloudless heavens. I, 516). But time cannot be annulled or reversed here. There follow immediately betrayal, darkness, and death as the woman denounces him to the police for the sake of the reward and he shoots himself. As if that moment of blazing anticipation—the last and most intense of several—had been too much for the wiring, the policeman matter-of-factly pronounces the play's last words: "Ein Kurzschluß in der Leitung" (A short circuit in the wiring. I, 517).

I suggest there are two things Kaiser wants to lay bare and attack. One, as Kessler saw, is the "Primanerphantasie," or our easily corrupted and potentially dangerous faculty of imagination. This is the timeless human element. The other is a set of beliefs and accepted ideas that informed and inflamed the daydreams of Wilhel-mine Germany. The play's action reveals the structure of phantasy, demonstrates what happens when it is empowered to change reality, and makes it something closely akin to original sin.

What then are some of Kaiser's signals to the reader or spectator that the play is to be reconstructed as acid, Swiftian satire? One is the rhythm of purpose-passion-anticlimax governing the whole play and each major episode. The cashier embezzles 60,000 marks and abandons his family for the sake of a supposed adventuress. He goes to her, suffers the pain of rejection, but draws no lesson from the experience. The episode ends rather with a bad joke or a dirty trick of fate. The woman is a respectable matron, mother of an art historian. Similarly, the Crown Prince's entrance into the royal box spoils the fun at the bike race; and the girls in the chambre séparée are too drunk or repulsive to effect a sexual resolution.

Each episode and the overall action as well follow a circular course. The circle, that symbol of futility, is the play's central image and is impressed on us by its most memorable scene, the six-day bicycle race or, as the cashier, now suddenly exuding self-assurance and wit, would have it, the six-day sleep (of the resting member of each two-man team). The race and the circle remind us that our achievements are futile, lead nowhere, that we are caught in a vicious circle. Moreover, Kaiser packs the situation with further signals and satiric charges. The cashier is at once cynical about the senseless folly of the sport and excited by its potential effect on spectator phantasy. And here too there are uncertainties. Does he gain his ecstatic sense of life from crudely erotic details like the derby hat as it falls from the top to the middle balcony and is there crushed against the rail by a large bosom? Or is it the prospect of seeing the crowd fused into one impassioned mass? Or does the greatest thrill come when one spectator plunges from the middle to the lower balcony and is trampled to death? "Es geht nicht ohne Tote ab, wo andre fiebernd leben," (A few dead are unavoidable when others are living passionately), he comments with a certain sang-froid (I, 496).

When he offers his outlandish prize of 50,000 marks, further doubts arise as to whether he really wants to set the crowd free: "No balconies—no levels—no classes. Release sweeping into the infinite" (Keine Schichten—Keine Klassen. Ins Unendliche schweifende Entlassenheit), or whether he takes more delight in the expectation that the racers may collapse and die and that more spectators are sure to be killed (I, 498). Is, in other words, the cashier a utopian visionary, a cynical clown, or a murderously perverse madman?

All three of these qualities are there in him, no matter how incommensurable they may seem; and they are inextricably linked. The cult of vitalism, taken to extremes, has inhumane and deadly consequences. The cashier, playing the ambiguous role of satirist on stage, perceives some follies and dangers and acts as Kaiser's admonishing spokesman. Yet he is far from all-seeing and quite unaware of the extent to which he is responsible for corruption and destruction.

Once he has the 60,000 in pocket, he becomes cocksure and voluble, a prankster and show-off. As he embarks on his new life, he delivers a three-page monologue that distorts reality by jumbling, magnifying, and belittling. Yet the speech has a peculiarly decisive, businesslike tone. Insignificant things like shirt cuffs and simple actions like lifting a handful of snow assume cosmic import. The speech is an unconcealed travesty on the invocation of the Earth Spirit, one of the high points in Goethe's *Faust I.* The periods are a clutter of bank jargon, militaristic bravado, titanic pathos, underworld slang, and outpourings on nature and springtime. Here is a segment of the speech ending with the grandiose Faustian effort to conjure not the Earth Spirit but fair return for money spent.

> *Er holt das Banknotenbündel aus der Tasche und klatscht es auf die Hand.* Ich zahle bar! Der Betrag ist flüssig gemacht—die Regulierung läuft dem Angebot voraus. Vorwärts, was bietet sich? *Er sieht in das Feld.* Schnee. Schnee. Sonne. Stille. *Er schüttelt den Kopf und steckt das Geld ein.* Es wäre eine schamlose Übervorteilung—mit dieser Summe blauen Schnee zu bezahlen. Ich mache das Geschäft nicht. Ich trete vor dem Abschluß zurück. Keine reelle Sache! *Die Arme aufwerfend.* Ich muß bezahlen!! — — Ich habe das Geld bar!! — — Wo ist Ware, die man mit dem vollen Einsatz kauft?! Mit sechzigtausend—und dem ganzen Käufer mit Haut und Knochen?! — — *Schreiend.* Ihr müßt mir doch liefern — — ihr müßt doch Wert und Gegenwert in Einklang bringen!!!! *Sonne von Wolken verfinstert. Er steigt aus der Gabel.* Die Erde kreißt—Frühlingsstürme. (I, 483).

(*He takes the bundle of banknotes out of his pocket and slaps it on his hand.* I'm paying cash. The sum is liquid. The settlement is running ahead of the offer. Forward. What is offered? *He looks into the field.* Snow. Snow. Sun. Quiet. *He shakes his head and pockets the money.* It would be a shameless fraud—to pay for snow with this amount. It's no deal. I'm backing out before it's concluded. Not a safe transaction. *Throwing up his arms.* I must pay!! — — I have the money in cash!! — — Where are the goods one buys with total commitment?! With sixty thousand—plus the whole purchaser from top to toe?! — — *Screaming.* You must deliver — — you must bring value and countervalue into balance!!!! *Sun darkened by clouds. He climbs down from the fork of the tree.* The earth is in labor. Springtime storms.) The cashier's conjuring is effective, but he invokes not the dynamic source of all life, but rather the apparition of death—reduced through his choice of words to "die Polizei des Daseins" (I, 484)—which he recognizes as an integral part of himself.

Karlheinz Martin, director of the 1920 film version of *Von morgens bis mitternachts,* chose to give the motif of death, present in almost every episode of the play, added emphasis. For one thing, his cashier moves in an unnaturally accelerated and violent fashion with chalky face, bared teeth, and rolling eyes. For another, he gives the movie the quality of a dance of death by means of "repeated hallucinatory transformations and dissolves when the cashier stares into the faces of women and sees the shell of a Death's Head."[12]

The monologue comes to its inappropriate, anticlimactic conclusion with a string of phrases from the stock used in business letters. The cashier bows and addresses the specter: "Ich sehe, wir haben bis zu einem annehmbaren Grade eine Verständigung erzielt. Das ist ein Anfang, der Vertrauen einflößt und im Wirbel kommender großartiger Ereignisse den nötigen Rückhalt schafft. Ich weiß das unbedingt zu würdigen. Mit vorzüglicher Hochachtung— —" (I see we have reached a reasonably acceptable agreement. That's a start that inspires confidence and will provide the necessary support in the whirl of magnificent coming events. I can appreciate that absolutely. Respectfully yours— —" I, 484). So at the expense of great verbal and theatrical effort—the scene places great demands on stage designers and actors—we arrive at nothing. The cashier ends with a postscript to the effect that he knew all along this was only a transient phenomenon. The speech has further, uncannily prophetic implications when compared to those Hitler was to make. It bears the marks of Nazi rhetoric, as Walter Jens has described it: "An analysis of Hitler's speeches will show whether the stilted writing style, a bureaucratic German in combination with dime-novel elements, informed the rhetoric of the Nazis."[13] The false bravado of Sternheim's Wilhelm Krey exposed the inanity of the language used by the nationalistic youth movement and, in the 1960s, reminded audiences of phrases they had heard at convocations or on the radio in the Nazi time. In Krey's case it is a matter of content and tone. Kaiser's cashier anticipates the style, or rather the absence of style that characterized "brown" rhetoric. Like Hitler he gains his effects by exaggerated gesture and screaming. This sort of speech making is not peculiar to 1912 or to National Socialist harangues; it is a universal phenomenon. The action of Kaiser's *Von morgens bis mitternachts* shows that people who speak, and consequently think in this way not only lack acquaintance with humane letters, they can perform inhuman acts.

After the monologue, the cashier sets forth into the world debasing everything he encounters, reducing it to nothing, or next to nothing. The Cranach painting of Adam and Eve becomes pornography; persons become expendable instruments of his pleasure.

Karl Kraus is therefore by no means the only satirist to focus on the abuse of language as a portent of moral disorder and violence. Wedekind and Sternheim do the same. The diction of Kaiser's cashier is characteristic of modern satiric theater in general; it is inauthentic, mindless, and yet all too familiar. Through his words, the cashier transforms the vital into the mechanical, humanity into bestiality, and beauty into obscenity. In the end he is even worse than the salacious bank director who dominated the opening scene. Both reduce people to objects or balance sheets. But the cashier is by far the more dangerous of the two; he has an ideological mission and thinks in absolutes. In his pursuit of liberation and vernal beatitude for himself and, he would like to believe, for all mankind, he only destroys.

Even his well-intended actions in the dance hall and at the Salvation Army backfire; they end in an anticlimax that is both morbid and ludicrous. The form of the final scene, for example, follows the ritual of the revival meeting. Several figures testify to their repentance for sins very much like the cashier's; and the scene builds toward a grand climax as the cashier himself stands and confesses. In a grandiose gesture of Christian contrition he throws away all the cash he has left and turns the meeting into a frantic scramble to pick up the coins and bills. As at the bike races he manages to break down the barriers between human beings but accomplishes this by turning them all, soldiers and repentant sinners, into a greedy, violent mob, "ein kämpfendes Knäuel" (a battling crowd). This penultimate episode concludes with the vivid but impractical stage direction: "Vom Podium stürzen die Soldaten von ihren Musikinstrumenten in den Saal. Die Bänke werden umgestoßen, heisere Rufe schwirren, Fäuste klatschen auf Leiber. Schließlich wälzt sich der verkrampfte Haufe zur Tür und rollt hinaus" (The soldiers abandon their instruments and plunge from the podium into the hall. Benches are overturned, hoarse shouts are buzzing, fists slap against bodies. Finally the convulsed mob rolls to the door and whirls out. I, 515).

M. F. Cyprian, reviewing the world première for *Hochland,* a conservative Catholic periodical, judged the play worthless because totally lacking those constructive elements that he considered essential to all great art.[14] One can disagree with the evaluation, but the observation is accurate. The drama is a reductive model, but it is scarcely "wertneutral." It is designed to inspire indignation and horror as well as scorn. The picture it paints is clear and critical. Something is, and always has been, wrong with the wiring.

The satiric points are age-old, but the currency is that of the early 1900s. Germany in 1912, to the satiric eye, differs only superficially from Wedekind's turn of the century, Brecht's 1920s, or Dürrenmatt's Cold War and age of affluence. In each case we see individual and collective phantasies run wild and identify the fatal spiral as the addiction worsens and ever more lurid images and sensations are required. Each collision with reality, each ineluctable anticlimax, or short circuit, intensifies the yearning to escape to a higher reality and brings the dream closer to nightmare. The ultimate breakdown in the wiring is an explosion of suicidal violence when the cult of sensation and dynamism is shown to be tied to the death instinct.[15]

> *this opera [...] to put an end to all operas*
> Klaus Pringsheim

Bertolt Brecht's most uncompromising satire, the opera *Aufstieg und Fall der*

Stadt Mahagonny (1929) with music by Kurt Weill, tells approximately the same tale as *Von morgens bis mitternachts* but with important differences, of which the music is the most obvious. Paul Ackermann, enterprising lumberjack with money and time on his hands, proposes to throw off all restraints and enjoy himself after ten years working in Alaska. Finding the rules of the establishment too constraining, he institutes the new order of perfect freedom, or better complete license in Mahagonny, the Las Vegas of Brecht's mind. Under the new dispensation one lumberjack eats himself to death, and another is killed in a boxing match. As Paul Ackermann is about to be executed, he pronounces the sum of his wisdom: No one has benefited, and the project was doomed from the beginning. The initial episode, the founding of the city, also shows the failure of an enterprise. Widow Begbick and her entourage of whores and strong-arm men are fleeing from the authorities and heading for the gold fields. But the car breaks down, and the desert blocks their way. So they have to settle for less and build here. "Alle wahrhaft Suchenden werden enttäuscht" (All true seekers are disappointed.) stands as the title for Scene Eight (192). With its ironic tone, this statement sums up the basic plot of the opera and its episodes.

The searchers in this case are pursuing something considerably more mundane than was Kaiser's cashier. We hear no mention of a new humanity. Although biblical tones are sometimes struck, the general tenor is intensely vulgar. The opera's theme is the human yearning for distraction. According to Brecht's notes, the piece itself is intended as fun ("Spaß").[16] The anarchic, antisocial, unquenchable thirst for pleasure is a dominant theme in most of Brecht's dramas.

"Was ist der Taifun an Schrecken/Gegen den Menschen, wenn er seinen Spaß will?" (What terrors does a typhoon have compared to a human being when he wants his fun?) sings Paul Ackermann in the axial scene, just before he declares that nothing is forbidden (204). The new order is instituted in Mahagonny with the express understanding that it will turn men into wanton destroyers. One can say this regard and in general that Brecht's satiric statement is an intensification and exaggeration of Kaiser's. Not merely one man, but an entire city goes under.

This holds for the level of phantasy as well. The governing imagination in *Von morgens bis mitternachts* was immature, a "Primanerphantasie." In *Aufstieg und Fall der Stadt Mahagonny* it is childish, at times infantile. It creates an unreal, comic-strip world where childhood dreams of omnipotence seem to come to fruition, women are utterly compliant, liquor and food are accessible in quantity, there's lots of entertainment, time can be annulled, and distances erased as if by magic. One can even jump on the billiard table, play boat, and escape by sea to Alaska. Or at least it's worth a try. Everything seems possible. Theodor Adorno read the sequence, incidentally, where Paul and his friends, all quite drunk, pretend to be sailors, as an anticipation of the classless society.[17]

But the boat game is brief, and the point is soon made that there is no escape and the day of reckoning has come. Paul has to pay his bar bill or die. This is the other half of the picture in Brecht's plays. Just as Kaiser's cashier crashes into the figurative cement wall, Brecht's pleasure-bound lumberjack collides with the suppressive rules of society and with the laws that he himself has carelessly formulated. The comic-strip takes on the aspect of those late medieval woodcut *Totentanz* series with their captions. According to the director's script for the *Mahagonny Songspiel* (1927)—a kind of Urmahagonny consisting mainly of songs and choruses without the continuing action—the piece is a "Totentanz."[18]

The reality principle in this very primitive play is represented by a corrupt kangaroo court. Paul Ackermann's conviction is assured before the proceedings begin, but the ritual is preserved, making the sentencing and execution communal acts. The banally mechanical quality of it all makes the victim's lot the more nightmarish, the fulfillment not of wishes but of deepest fears. Kafka knew the effectiveness of this kind of trial scene, and so do the directors of horror films. Mahagonny's lights don't go out, to be sure, but the city goes up in flames.

At its founding the city arises out of contradictions and frustrated aims. It is at once the "Netzestadt" (city of nets), a trap designed to bleed money out of its customers, and also the "Paradiesstadt" because it promises freedom from work, unadulterated pleasure, and a cure from "Zi-zi-zi-zi-zivilis" (a pun on Syphilis and "Zivilisation"), that ambiguous social disease. It is a fool's paradise founded on money and the principles of greed and lust. According to Arnolt Bronnen, in 1923 "Mahagonny" was Brecht's private code word for a petty bourgeois utopia with Nazi, or brown, coloration. But in 1930 Brecht thought it important to note in the director's script for the first Berlin performance, "The name Mahagonny designates nothing more than the concept of a city. It was chosen for acoustic phonetic reasons. The geographic location is unimportant."[19] This and other script revisions seem to have been undertaken to make the opera less exotic and more universal.

Widow Begbick, the *maîtresse de plaisir,* soon discovers that the simple pastimes of sleeping, smoking, fishing, and swimming do not suffice. Mahagonny quickly begins to lose customers and money. Though the miners and lumberjacks should be enjoying a relaxing vacation, the pressure of boredom and dissatisfaction steadily increases. Then all is temporarily saved when Paul Ackermann, prophet and savior, announces the new anti-Mosaic dispensation: nothing is forbidden; you can do as you please—provided you pay for the privilege. Once the management and guests accept this principle, the Saturnalia begin, and there follows a series of scenes demonstrating what happens when a man is given free rein to enjoy himself. Just as in *Von morgens bis mitternachts,* money is here the license and lubricant. What was in Kaiser's play a spree for one man with lots of cash in hand is broadened here to an experiment affecting a whole collective, or a whole society.

The demonstration consists of four episodes dealing with the pleasures of eating, sex, sport, and drinking. Their pursuit, it is shown, does not lead to happiness. With shocking suddenness we see each time that there is no joy in any of these activities practiced for its own sake. In a manner both comic and gruesome we are shown that the wages of sin and licentiousness is death. These true seekers are not merely disappointed: the eater, the boxer, and the drinker die. By the same perverse logic, love leads to separation, betrayal, and the electric chair.

This new world—"des lieben Gottes billiger Salon" (God's cheap saloon)—turns out to be hell. The common assumptions which held true in the first half of the play are no longer valid; they are in fact expressly contradicted. Money does not titillate the senses, and the winner gains nothing for his pains.[20] And in accordance with this new and strangely just world order, Paul Ackermann, who promulgated the laws of happiness, is sentenced to death for failing to pay for a round of drinks and a curtain rod. This is conclusive proof of the axiom sung to a tango melody and omnipresent in the opera: You must lie in the bed as you made it.

In accord with satiric convention, *Mahagonny* ends with a disorderly crowd scene. The words of the title, "Rise and Fall," point to another sort of movement that can be seen in the course of the action. Mahagonny's permissive new order makes it prosper briefly but leads then to its burning. Paul Ackermann's rise to Messianic prominence is a station on the way to the electric chair.

In speeches and dramatic situations high and low are often mixed. The great display of legal rectitude in court is patently criminal. The trivial is inflated, and important matters are reduced to trivia. Paul Ackermann is tried and condemned for a minor offense. And whereas Kaiser used a wildly jumbled rhetoric, Bertolt Brecht gives us contrariness and flat contradictions. Here are two of many: In Scene 14 the men waiting in line for their turn with the prostitute sing, "Liebe, die ist doch an Zeit nicht gebunden/Jungens, macht rasch, denn hier geht's um Sekunden" (Love isn't bound by time/Hurry up, boys, for here seconds count. 215); and money both turns you on (190), and it doesn't (215).

Like Brecht's pairing of the words come and go, must and may, win and lose, net and freedom, everything seems at odds with something else. People move back and forth and against one another. They are at cross purposes with themselves and in the finale as parties in the city. The various processions of demonstrators in the final scene bear self-contradictory signs and march "durcheinander und gegeneinander" (in confusion and against one another, 254).

Kaiser has his concrete wall unseen around the bend in the highway; Dürrenmatt sees to it that events take the worst possible turn; and Brecht has his big NO. Seek and ye shall not find; all true seekers are disappointed; we can not help ourselves, or you, or anyone else: these are key phrases from the libretto and are all the more striking because Paul Ackermann's new rules promulgated at the Do-as-you-like Pokerdrinksaloon would seem designed to make the city a place of freedom and happiness.

Yet the NO grows louder as the opera proceeds from that turning point to its end in conflagration and chaos. It is underscored in the "Benares Song": "Is here no Telephone? Oh sir, God help me, no." There is no whisky, no money, no boy, and ultimately no Benares.[21] In "Das Spiel von Gott in Mahagonny," Brecht's last word before the production number, the trio of men answers God's first three questions with Ja. The fourth and crucial one elicits a loud Nein, repeated three times over: You cannot send us to hell because we have always been there.

Brecht's "No" is the third, frustrating beat of the satiric rhythm: purpose, passion, anticlimax. The sequence can be found in the action over all and in the smallest units of dialogue. It happens five times in the opening fifteen lines of the opera:

> Willy der Prokurist: Hallo, wir müssen weiter!
> Dreieinigkeitsmoses: Aber der Wagen ist kaputt.
> Willy der Prokurist: Ja, dann können wir nicht weiter.
> *Pause*
> Dreieinigkeitsmoses [His turn to try]: Aber wir müssen weiter.
> Willy der Prokurist: Aber vor uns ist nur Wüste.
> Dreieinigkeitsmoses: Ja, dann können wir nicht weiter.
> *Pause*

And so on, three times more, ending finally with

> Dreieinigkeitsmoses: Nein. (173-74).

(Willy the Head Clerk: Hello, we've got to move on!
Trinity Moses: But the truck is broken down.
Willy: Well, then we can't move on.
Trinity Moses: But we have to move on.
Willy: But there's nothing but desert in front of us.
Trinity Moses: Well, then we can't move on.
Pause
. . . .
Trinity Moses: No.)

The distinguished critics Alfred Polgar and Theodor Adorno reviewed the Leipzig première of September 9, 1930. Both agreed that *Mahagonny* was caustic satire—the "signals" were clear, and the performance excited a "Theaterskandal" like few others—but they disagreed on its intent. The conservative Polgar understood it as a comment on the human animal and wrote with sarcastic wit:

"In Leipzig one gets books, furs, thoughts of escape, and at fair time no hotel room, in Mahagonny whisky, singable ironies, whores, catchy allusions to human nature and order, as well as acerbities in various flavors."[22]

Adorno, on the other hand, makes no mention of irony and reads the play as a critique, from an Olympian Marxist standpoint, of capitalist society. He begins, "The city of Mahagonny is a representation of the capitalist world, sketched from the elevated perspective of the classless society."[23] In Jimmy Mahoney, later renamed Paul Ackermann, he sees a dialectical Chaplin. Then, as if anticipating objections to this ideological distortion, Adorno backs off a bit and concedes that Brecht's anticipation of the classless society is not expressed outright but functions as the implicit counterpart to the ugly world of the opera.

For all its banal, juvenile, surface simplicity, the opera's text is full of contradictions and elicits contradictory responses from audiences as well as from reviewers. But once we observe the opera as a whole, libretto and music together, there emerge even more striking patterns of contradiction—simultaneous and sequential and between word and tone.

Music and operatic conventions, particularly in a work like *Mahagonny* that has next to no spoken dialog, place the literary satiric fiction at a second remove from reality. Even the hardships that lead to the city's founding—the proprietors' need to survive and the lumberjacks' instinctual cravings—come across in songs and recitative.

Brecht was well aware of the importance of the satiric travesty for achieving a strong satiric effect. The parenthetic sentence in this quote from the notes to *Mahagonny* recognizes the paradoxical relationship between the real and unreal: "The more indistinct and unreal reality becomes thanks to the music—there emerges a third element, something very complex and quite real in itself, which can produce quite real effects, but which is completely removed from its subject, from the reality employed—the more enjoyable the overall process will be."[24]

The circular course of the action is designed to underline this idea. In the opening sequence the audience sees and hears how the city of Mahagonny comes into being, or is constructed, from nothing, in the middle of the desert, in effect by the magic of wishing. Mahagonny is a city of dreams where pleasure reigns; and it has an autonomous history with strong mythical and religious overtones. The events taking place between its rise and fall are presented in exemplary and didactic scenes or model situations as a child might have created them in phantasy. The city is then destroyed as easily as it was created—the fire is of unexplained origin and merely painted on flats—and the opera falls back to the original level of fiction where hostile circumstance cannot be ignored. The conclusion is still altogether operatic. The music underscores the pattern of the vicious circle by repeating several times here in the final chorus and procession the phrase that opened the opera.[25]

Kurt Weill's music fits Brecht's text because it too has a primitive, childishly perverse quality. It distorts and destroys its sources and devices by juxtaposing chorale, fugue, and minuet with tango, march, and music hall songs. It is music constituted out of the rubble of old borrowed material used almost always in a manner inappropriate to its original intent. The I'm-all-right-Jack message of "Wie man sich bettet" is all the more jarring when sung in rousing chorus to a tango rhythm. The "Alabama Song" breaks into two halves: one full of yearning and sentiment, the other hard bitten and unmelodic.

The original intent of the cycle of poems Brecht entitled "Mahagonny Gesänge," published years before Weill set them to music and before they later collaborated on the opera, was to shock readers with a satanic travesty on a kind of devotional book, the "Hauspostille" (home breviary), designed for home use. Weill's music does the same with operatic tradition. A phrase from the "Brautjungfer" (Brides-maid) refrain in Weber's *Freischütz* can be heard twice in each strophe of the song that begins: "Auf nach Mahagonny/Die Luft ist kühl und frisch/Dort gibt es Pferd- und Weiberfleisch/Whisky und Pokertisch" (Off for Mahagonny/The air is cool and fresh/There we'll find horse- and female flesh/Whisky and poker games).[26] The ninth scene also quotes a piece of nineteenth century "Salonmusik" schmalz called "Gebet einer Jungfrau" (Virgin's Prayer), and scene one has reminiscences from Wagner's *Tristan und Isolde*. In scene thirteen Jack gorges himself to death on the meat of three calves to sentimental Viennese "Heuri-genmusik"—zither and all—in a *valse lento* tempo. Particularly incommensura-ble is the plagiarized refrain from the nineteenth century song *Seemannslos* [The Lot of the Sailor] as it is used in Weill's "Stürmisch die Nacht" [Stormy the Night]. It is the least appropriate music to cite in order to keep one's courage. The old song says, "Nichts half das Kämpfen mehr" (No use in struggling any more), and the rest tells how the ship went down with all hands.[27]

As the last episode before Paul Ackermann's execution, Brecht offers a play with-in the opera and calls it "Das Spiel von Gott in Mahagonny." The role of God is played by the least likely figure, the bouncer Dreieinigkeitmoses. The "play" builds toward an outbreak of anger and aggression at about its midpoint as God becomes more querulous and the men of Mahagonny surlier. The musical signal for the outburst is the striking up of a noisy waltz. Then, after the men of Mahagonny have told God to go to hell, where they have always been anyway, the opera moves rapidly to its close with Paul Ackermann's last words of despair and the chaotic processions of the still unconverted, incorrigible survivors.

A further example of Weill's satiric musical technique is the synchronic mix-ture of despair, aggressive rage, and cynicism in scene eleven, the axis of the opera. It begins as the men of Mahagonny sing a chorale-like verse reminiscent of the song of the armored men in Mozart's *Magic Flute*. The men are saying it is senseless to be afraid of the typhoon; better to resign yourself to death. Jenny joins them singing the refrain of the "Alabama Song," recommending whisky as an alternative solace. Then Jack's voice is heard countering Jenny's with the opera's basic statement on human nature: The natural world is ruled by destructive forces, and so is mankind. "Gerade so ist der Mensch:/Er muß zerstören, was da ist./Wozu braucht's da ein Hurrikan?/Was ist der Taifun an Schrecken/Gegen den Menschen, wenn er seinen Spaß will?" (That's exactly the way humans are:/They have to destroy what's there./Who needs a hurricane?/What terrors does a typhoon have/Compared to a human being when he wants his fun? 204).

Advice to calm down is contradicted by incitement to riot. The scene ends with the mixing of the distant chorus's "Fear not" chorale with the peppy, almost joyous reprise of "Wie man sich bettet," every man for himself, the doctrinal basis of Mahagonny's new order. In his review of the Washington, D. C., performance of *Mahagonny* in 1973, Andrew Porter cites a professor at London's Royal College of Music who used to speak of the opera "as an instance of positively *evil* music," in part because of its insidious attraction.[28] Adorno and Gottfried Wagner too are struck repeatedly by its demonic and aggressive tenor.

The early stage history of *Mahagonny* is misleading if one wants to draw conclusions from it concerning the effect of dramatic satire on normal theater audiences. Performances of Brecht plays had been disrupted off and on since 1923 by demonstrations organized by ultraconservative groups.[29] This made his plays appear uncommonly provocative. During the world première of 1930, at the end of the first act, *Mahagonny* elicited loud disapproval from the bona fide constituents of the audience. But then from among the spectators organized bands of university students, members of dueling fraternities, together with right-radical street fighters completely disrupted the performance by carrying out a planned demonstration. To make things worse, the parties of the left had gotten wind of this scheme and had sent members of their youth groups to demonstrate in favor of the opera. The consequence was not a "Skandal" but a battle. The actors stopped playing to watch the fights in the orchestra.[30] Later, when the opera was to be broadcast over the radio, policemen were stationed along the cable to make sure no one severed it.[31]

The few productions after the première and up until 1933, on the other hand, provoked scarcely any response at all. The audience at the first Berlin performance in 1931, directed by Caspar Neher, found the opera too dry and banal. The music impressed them, but the libretto seemed weak. The Vienna performance of 1932, according to one reviewer, was no more than a mockery of the concept of art. Both music and libretto were for him nihilistic, and the music alone a torture for anyone accustomed to the great masters.[32]

One reason for the silence of later audiences—at a Kassel première most spectators quietly departed during the course of the performance—may be that

Brecht revised the book after the Leipzig riot. People came to the theater expecting rude shocks and were disappointed. In the Leipzig version of the opera, Paul Ackermann's closing speech shows him unrepentant and incurable in the face of death. He says: "Ja, ich wünsche, daß ihr alle euch durch meinen schrecklichen Tod nicht abhalten laßt, zu leben, wie es euch paßt, ohne Sorge. Denn ich bereue nicht, daß ich getan habe, was mir beliebt. Hört meine Anweisung!" (Yes, it is my wish that my terrible death not deter you from living as it suits you, without care. For I do not regret having done as I please. Hear my instructions).[33] The episode then reaches its climax with his instructions couched in the words of the song "Laßt euch nicht verführen/Es gibt keine Wiederkehr" (Don't let them mislead you/There's no return).

In the final, authorized version, as revised in 1930 for the Berlin performance and published in volume two of the *Versuche* in the same year, Brecht replaced the crucial speech with Paul Ackermann's confession of error and guilt, suggesting that his great mistake was to use money. Also, the revised speech now ends, in however twisted a fashion, on the faintly blasphemous note: "Ich aß und wurde nicht satt, ich trank und wurde durstig. Gebt mir doch ein Glas Wasser!"[34] Since 1945, *Mahagonny* has enjoyed great success in Germany, the U. S. A., and elsewhere. Its anticapitalist strictures and Weill's music have been uniformly applauded by liberally inclined audiences.

Von morgens bis mitternachts, on the other hand, received far better and fairer treatment once theater censorship was abolished in 1918. Between 1919 and 1924 Berlin theaters mounted four major productions. From the time of its Munich première under the direction of Otto Falckenberg on April 28, 1917, it was recognized as a theatrical milestone. Even "P.S.," reviewer for the *Frankfurter Zeitung,* who objects to the play's confusion, and to the attempt to render psychotic confusion by psychotic confusion, acknowledges the play's suggestive and immediate affective power.[35] Richard Braungart, critic for the *Münchener Zeitung* speaks of a near riot at the close of the play as evidence of Kaiser's uncommon strength. One part of the audience applauded and cheered hysterically; another tried to drown it out "brutally" with catcalls and whistles.[36]

The most discerning review of this performance was written by Joachim Friedenthal. He notes the dramatic tradition—Lenz, Grabbe, Büchner, Wedekind, Sternheim—in which Kaiser stands and then describes the excitement in the theater: "The performance at the Kammerspiele was interrupted by an aroused audience with shouts, laughter and hissing, then toward the end elevated by stormy applause to the level of a special theatrical event."[37] This response was all the more unexpected because the Kammerspiele stage was too small to encompass the action properly, and Erwin Kahler as the cashier was not altogether up to the role.

The first of the four Berlin *mises en scène* between 1919 and 1924, directed by

Felix Hollaender, again excited aggressive audience participation and indignation. According to an anonymous reviewer, "The audience responded to the crass effects with whistles and howls, people got involved in lively personal arguments, offered each other a slap in the face, and joined in the play. The director Hollaender appeared at the end and declared he would report to the author on the play's lively reception."[38]

Fritz Engel wrote in the *Berliner Tageblatt:* "The play found a restless and increasingly aroused audience. They clapped, hissed, whistled cat music on big house keys. They screamed, clenched fists, and insulted one another."[39] Engel describes the audience as overwrought—"überreizt"—and suggests that the cause might be sought in the anticlimaxes and disappointed expectations the play's action provides for. Siegfried Jacobsohn was also struck by the number of ironic and frustrating episodes.[40]

Opinion was, to put it mildly, divided on the merits of the play but unanimous in applauding the performance of Max Pallenberg. Pallenberg had a reputation as an interpreter of comic roles but did not play the cashier consistently for laughs. He kept the spectators off balance. One reviewer wrote: "Pallenberg plays, and people are inclined to laugh. But they are taken aback when the little bearded man's uncanny covert glance moves back and forth; and they get an icy chill when he walks through the lady's hotel room on his weak legs and begins to rave in indignation. Nothing overdone, nothing burlesque. A bitter, scarcely human earnestness that undercuts all the broad comedy, a lurking terror that breaks out wildly in the Salvation Army scene and is as gripping as if this penitent were Moissi and not Pallenberg."[41]

Both these early productions, the openings in Munich and Berlin, touched a nerve. They excited and aggravated audiences to a degree never again matched. The police were present at the first night of the second Berlin production in 1921, but they needn't have bothered to come. The audience was polite and enthusiastic. The director, Viktor Barnowsky, and the leading actor, Alexander Granach, who came from Munich to play the main role, made the production into a classic example of Expressionistic tempo, intensity, and pathos. In doing so they seem to have erased all traces of comedy and slapstick. One reviewer describes Granach's performance as follows: "The audience saw a man cheated and disinherited suddenly wake up but then fall victim to a kind of demonic insanity and race around like a maniac. A hollow-eyed, emaciated, creased face, wasted hands with spidery thin fingers, a worn out, loose fitting coat: these characterize his appearance. From inside, however, there came a scream of hoarse, hungry misery in hard staccato tones."[42]

Granach's interpretation set the style for those to follow. He played the role once more in Berlin in a Jessner production that was greeted with hisses. A reviewer interpreted this response as an expression of moral indignation as well as a comment on poor direction and acting. Granach apparently started off with the berserk tone he should have reserved for the second half of the play.[43] Nevertheless Granach became identified with the role; and he was invited to New York in 1931 to act in a Yiddish version of the play performed at the Public Theater just after Yom Kippur.

The decline in the popularity of *Von morgens bis mitternachts* can be explained, I believe, in two ways. First, the play became famous as *the* Expressionist drama and was played accordingly in the unrelievedly hysterical, intense fashion people had associated with Expressionism. Second, many newspaper reviewers began to read up on Kaiser and began to judge performances in the light of what literary critics were writing about the text. One of the latter coined the designation "Denkspieler" (intellectual player), the reviewers picked it up, and Kaiser has been so categorized ever since. He originated the idea himself in an essay from 1917 entitled "Das Drama Platons" (Plato's Drama), in which he praises Plato's dramatic skill and concludes, "We are drawn into the intellectual game and have already learned to appreciate blissful think-pleasure over meager spectator pleasure."[44] Yet all Kaiser's admiration for Plato does not change the fact that his own plays remain rather disordered, passionate, uncalculated pieces, and not "mere" think-plays.

That *Von morgens bis mitternachts* can make very good theater is evident from its reception in other times and in places outside Germany. The Theatre Guild of New York, with Frank Reicher as director and leading actor, staged it at the end of its 1921-22 season as an experiment for the delectation of subscribers. The reception was so enthusiastic that the run was extended and the play was moved to a larger theater to accommodate the general public. Working with the translation made by Ashley Dukes in 1919, which had trimmed away some of the hyperbole, Reicher wisely relieved the monotony by exploiting the play's comic and slapstick potential and so earned cheers from the audience, which, like the Berliners in 1919, laughed even during the Salvation Army scene. In London, on the other hand, staid spectators and critics dismissed the production of Dukes's version as "a regrettable breach of taste."[45]

More recent productions at the University of Leeds—a 1977 amateur effort with tricks to involve the audience—and in 1974 in Cologne with an all-star cast under Robert Ciulli's direction got near unanimous critical acclaim and applause.[46] The sole negative vote on the latter performance comes from Werner Bruck in the *Mosaik* [Hadamar] issue of 4 October 1974. Bruck notes the audience's approval but then records his own disappointment that the play's promise of "Kapitalismuskritik" is not fulfilled; it gets sidetracked into realms of morality and idealism.

Georg Kaiser's play was completed at roughly the same time as Sternheim's *1913*. Yet they are radically different. Kaiser's piece represents a new departure in style and material. *Von morgens bis mitternachts* is constructed more like a film than a stage drama. Whereas Sternheim's characters belong to the power elite or upper middle class and his scenes are laid in drawing rooms, Kaiser puts an average man and a crowd on stage in locations like banks and cafés. Both authors were writing on the eve of Germany's entrance into war. *1913* develops the consequences of the nation's self-deception and fatal obsession with prestige. *Von morgens bis mitternachts,* on the other hand, prefigures the great adventure, the move to greatness, and its end.

Kaiser and Brecht also exploit the sociological problems of their time. Kaiser's cashier is typical of the majority of Germans in that until his escape he lived and worked in a provincial city. Some of the play's comic effects are developed from his ignorance of sophisticated urban ways. He travels to Berlin in search of the "philistine's paradise," as Brecht described his Mahagonny. The metropolis—Petronius's Rome, Pope's London, Nathanael West's Los Angeles—has from the start been the favored satiric backdrop. Kaiser and Brecht give us Berlin and the Berlin experience; the effect of the big city on mind and soul, the problems of mass culture, and the spread of the American way of life (jazz, sport, speakeasies, free love) lie at the heart of the two plays. Brecht's vacationers are weary of city life and want to escape civilization. Their song "Auf nach Mahagonny" calls it "die Zi-zi-zi-zi-zivilis" perhaps in recollection of the epidemic of venereal disease in Berlin in the early 1920s.[47] Their flight actually takes them not out of the city but rather to its entertainment district.

Both plays draw on urban fads and obsessions: pornography, "liberated" sex, operetta, professional sport, including boxing. We are shown the new barbarism and the devices by which people hoped to escape from reality into a land of pure pleasure. Tabloids, films, illustrated magazines, the mass media provided inspiration and material for these daydreams, and both plays show their effect on the mind and mood of the time.

The cures for "Zivilis" as prescribed by the cashier and Paul Ackermann are ill-conceived. They only create worse problems. The cashier's vision of an amalgamated, ecstatic humanity is a travesty on the views propounded in earnest by critics of culture and by serious advocates of the new barbarism. I have in mind here the renewed interest, during the twenties, in the ideas of Paul de Lagarde, Julius Langbehn, and other prophets of nationalism and racism. Spengler's *Untergang des Abendlandes* [*Decline of the West,* 1918-1922] at the beginning of the Weimar period and Ludwig Klages' equally weighty *Der Geist als Widersacher der Seele* [The Mind as Opponent of the Soul, 1929-1932] at the close are symptomatic of the prevalence and respectability of antirationalistic, vulgar-vitalist ideas. Both give a sweeping overview of human history in order to show the present day in decline. Klages is the more radical, foretelling the end of all natural life brought on by the abuses of technical civilization.

These terrible simplifiers are close kin to the cashier and Paul Ackermann in their messianic costume. Their message is like the fatalistic siren call of Brecht's Jenny: forget work, discipline, thought, and let go. In abstract fashion the political scientist Kurt Sontheimer describes the same intellectual regression and consequent disaster that Brecht dramatizes:

> By simply damning reason, "subjugating mind to life" (Thomas Mann) they opened the door to the subjective caprices of ideological assumptions; worse still: they purposely opened the safety valve on drives and passions and—imitating Sorel—thought it wonderful to suggest to these drives and passions mythic images and symbols to take the place of the thinking mind. The abdication of the mind in the face of forces of the depths therefore actually characterizes the situation. But this means that when social relationships become troubled, then the ordering and culturally creative functions of the mind are delivered over to the dark forces of life. Whoever preaches irrationalism must expect irrationality and evil to gain power. Whoever refuses to impose any limits of reason and morality on life must anticipate that life in its most inhuman form will seize power and won't give up so quickly.[48]

With simulative irony and satiric intent, Kaiser's *Von morgens bis mitternachts* speaks the antirational language of an earlier era. It quotes the litany of the cult of sexuality, fertility, and the dynamic life force that resounded in Wedekind's plays. Not yet sunk to the level of the lumberjacks' naked pursuit of intoxication as escape, this exalted and overheated sensualism nevertheless followed the same path. Gunter Martens, in his book on the period from 1890 to 1910, speaks of how the striving for an ever more intense capacity to feel—Sternheim's *1913* says "Sensationen"—leads toward a hunger for sensual intoxication that no stimulus, however strong, can satisfy. "The whole era," he continues, quoting an essay from 1926, "presents the picture of a narcotics addict who requires increasingly strong doses of a stimulant in order to stir his enervated senses and blunted nerves again."[49]

Writing in 1912, the year in which Kaiser's play originated, Walter Rathenau used the same metaphor of narcotic addition to describe the workings of city life and the communications media on the human psyche. Stunned by the speed and incoherence of ideas and images from the newspapers and magazines as well as the world around him, Rathenau writes in his much read essay *Zur Kritik der Zeit*, the city dweller has no time to compose himself. He continues:

> In the hail of facts, the capacity for wonder, respect for action, receptivity die out, and at the same time the lust for new facts, for intensified experience grows greater. If these desires are not satisfied, then depression and exhaustion ensue, which make the time of one's own life seem hateful and are called for that reason boredom ("Langeweile").
> From a mechanical viewpoint, boredom is the warning signal whispering to a person that he is for the time being excluded from the action and spurs him to seek the compulsion of work or pleasure.[50]

This neophiliac disease of the hypertrophied imagination that runs its cyclical course from ecstatic anticipation to anticlimax and frustration Fritz Stern identifies at four points in German history between Bismarck and Hitler. His four upheavals are: the youth and emancipation movements of 1890, the euphoria of August, 1914, the mystical, comradely wartime front experience, and "the idealistic brutality of the postwar years."[51] Stern also emphasizes the "deep national frustrations, galling discontents which inspired nationalist phantasies and utopias which found easy assent among the German elite." These phantasies drew their form and content from the work of prophets of cultural despair—Julius Langbehn, Paul de Lagarde, Arthur Moeller van den Bruck, and the others—who like Paul Ackermann and the cashier proposed to destroy the present order "in order to usher in a future Reich."

This recurrent, cyclical historical phenomenon of repression, new departure, and anticlimax is best analyzed and presented in Christopher Booker's *The Neophiliacs*.[52] Booker gives us the plot of these and other satires in psychological and social terms, using England in the period from 1956 to 1965 as his model on which to demonstrate the working structure of phantasy and to define the cycle's course. This is coincidentally the euphoric time of the German Economic Miracle reflected in Dürrenmatt's *Besuch der alten Dame*. Booker's scheme is not only widely applicable; it integrates most of the threats and evils that have been identified as the targets of modern German satiric drama.

The germs of neophilia were spread first by the media, Booker argues. The publicity industry, giving the word "image" new weight and content, developed new ways of engaging the eye and mind. Through the titillating arts of advertising, the public gained a sense of sweeping change. Once the initially vague but potent phantasy was implanted, it created an aggressive group solidarity, out of touch with reality, and inhuman because it could see the world only in terms of unreal images. "Every phantasy requires a constant supply of new images and sensations," according to Booker, and in the decade 1956-1965, as on many earlier occasions in the history of the race, these took the form of dreams of vitality, nourished by the contemplation of disorder or of violations of order. The entire British nation suffered from a sense of constriction and longed to escape to a "dimly sensed heightened reality" somehow associated with sex and violent aggression.

The trouble with these images is that they excite but do not satisfy. This fact explains what Booker terms the phantasy spiral, which "feeds on a succession of sensations or unresolved images, each one of which arouses anticipation, followed by inevitable frustration, leading to the demand for a new image to be put in its place." This intensifying desire grows ever more chimerical and violent, and the fantasy moves ever "further from reality until it is actually bringing about the very opposite of its aims, the dreams producing the nightmare, the vision of freedom producing the slavery" of the addict; and one could add here, with Georg Kaiser, the cult of vitalism leading to death. Booker sees the same connection and notes: "[...] behind the glittering dream of life and vitality lies nothing less than the death wish." According to Booker's scheme, the psychic epidemic proceeds through five stages on its way to the culminating "apparently senseless explosion of destructive or self-destructive violence." These stages are: anticipation, dream, frustration, nightmare, and finally the collective death wish.[53]

There are two main ingredients that constitute this dream. One can be seen in Paul Ackermann's promise of liberation and joy. The other is the technological dream of power, freedom, and silent efficiency best represented by Christian Maske and later by the citizens of Güllen in Dürrenmatt's *Besuch der alten Dame*. Both are inextricably entwined with aggression.

Finally, the idea of a forfeited paradise, still worse, the feeling of being right now in hell, as well as the destruction of human life and the body politic, with which these plays make their most striking statements, Booker integrates into his mythical religious pattern of phantasy. Toward the end of *The Neophiliacs* he writes:

> All the great religions contain some version of the Fall, or man's 'separation' from his true existence, usually pointed up with a picture of some paradise or golden age before he became thus separated—as in the Greek myth of Pandora's Box which, when opened, released evil into the world. Similarly, in their different versions of Hell and its punishments, all religions contain their own projections of the nature of fantasy and its consequences, whether the fate of Sisyphus and Tantalus, doomed for their offences to the eternal affirmation of anticipation and frustration or simply the straightforward nightmare-cum-death-wish culmination of hellfire and eternal damnation. Again, all religions contain their mythical projections of fantasy in a straightforward worldly sense, such as the story of what happened to Sodom and Gomorrha, or the fate of the tower of Babel, or the nemesis that overcame the world when it had become wicked in Noah's time.[54]

Common to all these stories is that "mankind had become so evil that it had brought upon itself an unparalleled disaster, from which a tiny handful survived to carry on the chain. For of course the essence of the death wish that lies at the heart of all fantasy is that it is not just personal, but that it also comprehends the death of the species as a whole, of all life."

This quotation with its fire and brimstone rhetoric and with its reference to the tower of Babel will be worth keeping in mind as we examine Friedrich Dürrenmatt's satiric dramas.

In 1949 Friedrich Dürrenmatt destroyed the manuscript of a play entitled *Der Turmbau von Babel* [The Tower of Babel]. Yet the idea has continued to preoccupy him. He has recently published a series of Tower drawings, "Turmbau I-IV,"

Dürrenmatt, "Turmbau IV: Vor dem Sturz" (1975). Plate 15 in:
Dürrenmatt: *Bilder und Zeichnungen.*

from the years 1952-1978 in his *Bilder und Zeichnungen* [Pictures and Draw-ings].[55] And in the notes accompanying the drama *Ein Engel kommt nach Babylon* [An Angel Comes to Babylon, 1953], he suggests the point of that play: "Everyone is against the tower, and it gets built nevertheless."[56] The construction of the Tower, symbol of human folly, pride, confusion, thwarted schemes, aggression, and division, stands behind most of Dürrenmatt's satiric work. In *Die Physiker* [*The Physicists*, 1962] Möbius wants to prevent the military and industrial exploitation of his discoveries. Nevertheless all his efforts serve to accomplish the opposite, and he sees them exploited in a way that assures the end of life on Earth. In *Der Besuch der alten Dame* (1956), the townspeople of Güllen reject the idea of killing Alfred Ill in order to restore the city. But they cannot help but murder him and live on in affluent misery. In other works as well, even Dürrenmatt's most civic-minded people, acting as members of a collective, deceive and defeat themselves, bringing disaster to the broader human community. Dürrenmatt's great accomplishment is to make this process of seemingly inevitable failure vis-ible to reader and audience.

One can gain an initial sense of the way Dürrenmatt's satire works from a comparison of one of his early radio plays, *Der Prozeß um des Esels Schatten (nach Wieland aber nicht sehr)* [The Lawsuit over the Ass's Shadow (After Wie-land but not very)], completed in 1951 and published in 1956, with book four of Christoph Martin Wieland's *Geschichte der Abderiten* ([History of the Abder-ites, 1781]. The earlier version, *Die Abderiten*, appeared in 1774), which bears the same title and on which Dürrenmatt's radio play is based.

Wieland's novel, of which this episode is the best known part, stands as a master-piece of comic-satiric writing. It tells how the Republic of Abdera—known in the literature of late antiquity as a community of narrow-minded dunces—brought itself to the edge of destruction. Dürrenmatt, on the other hand, does not avert the catastrophe. His Abdera goes up in flames.

The city of Abdera at some unspecified ancient time is the scene of Wieland's chronicle. He builds a consistent fiction and maintains an even, urbane narrative tone. His Abdera is at the same time a model polis, and its politics bear a strong resemblance to those of certain central European petty principalities of the eighteenth century. One of Wieland's main points is that people and institutions of all places and times are much the same. "What fools these mortals be," the reader thinks as he sees the quarrel over the cash value of an ass's shadow bring out the worst in everyone, divide the city literally into two armed camps, and finally resolve itself in the nick of time as both parties vent their rage on the ass. The whole incident ends with the Abderites' Homeric laughter, an expression at once of relief and recognition: "The Abderites were laughing themselves now at their folly as an attack of feverish madness, which, thank God!, was now over."[57] Their great comic dramatist, Thlaps, immortalizes the escapade in a popular play and so renders it harmless.

The potential for aggressive violence is present in Wieland's novel, but the participants are too civilized to "set the city in blood and flames."[58] Wieland's characters are guilty of real evils: the debauching of innocents, corruption among those entrusted with high office, sexual bribery, and religious hypocrisy. His women are fickle, the men venal and obsessed with power. The whole city becomes infected with the fever, but explosion into civil war is averted. Wieland's liberal, witty tone prevails. His tongue-in-cheek, allusive style makes the villainy and folly seem no more than a temporary aberration, human foibles we can all understand and excuse. The Abderites are none the wiser, to be sure, but no harm is done, except to the ass.

Dürrenmatt sets his accents differently. He devotes far less attention to the complicated intrigues set off by the litigation over the shadow. Nor is he much interested in the private lives of his characters or in the intricate relationships between the two churches and the state. He gives us only two of the several set speeches Wieland has his attorneys deliver before the court.

Dürrenmatt's Abdera is located in history by ominous references to the Peloponnesian War and the beginnings of the disastrous Athenian campaign against Sicily (413 B.C.). On the other hand, the language spoken is a very colloquial modern German, and some of the characters—firemen, the managing director of Marble Inc., the head of the Tourist Office, and the leader of the S.P.C.A.—seem out of place in ancient Greece. Mundane details: garlic, wine, schnapps, wife beating, dentistry, and poultry give the radio play an earthy, vulgar quality.

Matters follow the course laid out by Wieland until shortly beyond the midpoint of the action, where Dürrenmatt's chief concern emerges. No one wants it to happen, but things take a turn for the worse when the lawsuit becomes the occasion for an ideological battle, a miniature Cold War. Judge Philippides, Dürrenmatt's satiric spokesman, complains that the leaders of the opposing factions have done great mischief, "aus diesem Prozeß eine Angelegenheit der Philosophie, der Ideale und weiß Gott was für heiliger Güter zu machen" (by making of this lawsuit an issue of philosophy, of ideals, and God knows what sacred things).[59] Abdera's doom is sealed when people turn the original insignificant issue into a matter of principle. Party lines—bourgeois right and proletarian left—harden. Thykidides, director of Weapons Inc., makes the situation literally more explosive by offering arms to both sides. And if this were not bad enough, things take the worst possible turn when representatives of each party approach Captain Typhis and buy his help in their good causes.

Typhis is altogether Dürrenmatt's creation. There is no similar figure in Wieland's novel. At the outset he appears a rough and ready, drunken sea captain with a girl in every port. He identifies himself to listeners by singing the "Ballade von den Seeräubern" (Ballad of the Pirates) a song from Brecht's *Hauspostille* (1927). But when the opposing factions each hire him to set fire to the other's temple, Typhis is transformed into something like the hundred-headed, fire breathing Typhon of Greek myth. He completely dominates the closing pages of the play. He is no longer merely larger than life but a grotesque monster, Abdera's Nemesis. Once he is set in motion there is no stopping him. Through this figure Dürrenmatt gives his play a nightmarish conclusion and an unforgettable satiric symbol of human aggression and violence. In his role as avenger, in his ruthless use of force, and with his internal contradictions, Typhis is a prefiguration of Claire Zachanassian in *Der Besuch der alten Dame*. Through him are revealed the true nature and the consequences of the Abderites' wishes and daydreams. "Bist du zu mir gekommen, Mann, nun hast du mich bekommen, den Kapitän Typhis, dessen blutige Hände deine Gedanken ausführen" (You came to me, man, and now you've got me, Captain Typhis, whose bloody hands are carrying out your thoughts), he says.[60] He is the incarnation of Freud's destrudo.

In his final prophetic speech, delivered as he sails away and addressed more to the listener than to Abdera, he makes the same point with greater force: "Ich wurde der Feuerhauch, der eure Vergänglichkeit sengte, die Gerechtigkeit, die über diese Stadt kam und immer wieder kommen wird, ich wurde die Hölle eurer Taten, die ihr selbst begangen, die ihr selbst in euren Träumen herbeiwünschtet" (I became the breath of fire that singed your frailty, the justice that came over this city and will come again and again, I became the hell of your acts that you committed yourselves, that you yourselves wished for in your dreams).[61] Dürrenmatt offers no comic, humane resolution on the order of Wieland's but rather the hell and bonfire of human aggression, disguised as an ideologically inspired battle for freedom or for the homeland. This is the apocaplyptic vision of the conservative and prophetic—in the biblical sense—satirist Friedrich Dürrenmatt.

The picture of a society burning in an Inferno of its own making is not new to satire, but Dürrenmatt makes it particularly vivid and up-to-date. In a short prose sketch entitled "Zu den Teppichen von Angers" (On the Tapestries of Angers) he muses on the meaning for today of these fourteen century tapestries illustrating the Apocalypse of St. John. It was composed in 1951, the same year as *Der Prozeß um des Esels Schatten* and reads like a gloss on its conclusion. For contemporary Western man the Last Judgment has become identical with a nuclear disaster, after which a burned out Earth will continue to circle meaninglessly about the sun. The essay continues:

> The consolation that even the collapse of all things is Grace, that it is the angels themselves who kill, has been replaced by the certainty that mankind is capable on its own of setting off an inferno of elements that people formerly dared ascribe only to God's anger; and cruelties are being perpetrated that surpass the devil's. So that which was revelation has actually taken place, but it is no longer a fight over Good and Evil, no matter how eager each party is to portray it thus. Humanity as a whole has become guilty, everyone wants to rescue ideals along with the opposite: Free-

dom and business deals, justice and rape. The human being who once trembled before hell has erected a secular world that has produced hells which devour the guilty and the innocent without distinction.[62]

This static picture of hell on earth has remained a part of Dürrenmatt's *Weltanschauung* up to the present. He has altered it only to make it into one phase of the process he calls the dramaturgy of world history. The cast may change but the action is always the same. Most people, he says, accept this situation resignedly as the inevitable consequence of the human condition, "the condition inherent, sad to say, in all human beings in all their recalcitrance, wildness, sloth, luxury, in all their hunger for goods and power, but also in all their unconscious selves."[63]

Of all the playwrights in this study, Dürrenmatt has taken the greatest pains to help readers, audiences, and theater people understand his plays and his intentions. And he comes closer than any of the others to claiming the designation satirist. In his two-page autobiography he writes of his Swiss childhood and antecedents, one of whom, his paternal grandfather, was an irascible politician, poet, and newspaper publisher, proud of his ten days under arrest for an impious poem on the front page. And with oblique reference to his clergyman father, he says elsewhere: "Ich bin Protestant und ich protestiere" (I'm a Protestant, and I protest).[64]

Dürrenmatt makes no effort to disguise his aggressive temperament. He recognizes it as the motive force behind his writing. He generalizes from this personal conviction on the mission of all writers: "The writer can fulfill his moral obligation only if he is an anarchist. He must attack but not be involved."[65] Malice, he says in the same conversation, is the duty of every dramatist. His anger, consternation, and distress on being misunderstood, and his conception of his mission as writer emerge clearly from what would have to be called the parable of the woman driver:

> Today's humanity resembles a woman driver. She is driving down her road with increasing speed and carelessness. But she doesn't like it when her passenger cries in consternation "Look Out!" and "Here's a danger sign," or "Put on the brakes now," or "Don't run over that child." She hates it when anyone asks who paid for the car or provided gas and oil or when he has the nerve to ask to see her license. Uncomfortable truths could come to light. The car could have been taken from a relative without permission, gas and oil extorted from the passengers and not really gas and oil but the blood and sweat of all of us, and the license could possibly not exist at all; it could even turn out that she is driving for the first time. It would be painful of course if one asked about such obvious things. She loves it when one praises the beauty of the countryside she's driving through, the silver of a stream, the glow of the glaciers in the distance, amusing stories too she loves to hear whispered in her ear. It is no longer really possible, however, for today's writer to whisper those stories and praise the beautiful countryside with good conscience.

But unfortunately he can't get out of the car to satisfy the demand for pure poetry that all the non-poets are making on him. Fear, worry, and above all anger force open his mouth.[66]

The language Dürrenmatt's parabolic writer speaks is the discomfiting language of satire. Dürrenmatt may apply other terms—comedy, the grotesque, serious humor—to his work, but with each he means something that is both dangerous and moral, unmasking and demanding.[67] And what dismays him most is to observe how his audience and the critics go about dulling or removing the sting in his plays merely by denying them validity as works of art. By attributing the unfavorable reception of his later plays to this practice of anaesthetic criticism and also by unsparing attacks on people who think of themselves as progressive intellectuals, Dürrenmatt has himself placed some barriers in the way of understanding.

His expressions of admiration for Aristophanes and Jonathan Swift as well as his unspoken but implied claim to be their heir give clues to the way he sees himself.[68] Other authors in what Dürrenmatt calls the "comic" tradition include Wedekind, Brecht, Karl Kraus, Gogol, Rabelais, and Cervantes.[69] They all attack with some degree of outrage the evils and follies of their time, and so can be said to practice socialized aggression. But what sets them apart from run-of-the-mill social critics is the power of their aesthetic imagination to transform the real world through satiric fictions, "Einfälle" ("Einfall" is Dürrenmatt's word meaning roughly idea, inspiration, brainstorm) or grotesque deformation—an imprecise term often used to describe Dürrenmatt's work.

The three terms—satiric fiction, "Einfall," and grotesque deformation—are so closely related that they are practically interchangeable. "Einfälle" are the missiles Dürrenmatt fires at reality, and their effect is to raise it to the imaginative level of the grotesque. Once in this state, its true condition becomes apparent, and it becomes the vehicle of undirected satire, beyond reportage and tendentiousness. The concluding sentences of his essay "Anmerkungen zur Komödie" (Notes on Comedy, 1952) bring together on the example of *Gulliver's Travels* the concepts of satire and the grotesque as well as the three components of satire: sadistic, moral, and artistic:

> The grotesque travels of Gulliver are like a retort in which the weaknesses and limitations of mankind are demonstrated in four different experiments. The grotesque is one of the great opportunities for being accurate. It can't be denied that this art possesses the cruelty of objectivity, but it is not the art of the nihilist but sooner of the moralist, not the art of rot but of salt. It is a matter of wit and sharp intellect (that's why the Enlightenment was good at it), not of what the public understands by humor: a sometimes sentimental, sometimes frivolous geniality. It is bothersome but necessary.[70]

As the years have passed, Dürrenmatt has moved farther and farther away from the genre of ironic comedy. Even though it withholds resolution and reconciliation, *Romulus der Große* [Romulus the Great, 1949] has remained popular because of the preponderance of comfortable, often serene and humane humor over anger and violence. It is a comedy tinged with satire.

Since the late 1950s, however, beginning with *Frank V* (1959), his plays have grown blacker and blacker; the grotesque "Einfälle" have become less comic and more bloody. The fools have declined and the knaves increased in number. Aggression and moral indignation remain strong, but the fictions have grown thin. His dramas, as *Play Strindberg*, his adaptation of Strindberg's *Dance of Death*, suggests, have acquired a morbid, obscenely violent quality. Betrayal, murder, mass slaughter on the battlefield have become central images, and we find ourselves in Northrop Frye's sixth and last phase of satire, which "differs from a pure inferno mainly in the fact that in human experience suffering has an end in death."[71] This change has lessened his popularity with directors and theatergoers.

His most successful drama, now become a theater classic, is *Der Besuch der alten Dame* (1956). It is at the same time his best made dramatic satire. In its compressed, watch-like intricacy everything counts. Like a Kafka novel, it cries out for interpretation. One discovers on each reading new interrelationships and patterns of meaning, ironies, allusions, ambiguities. It is also eminently playable, carried by a sure sense for theatrical effect and a wealth of comic-ironic-grotesque ideas.

The plot is simple and the action realistic with the qualification that it is governed and propelled by the outlandish figure of Claire Zachanassian. She embodies Dürrenmatt's satiric fiction and his most explosive "Einfall."

Forty-five years before the play opens she lost a paternity suit against her lover Alfred Ill, on the basis of false testimony by bribed witnesses. She left the small town of Güllen, pregnant and in disgrace. Perforce she became a prostitute, then married an Armenian billionaire, and has since become the richest, most powerful, most envied and notorious person in the world. She has divorced husbands and taken new ones so often she has lost track. The sole survivor of a plane crash in Afghanistan, she has an artificial leg and a hand made of ivory. She has used her wealth and power secretly to buy out Güllen's industries, close them, and so bankrupt the town. The play opens as she returns to visit her old home. There she announces the true purpose of her homecoming: to buy justice for the wrong done her. At the end of act one she offers the town one billion (in an unspecified currency) on the condition that someone kill Alfred Ill. In the name of humanity and humanism, the citizens indignantly reject the offer.

Acts two and three show how the Gülleners, precisely because they are only human, lose their resolve, succumb to the temptation to buy on credit, and so are forced to commit the murder no one wanted. The way in which this comes about, the rationalizations and devices the townspeople contrive to justify and carry out the act, the corruption of Güllen in other words, compose the substance of Dürrenmatt's satire.

Like his predecessors, Kaiser's cashier and Brecht's Paul Ackermann, Alfred Ill is both savior and scapegoat; and he rises to near tragic status just before his aggravatingly inappropriate murder, or execution. The figure of Ill takes on other aspects as well and is more complicated than the others. He is a villain, guilty of a cruel and thoughtless crime in his youth, recognizes this in the course of the play, and accepts his death as expiation. Through two thirds of the drama, however, he behaves like a mediocre, morally obtuse shopkeeper, no less unscrupulous than the average citizen. Because of his betrayal of the young Claire Zachanassian, reader and audience, like the Gülleners, can accept his punishment as somewhat harsh, to be sure, but justified. This is so until the beginning of the third and last act, when Dürrenmatt pulls the rug out. A wholly transformed Ill takes the stage. He is ennobled by his acceptance of guilt and remains to his execution serene, dignified, and yet humane and understanding.

What seemed a feasible resolution to the city's problems is now a murder out of greed. Alfred Ill rejects the mayor's suggestion that he commit suicide and so forces the fatal decision on the community. He is the dramatic satirist in act three. He, together with the audience, watch in dismayed awareness as the morally numbed Gülleners develop the elaborate hypocritical ritual that will bring them the billion.

Dürrenmatt also closes off the last avenue of escape left the audience, namely the identification of Claire Zachanassian as the villain. If he showed us her vengeful, misanthropic, cynical side alone, it would be easy to generate indignation against her as the embodiment, say, of the capitalist power elite. But enough of her softer, human, sentimental qualities—recollections of youthful love, the dead baby, the death of the heart—emerge more strongly toward the play's end. Consequently one is confronted with the devious immorality of the Güllners' deed, and if one finds no effective rationalization, he must accept his role as potential accomplice, or "Mitmacher."

Dürrenmatt is a master of the art of withholding resolution. The play's end brings no real satisfaction for any of the three parties. Claire's "justice" takes the form of Ill's corpse and proves in reality only an act of revenge. Her life has no further purpose, and she has lost all contact with the living world. Ill's hope that his death will mean the carrying out of justice and will also, perhaps, awaken the townspeople to their moral depravity, is deceived by the coalition of Gülleners and newsmen. The play's coda, the closing chorus of townspeople, is a parody on a passage from Hölderlin's translation of Sophocles's *Antigone,* lines 332 and following. Both begin "Ungeheuer ist viel [...]" (Much is monstrous). Sophocles continues, "[...] und nichts/Ungeheurer als der Mensch" (And nothing more monstrous than man). Dürrenmatt's Gülleners, on the other hand, dressed in evening clothes and standing before a renovated city gleaming in neon and chrome, sing of their earlier poverty and the comforts of affluence. Their words are directed at the audience and are, despite their stiff archaic tone, a plea for understanding that cannot fairly be rejected.

Dürrenmatt leaves little doubt that this prosperity is rotten and will not last. As Claire Zachanassian brought doom to Alfred Ill, so Güllen's Nemesis is sure to come. Güllen's rise is its fall. Further support for this reading comes from the final speech of *Ein Engel kommt nach Babylon* (1953), delivered in the rhymed prose of the Arabic maqamat. Dürrenmatt's spokesman, the beggar Akki, says: "Babylon, blind und fahl, zerfällt mit seinem Turm aus Stein und Stahl, der sich unaufhaltsam in die Höhe schiebt, dem Sturz entgegen [...]" (Babylon, blind and fallow, crumbles with its tower of stone and steel, which is pushing its way irresistibly upward, towards its collapse. I, 262). Like the chorus at the end of *Mahagonny,* this collective is unrepentant and none the wiser. "For a society, however it is ordered, is not threatened by individuals but by itself," writes Dürrenmatt in the foreword to *Der Mitmacher: Ein Komplex* (1976).[72]

What seemed at the beginning of *Der Besuch der alten Dame* like a perfect partnership promising to restore the city to health very soon takes on a threatening aspect. The citizens of Güllen, through the mediation of Ill, expect to regain the prosperity that is their due. And Claire can look forward to achieving perfect justice. Yet things don't work that way. The play consists in a series of frustrated efforts to resolve the problem presented by Alfred Ill. The elaborate preparations for Claire's reception go for nought as does the economically attractive scheme intended to buy back Ill's life.

The uncanny high point of the action is reached at the end of act two where Ill stands on the steps of the train that may carry him to safety. The Gülleners are crowded around him. He wants to leave, and the Gülleners too wish he would board and be off. In sincerity they implore him to get on. He is paralyzed, however, by the fear that they will do him harm. And so the train departs without him. By its mere presence the town has inadvertently brought itself a step closer to catastrophe.

This seemingly unstoppable course of events is set in motion by Claire Zachanassian, who knows well what will happen, and watches with cynical patience as the action unfolds. She shares Dürrenmatt's low estimate of mankind's moral fibre. But the play is so constructed that reader and audience perceive things from Alfred Ill's perspective. They should ideally share his fear and dismay and echo his cry of "Mein Gott!" at the travesty of justice his trial represents.

The crucial question Dürrenmatt's audience must ask itself is: How is it possible for the decent citizens of a civilized democratic community to murder one of their number? At first glance it is inconceivable that this group of well meaning people could kill. Yet Dürrenmatt makes it all too plausible. The lethal danger lies in the human psyche and in the moral realities of individual and collective existence, of which the play constructs a rather spare model. Human weakness, a natural moral lethargy, understandable aversion to poverty, a preference for creature comforts: these are the things that make it necessary to commit murder. The play is a demonstration of the banality of evil.

The outcome is less horrifying in its effect—Ill's execution takes place in the dark and in silence—than the process that leads up to it. This process is guided by the workings of the collective mind, which Dürrenmatt translates vividly into speech and action. The Gülleners betray their unconscious selves by the way they cheer and applaud, by their turns of phrase, by the way they handle knives and guns, by buying on credit, by their choice in brands of chocolate and brandy, and by their new yellow shoes. As they leave the reception for Claire at the train station, they fall in line behind the coffin she has brought with her (I, 282). On two occasions, one at the beginning and the other at play's end, the cue for their jubilant cheer is not the offer of a billion but the condition attached (I, 292, 347). When they assure Ill of their support, they reinforce the statement with "Todsicher"—sure as death (I, 301)—or "[...] da können Sie Gift darauf nehmen" (You can take poison on that. I, 305). Even the radio is involved; from it come forth tunes from *The Merry Widow*. The policeman inadvertently aims his rifle at Ill (I, 307). And the press photographers ask him to pose bent forward over his shop counter as the butcher in front of him weighs a big cleaver in his hand.

All these slips and ironies are evidences of aggression, and they are contradicted by protestations of innocent good will right up to the final episode. As their dreams of affluence are realized, the Gülleners develop a startling capacity for argumentation and for moral indignation at the vices of others. For protective purposes they grow insensitive and sure of themselves. Ill gets nowhere with his appeals for support and mercy. The Gülleners barricade themselves behind an infallible moral system as tight as Claire's monetary logic.

Dürrenmatt erects other signposts pointing to his chief concern. These are the structural traits normally found in a satire. Trivial items—yellow shoes, a typewriter, cigars—acquire crucial importance. On the other hand, Claire over and over again reduces the great to the petty, be it the leadership of world powers or venerable concepts like humanity and justice. Dürrenmatt's ideas for mixing incommensurate ingredients are as imaginative as any of his predecessors'. Most often he brings together vaudeville comedy and blank horror. The two little men, like Tweedledum and Tweedledee and named here Koby and Loby, blinded and castrated some time back at Claire's order in punishment for their perjury at her paternity hearing, are laughable as long as they speak in their ridiculous tandem fashion and as long as one forgets their condition and what led to it. The architecture of Güllen is represented in the play by two structures: the gothic cathedral and the public toilet erected by Claire's father (I, 277, 279). Only the latter is visible on stage. It is also of greater importance to the play. Two serious scenes between Claire and Ill in the Konradsweil woods are leavened by the presence of four actors, earlier on stage as citizens of Güllen, playing the roles of trees, birds, and animals.

Claire returns to the woods because they were the scene of her trysts with Ill. He is not content with memories; he seems to want to annul time and return to the days of youthful paradisal bliss. But as in earlier instances, Paul Ackermann's and the cashier's efforts to restore innocence and return to Eden, Ill's project backfires. Claire obliges him, to be sure, by returning to the past, not to relive their love affair, but to restore the balance of justice. This time she buys the judge and the executioners. In fact she goes much further than this. She corrupts a model town and with it the ethical standard of Western civilization. In satire, attempts to regain Eden result in intensified recurrences of the Fall. With each cycle, guilt and punishment grow more severe. This is what lies in store for Güllen after the curtain falls. "Noch weiß ich, daß auch einmal zu uns eine alte Dame kommen wird," prophesies the teacher to Ill in his last moment of illumination, "und daß dann mit uns geschehen wird, was nun mit Ihnen geschieht [...]" (Yet I know that one day an old lady will come to visit us too, and what is being done to you will be done to us. I, 334).

The inescapable, rigid quality of this scheme of events is reinforced through the play by repetition, by ceremonial and ritual. Almost every scene has its counterpart somewhere else in the play. There are two meetings in the Konradsweil woods. Acts one and three end with a formal trial and sentencing of Alfred Ill. The choric crowd movement in the train boarding episode at the end of act two is very much like that at his execution at the close of the final act. Over the potentially chaotic violence of the collective is imposed a frozen ritual pattern that produces a symmetry of terror; so many scenes and situations share the formal structure of the whole and anticipate the killing of Alfred Ill.

The series of parallel choric scenes finds its climax in the play's most powerful and troubling episode, the community's great concluding ceremony preparatory to the murder. In its labyrinthine ironies and compounded falsehoods it is at once the most beautiful and the most terrible demonstration of the betrayal and corruption of all that Dürrenmatt understands by "Geist": the ethical and cultural Judaeo-Christian, Western tradition. The Gülleners cite these things to distract from their blood guilt. They want to have it both ways, to live at ease in affluence and to have an easy conscience.

The whole travesty of piety and justice is conducted on a stage within a stage. On the proscenium arch is inscribed the slightly distorted, oft cited last line from the prologue to Friedrich Schiller's *Wallensteins Lager* [Wallenstein's Camp, 1798]: "Ernst ist das Leben, heiter die Kunst" (Life is earnest, art serene. I, 345). In actuality it is hard to imagine anything in real life blacker and more distressing than what takes place beneath that inscription. Then at the close of the episode, a newsman glosses the official announcement that Ill has died of a heart attack brought on by the joyful excitement with the hackneyed phrase, here the complete reversal of the truth: "Das Leben schreibt die schönsten Geschichten" (Life writes the nicest stories. I, 353). What is spoken in the space between these two clichés strikes reader and audience as even more perverted and mendacious.

Kaiser's Salvation Army revival meeting followed by the scramble for the cashier's money, and Brecht's blatant travesty of justice in the trial and execution of Paul Ackermann are comparable to this episode in nature and function. The ritualized crowd scene is a convention of recent dramatic satire. And here again Dürrenmatt's "Einfälle" give his version an impact far stronger than that provided by the others. His ceremony is part legal trial and part cultural event, since it is located specifically on the stage of the inn where Goethe once spent the night (I, 345). So Dürrenmatt, with great economy, is able to show the deadly perversion of all that is, or was, sacred not merely to Swiss but to Western audiences.

Viewed from a liturgical standpoint, the action follows a kind of order of service: public confession of sin, a ritual cleansing—here by the sacrifice of the scapegoat—, and then the announcement of forgiveness and grace in the form of Claire's check for a billion.

The Gülleners are patently sincere when they say they hunger for righteousness. Yet no reader or spectator can take their words at face value. Through the whole play they will have noted again and again that the Gülleners use words, rhetoric, and ritual to conceal their real, though often unconscious, thoughts and what is really taking place. The accumulation of impressions is so great that words like righteousness and grace eventually acquire a negative connotation.

The lying and distortion started in harmless fashion when the mayor had to twist the facts about Claire's youth in his welcoming speech and attribute to her virtues and accomplishments that were never hers. This is humorous and understandable under the circumstances. On the other hand, the Gülleners' initial rejection of Claire's offer is couched in suspiciously high-flown, trite language. By the middle of act three any reference to ethical and cultural values can automatically be taken to be hypocritical.

Yet Dürrenmatt is fair to his Gülleners. They are using this rhetoric to persuade themselves as well as others. So it is important to them to make it clear that Ill married Mathilde Blumhard out of love and not for money or that money alone does not bring happiness (I, 329). But Dürrenmatt has so worked it that their words draw attention to what they try to conceal. The actual content of speeches becomes insignificant. Dürrenmatt soon persuades us of "the unreality of a language frozen in convention."[73] Considering what is really happening in the play, the quote might be expanded to include the lethal quality as well of a language from which the spirit—"Geist"—has vanished. When the burgomaster's speech at the railroad station is drowned out by the noise of the train, we are not inclined to complain, for we knew beforehand what he was going to say. The Gülleners, and the audience too, think and speak alike with stock phrases and reactions. Nothing more than a cue is needed to set off automatically a sequence of associated ideas. The opening minutes of the play work this way. Four indistinguishable citizens of Güllen are seated on a bench before the public toilet. Whenever a train passes, they turn their heads in unison. And they speak, where not in unison, then in interchangeable fragments and staccato sentences, repeating with slight variations the sense of the preceding speech and providing the cue for the following one. Their language and thought are the homogenized currency of the collective.

In act three the rhetoric of Güllen becomes wholly spurious thanks to the presence of the media. Cameramen for newsreel and television as well as reporters from all the world first gather to cover Claire's ninth wedding, an event staged in the Güllen cathedral for their benefit. Then they stay on to report the ceremony the town stages in order to mask the murder and get the reward of a billion. With or without the newsmen, this would have been a false ritual. But by the mere presence of reporters the Gülleners are inspired to supply them with appropriate material, the kind of thing they are used to seeing and hearing in tabloids, illustrated magazines, and over the air. It is for the press that Frau Ill says her husband married for love; and, more grotesque, the entire Ill family poses beaming with happiness—"Das gibt ein Titelbild für die Life" (That will make a cover picture for *Life*)—though they all know that Alfred is about to die (I, 332). The press too imposes its false interpretation on reality. Reporters call Claire's grant to the town the greatest social experiment of our age (I, 346), and their running commentary on the final ceremony is so utterly at odds with real events, so unctuous, and yet so familiar in tenor, that it evokes the shudder one feels on experiencing something grotesque.

Dürrenmatt's most telling "Einfall," the unforgettable feature of act three, is to have the climactic litany, led by the burgomaster and repeated phrase for phrase by the community, done a second time in toto. Because the lighting broke down, the cameraman asks them to do it once more. Treated like actors in a film, the Gülleners respond as such and go over the whole thing again verbatim, so that we hear their phrases about purity of motive, justice, conscience, and our most sacred values four times over (I, 349-50).

If this were not sufficient, Dürrenmatt has sharpened our ears to pick up repeated and echoed lines and to attach a certain meaning to this kind of redundant dialogue. It is identified in our minds with the figures who first practice it early in act one: Koby and Loby, the blind eunuchs (I, 282-83). They appear again near the end of the first act and once more in act three and are at any event unlikely to be forgotten. The reporters also repeat memorable phrases as they write them down; and the customers in Ill's shop early in act two show a tendency to say things twice. What might seem primarily a comic device at first is used to eerie effect in the final scene of act two, which is in turn a rehearsal for the great ceremony at the end of act three. The crowd gathered around Alfred Ill by the train utters several times within a few minutes a single and often a double choric echo to words spoken by one of their leaders: the burgomaster, the doctor, or the teacher.

Mindless repetition works here as a signal to the audience and to Ill. Spectators are likely to associate the Gülleners, now also in Claire's thrall, with Koby, Loby, and all the -obys in her retinue, people without will or identity. Ill of course is reminded, as he tries to get up courage to climb aboard the train, of the punishment Claire inflicted on the pair; and this can be adduced as one reason why he does not try to escape. Koby and Loby had fled to Canada and then Australia, but Claire found them anyway.

Finally, in Claire Zachanassian, Dürrenmatt has embodied the essence of modern satire and of the satirist. In contemplating her vengeful nature we are reminded that satire itself is a form of aggression and that its words are designed to hurt and destroy. "Great satire reflects its own problematic nature," says Brummack, and this surely holds for *Der Besuch der alten Dame*.[74] Like her very name, supposedly a montage of syllables from names of Levantine oil and shipping magnates, she is a mystifying mixture of traits and moods. She is mordantly ironic or sarcastic in her dealings with others, heartless, filled with hatred and scorn for the world. Yet she is sentimental about her early love and dead baby. She is the living realization of our wishes for wealth and power, the kind of notorious person who is celebrated in scandal sheet and tabloid. Her body is a composite of ivory, steel, and flesh. She is calculating, all-seeing, perfectly composed, and well able to manipulate others. But she lives like a parasite, exploiting her victims through sex, money, and publicity. As a child she spat on men from the roof of the railway pissoir and later vents her hatred in more direct ways, by castrating and blinding. She makes the entire citizenry of Güllen her dupes and slaves. Claire is seemingly omnipotent but also barren. Her efforts to restore the balance of justice go for nought because it is actually retribution that she is after. The town meeting, that bitter travesty of righteousness at work, is the fruition of her efforts.

Her peculiar softness in the last conversation with Ill stems from her self-understanding and from her realization that she has been motivated by grotesquely perverted feelings. Once Ill is dead, she will herself have no further reason to live. She speaks to Ill of her youthful love for him: "Sie ist etwas Böses geworden wie ich selber, wie die bleichen Pilze und die blinden Wurzelgesichter in diesem Wald, überwuchert von meinen goldenen Milliarden. Die haben nach dir gegriffen mit ihren Fangarmen, dein Leben zu suchen" (It turned into something evil like myself, like the pallid mushrooms and the blind root-faces in this forest, overgrown with my golden billions. With their tentacles they have been reaching for your life. I, 344). As satire and the satirist depict the dehumanization of our existence, so Claire's enterprise was undertaken in the cause of the death principle.

All three satirists: Kaiser, Brecht, and Dürrenmatt, depict the victory of death and aggression over opposing constructive and cohesive forces. Sigmund Freud's illusionless view of man as a wolf to man *(homo homini lupus)* underlies the three plays treated here. Brecht alludes to Freud's *Civilization and Its Discontents* in his notes to *Mahagonny* (275). While the other playwrights don't mention it, that essay applies equally well to them. These plays are more than anticapitalist satire; they are concerned with the nature of the human animal. But, as at the end of *Von morgens bis mitternachts,* it is hard to distinguish the words "Ecce Homo" from the death rattle.

Belief in a utopia is the ally of Eros, and some theorists suggest that satires presuppose or imply a utopian ideal when they castigate the stupidity and evil of the times. But one is hard put to discover, or even deduce, an ideal counterpart to the worlds presented in these plays. There is talk of paradise, Adam and Eve, the Golden Age of innocence, harmony, and happiness, but these prove to be delusions that only mislead and corrupt further. In the view of these authors, all efforts to redeem the world serve only to demonstrate that we are living in a hell organized on the principle of a whorehouse. In *Der Besuch der alten Dame* Claire Zachanassian puts it bluntly: "Die Menschlichkeit, meine Herren, ist für die Börse der Millionäre geschaffen, mit meiner Finanzkraft leistet man sich eine Weltordnung. Die Welt machte mich zu einer Hure, nun mache ich sie zu einem Bordell" (Humanity, gentlemen, is created for the millionaires' stock exchange, with my financial strength I can pay for a world order. The world made me into a whore, now I'm making it into a bordello. I, 325).

This differs little from the early Augustinian and radical Protestant view of this world as the devil's province. But the Lutheran promise to the faithful of resurrection and the Kingdom of Heaven is lacking. Only Alfred Ill manages simultaneously to surrender his flesh to Satan and keep his spirit free. But his Christlike sacrifice, like the cashier's suicide with the Cross behind him and Paul Ackermann's electrocution, is meaningless to any but himself; and even this private satisfaction is ambiguously qualified. The city and the world are still doomed. By allowing or, in the end, compelling the Gülleners to murder him and collect the reward, he lets them accumulate further guilt. They are incapable of living in the uncomfortable innocence of poverty and prefer to lose themselves in the dead life of wealth and power.

Sigmund Freud puts the actions of figures like these in a different light. Like all of us they are coping with a painful reality and seeking to avoid the suffering imposed by the presence of other people and the inadequacy of social institutions. In *Das Unbehagen in der Kultur* [*Civilization and Its Discontents,* 1930] he describes some radical procedures people may follow to accomplish this and provides, in effect, a plot summary consistent with all three plays.

People—i.e., satirists and the butts of their satire—who regard reality as the "sole enemy and as the source of suffering with which it is impossible to live" may, like the hermit, merely turn their backs on it. "But one can do more than that; one can try to recreate the world, to build up in its stead another world in which its most unbearable features are eliminated and replaced by others that are in conformity with one's own wishes. But whoever, in desperate defiance, sets out upon this path to happiness will as a rule attain nothing. Reality is too strong for him. He becomes a madman, who for the most part finds no one to help him in carrying through his delusion."[75] This is the course taken by Kaiser's cashier, Paul Ackermann, the citizens of Güllen, and Claire Zachanassian.

The cashier tries to remove all that separates the individual from his fellows and return mankind to a paradise of infancy and undifferentiated ego. Brecht's Paul Ackermann too wants to free himself and others from all artificially imposed bonds. Claire goes to great lengths to achieve perfect justice; and the Gülleners, with Ill's help, want to restore the polis to health. Not only are they frustrated in these undertakings because they use the enemy's weapons, but they aggravate the evils they want to cure, with disastrous results. Rather than unite their fellows, making them happy and free, they liberate the worst in them.

At the heart of each of these satires is the dynamic relationship between the central figure, or figures, and the collective. Kaiser's cashier exploits the people of B(erlin) in three encounters and ultimately, after trying to convert the mob to Christian contrition, he dies as a scapegoat for its sins as well as for his own. Paul Ackermann functions for a time as unofficial mayor of Mahagonny, until in the end the city puts him to death. Dürrenmatt's Alfred Ill and the town of Güllen act out a similar story.

Whereas Wedekind and Sternheim show us conflicts between individuals who represent a broader range of forces, the latter three playwrights bring the collective on stage and show us not only the pernicious consequences of certain beliefs but how these, together with the perverse workings of mass mentality, make a cataclysm seem inevitable. It has been noted in studies of mass-psychology that the crowd, once set in motion, gains momentum, rejects or kills its leader, and rolls on to its own destruction. Dürrenmatt's Anabaptists in *Die Wiedertäufer* (1967), like the German nation in the 1940s, blindly bring on their own end and the destruction of their city, believing firmly in an "Endsieg" to the dismay of their leaders who have long since conceded defeat. The few who see what is happening are helpless to prevent the debacle. In their suicidal folly, the people of

Münster cling to their faith in their leader, a flamboyant theatrical confidence man, and in ultimate victory.[76] Only as they are about to die do the satiric protagonists of these three plays perceive the morbid state of things and willingly take their punishment for their part in creating it. They are aware of the hopeless situation and stand by in isolation watching others continue on the road to destruction. "Können uns und euch und niemand helfen" (We can't help ourselves or you or anyone), is the last line of *Mahagonny,* sung by the entire cast. Kaiser's cashier looks back on his futile exertions and confesses his own stupidity: "Ein Fünkchen Erleuchtung hätte mir geholfen und mir die Strapazen erspart. Es gehört ja so lächerlich wenig Verstand dazu" (A tiny spark of illumination would have helped me and spared me the hardship. It requires such a little bit of intelligence). And he sums up his frenetic career with the words: "Von morgens bis mitternachts rase ich im Kreise" (From morning to midnight I've been racing in a circle. I, 517). The only way out of the vicious circle is death. Finally, Alfred Ill too pronounces judgment on himself: "Alles ist meine Tat [...]. Ich kann mir nicht helfen und auch euch [the city] nicht mehr" (It's all my fault. I can't help myself or you either any more. I, 333).

The première of *Der Besuch der alten Dame* received mixed reviews, but it quickly became a theater classic; it still finds acclaim in amateur and professional performance. On the other hand, none of Dürrenmatt's more recent serious satiric plays—this would rule out *Die Physiker* and *Play Strindberg*—have excited anything like the same response. The reason lies in their increasingly inhumane qualities. They deal more and more with naked fear, slaughter, and the process of dying. *Der Meteor* (1966), for example, is constructed like a medieval *danse macabre.* And in the foreword to *Porträt eines Planeten* (1971), whose action unfolds in a series of vignettes taking place in the moments before all earthly life is to be extinguished, Dürrenmatt speaks of a "Totentanz innerhalb eines Totentanzes" (A dance of death within a dance of death).[77] Sympathetic, transfigured individuals like Alfred Ill or Emperor Romulus are no longer to be found. Human beings function now primarily as members of a collective or of a "Gewaltsystem" (system of despotic violence) like the Politburo or the Mafia. Dürrenmatt maintains that the historians' figure of the great and influential ruler is a fiction. "Real history is the story of collectives and the power struggles that these have waged against each other and among themselves," he states but then reinforces his consistently conservative philosophy by arguing that the causes of these power constellations and struggles are sooner found in human nature than in social or political institutions.[78] Nevertheless his dramas concentrate on the machinations of one power elite or another. As the atmosphere of Dürrenmatt's plays grows progessively colder and more detached, not to say misanthropic, the language likewise becomes more laconic.

Impersonal murderers and their stoically resigned victims speak lines pruned of all rhetorical decoration. Dürrenmatt carries on Sternheim's war on metaphor ("Kampf der Metapher") with unmatched rigor. Hellmuth Karasek says in his review of *Der Mitmacher* (1973), "Compared to such dialog telegraphing shadows are pure chatterboxes."[79]

Dürrenmatt cultivates the compressed style even though he knows that it does not fit the formula for effective satire and theatrical success. In a long essay entitled "Dramaturgie des Publikums" (ca. 1970) he tells us in effect why *Der Besuch der alten Dame* works so well: "An audience can be influenced only by outwitting it. Directors should therefore make each play production simultaneously culinary and revolutionary, a problem that can be solved even with classic dramas. Anyone who wants to tell the truth today can only tell it in a covert way, and the truth is always revolutionary."[80] And indeed, *Der Besuch der alten Dame* has its share of culinary tricks or "Einfälle," some sentiment, some farce, and some wisdom. Dürrenmatt ignores his own advice, perhaps because audiences have become less important to him than the neat construction of prototypical models of power constellations.

The anticulinary tendency leaves its imprint also on the stage qualities of his later plays. In the foreword to *Porträt eines Planeten* he writes, "I am continually trying to make my dramas simpler and more economical, leaving out more and more, restricting myself to allusions." His characters and actors he treats like tiles for a mosaic or pieces in a complicated game: "I don't write my plays *for* actors any longer, I compose *with* them."[81]

The idea that culinary decoration and rhetoric are to be avoided is grounded in the moral perceptions emerging from *Der Besuch der alten Dame*. First, words are lethal weapons. From them are constructed the systems of concepts and ideologies which make absolute power possible. "Die Sprache ist die Sache" (Language is the thing), says Dürrenmatt in *Zusammenhänge* [Contexts, 1976], his essay on Israel.[82] There is no escape from the toils of language. And second, we tend to use it in order to persuade ourselves as well as others of our virtue and good intentions. That is, it is too easy to fall back on conventional phrases to hide the truth. "In the end we have to give reasons why there is so much bloodshed here below, otherwise it would look suspiciously as if it gave us pleasure."[83] Language is dangerous because it distorts and perverts and because it is an instrument of power. In both instances it serves the death instinct.

Dürrenmatt records impressions gathered one evening in 1974 at a Marxist kibbutz in Israel—theoretically as close as one might come to the ideal collective—and through them tells what has become his ultimate concern: human aggression. He writes:

> What grazed by me that absurd evening in the seemingly perfect world of a kibbutz was a whisper of what we all are afraid of, namely that after all the planning, after

all the effort, after all the concessions, after all the compromises, after all the bloodshed, after all the revolutions and wars, after all the failures and successes, people couldn't tolerate peace, a fear made worse by the fact that it could only be confirmed or refuted by peace. To give meaning to fighting is easy because we fool ourselves into believing that the meaning of fighting lies in peace; with this lie we locate meaning in a goal outside ourselves, we locate it in our opponent and so beyond our reach.[84]

And so it is with the private bank of the Frank family in Dürrenmatt's *Frank V* (1959). All its members justify their crimes with the excuse that they are perpetrated with the aim of escaping the bank and leading a decent life. All their efforts work to the opposite effect, and they become bound ever closer to the institution they despise. The bank is far from an ideal collective. It is organized to defraud and exploit, and is itself an arena for betrayal and bloodshed. Everyone is against the institution; yet it resists destruction and seems in the final scene destined to thrive. Contrary to all common sense and moral or juridical expectation, it is reorganized and strengthened by the state. It becomes ultimately part of a larger, state controlled system, even more pernicious than the old piratical bank because it is run on principles of honesty and order. The prologue, recited by Egli, the personnel officer, tells the story:

> Doch nun laßt den romantischen Quark
> Der Mensch ist nicht frei, er lebt im Geschäft
> Von Wölfen umstellt, von Hunden umkläfft
> Im Kollektiv gefangen
> Vom Nächsten beschattet, den er selber bewacht
> Mit allen gehangen
> Wird er über Nacht
> Um seine Menschlichkeit gebracht
> . . . .
> Wir sind die letzten Schurken weit und breit
> Nach uns nur böse, öde Ehrlichkeit.

(Just forget the romantic nonsense/Man is not free, in business he lives/Surrounded by wolves, barked at by dogs/Imprisoned in the collective/Shadowed by the neighbor he's spying on himself/At odds with all the others/Over night he is/Robbed of his humanity/. . . . . We are the last rogues far and wide/After us only evil barren propriety.)[85]

The reign of the ruthless entrepreneur—a perception anticipated in Sternheim's *1913*—will look attractive when compared with the methods of the new generation and the new dispensation in which Ottilie Frank, widow of Frank V, is damned to go on living. In the final scene, the Head of State rejects her confession of guilt and plea for justice and gives a compelling justification for the play's cruellest anticlimax: "Die Weltwirtschaft käme ins Wanken, griffe ich da ein, der Glaube an unsere Banken darf nicht durch ein verirrtes Kind erschüttert werden. Nein nein. Erwarte kein Gericht, erwarte keine Gerechtigkeit, erwarte keine Strafe, die wären allzu warm und menschlich für die eisige Welt der Ehrlichkeit, in die ich dich nun stoße: erwarte nur noch Gnade" (The world economy would become unstable if I didn't step in, faith in our banks must not be shaken by one errant child. No no. Don't expect a trial, don't expect justice, don't expect punishment, they would be far too warm and human for the icy world of propriety, into which I now cast you: you can expect only mercy. II, 278.)

Frank V is far more explicit and straightforward than *Der Besuch der alten Dame* in its pronouncements. There may be some ironic intent in letting Egli speak the prologue from his biased point of view. Yet generally speaking, Dürrenmatt does not involve his audience in the work of deciphering and reconstructing to the same degree. The "Oper einer Privatbank," as it was called in its 1960 version, was his first major stage play after *Der Besuch der alten Dame*, but in it he seems intent on overpowering, rather than outwitting the audience.

This is not to say that the play wants for culinary effects. It has its origin in a set of songs written by Dürrenmatt and set to music by Paul Burkhard (composer of that international hit of the 1950s, *O mein Papa*) in a two-week collaborative session.[86] Also some outlandish props give the play a touch of the fantastic. The outsized black marble Angel of the Resurrection over Frank V's grave at his sham burial as well as the gigantic soiled napkins around the necks of the guests at the funeral banquet, for instance, are characteristic of the comic alienation effects abounding in Dürrenmatt's earlier work. Comic too are two or three of the sequences in the opening scenes, which through paradox exemplify the laws of bank existence. To be a proper and decent bank employee one must remain deeply in debt, abandon one's pregnant fiancée, and suffer from ulcers. The trouble is that the world has changed and gangster banks are *passé*. The general manager, in a direct address to the audience about half way through the play, says: "Die Zeiten sind schlimm. Wir leben leider Gottes in einem Rechtsstaat. Uns fehlt durchaus der fördernde Hintergrund einer allgemeinen Korruption, auf die wir uns berufen könnten, unsere Geschäftsmaximen sittlich zu untermauern. Wir können mit keinen bestochenen Finanzministern oder obersten Polizeichefs aufwarten, nicht einmal mit bestechlichen Revisoren, nein, um uns herrscht die lauterste, brutalste Ehrlichkeit [...]. Der Hölle erscheint die Erde als Paradies" (The times are bad. We live under the rule of law, God bless us. We sorely lack the nurturing background of a general corruption, which we can cite to give our business maxims a moral foundation. We can't provide you with any corrupted ministers of finance or police chiefs, not even with corruptible auditors, no, round about us the purest, most brutal propriety prevails. Earth looks to hell like a paradise. II, 217).

The contradictions, inversions, and moral paradoxes are still amusing here, but the great threat, the omnipresent evil that makes this world a hell, moves gradually into view. The songs, the props, the humorous episodes that follow the robber-robbed scheme are the bait Dürrenmatt uses to lure us into his trap, to use a metaphor from the play. Like Claire's billion, the bank works like flypaper. The more strenuously one tries to escape, the more entangled one becomes in this collective that forces its members to commit crimes.

Everyone suffers under these circumstances and talks of change, but as the play continues the situation only grows worse and worse. Murder of colleagues becomes bank routine; guilt feelings intensify. All the accomplices in the enterprise have their good intentions and rationalizations. Each intends one day to let the bank go under and to escape to a better life of innocence and virtue. But the goal recedes faster than they can approach it. As the collective proves too strong for its members and as naked fear, killing, and voluntary dying begin to govern the action, one recognizes some of the reasons for the apparent helplessness of its victims. They want the impossible: to close big deals and remain free; to be at once affluent and morally blameless.

Frieda Fürst and Egli yearn to escape with enough money from the bank, to marry, and to found a normal family. Their love and longing ultimately bring them to the point where he is morally obliged, for the sake of the collective, to be her executioner and she, in full agreement, goes with uncanny willing passivity to her death, hoping thereby to spare him another attack of ulcers. The climactic, grotesquely paradoxical, and most horrifying in this series of killings is committed by Ottilie Frank. She injects poison into the veins of her good friend and loyal general manager to keep him from committing the "disgraceful sin" of confessing to a priest. As she methodically fills the hypodermic and carries out the murder, her husband, Frank V, sings in order to soothe the victim. "[...] dein bester Freund kann jeden Augenblick das Zeitliche segnen, erbaue ihn, gib ihm Trost, du hast eine so schöne Stimme und siehst, wie er leidet," says Ottilie (Your best friend can depart this life at any moment, edify him, give him comfort, you have such a nice voice and can see how he's suffering. II, 254).

The scene is comparable to the town meeting of Der Besuch der alten Dame in its angry power. To cover up the killing, the supposedly dead banker, disguised now as a priest, sings of his own repentance, of peace, of undying friendship. The sweet melodies and mendacious sentiments of the song achieve the same effect as the pious litany in the earlier play. Both belong to rituals of murder. Dürrenmatt tells only half the story when he says that these songs make the play endurable: "In this play, Frank V, the tolerable thing is the lying, the evasion, the specifically poetic atmosphere the play is steeped in. In Frank the people sing when they are lying."[87]

In the figure of Gottfried Frank, Dürrenmatt has incorporated the thing he most despises: the perversion of "Geist". Like the priest's garb, it is for him no more than a cover and an escape. He sings in hymnic verse, and he so loves the poetry of Goethe and Mörike that to be parted from them is the worst of punishments. He sings in the last verse of a song in which each bank employee describes his special form of suffering—constipation, impotence, insomnia:

> All die Klagen
> All die Plagen
> Nichts sind sie vor meinem Leiden
> Meinen Goethe muß ich meiden
> Und von Mörike gar scheiden
> Bin vom Bankgeschäft verreist
> Ihr leidet nur am Leib
> Doch ich am Geist! (II, 247)

(All the laments/All the miseries/Are nothing compared with my sufferings/I have to do without my Goethe/And even part from Mörike/I have left the banking business/You suffer only pains of the body/But I pains of the spirit ["Geist"]!).

The idea occupied Dürrenmatt for a decade before the publication of *Frank V.* Out of sloth and greed, postwar Europe had ignored the moral imperatives of spirit and mind while decking itself in their trappings, he says in an essay from 1951 entitled "Trieb." "So wendet es [Europa] sich ab," he writes in tones of Savonarola, "schöneren Dingen zu, mit dem besten Gewissen, in einer Welt, die den Geist nicht kennt, das seine zu tun, indem er für ihn Reklame macht und die Kultur der Vergangenheit als einen Check betrachtet, der berechtigt, um des Muts und des Opfers jener willen, die stets nichts neben den Bankaffären galten" (So it [Europe] turns its eyes away to look at prettier things, with perfectly clear conscience, in a world that doesn't know the spirit, to do its part by making much of it [spirit] and considering the past a check that grants privileges by dint of the courage and sacrifice of those who have always been held to be worthless beside bank affairs).[88] This resurgent Europe is "an abomination before the angry countenance of God."

Frank V finds a quiet end as he allows his son to lock him in the bank vault and bury him alive. His was a false resurrection in any event. And Dürrenmatt leads us to believe that the action will reach its resolution when Ottilie Frank finally breaks free from the trap and asks the president of the country, as highest judicial authority on earth, to put an end to the bank and punish her as well. For her efforts, however, she receives a medal and the advice, delivered in song to gavotte rhythm, not to take it all so seriously.

Once more events have taken the worst imaginable turn. The bank is restored and placed in the hands of the next generation of Franks. Frank V's lies, deceptions, and crimes—most committed out of weakness—were mild human errors compared to what is to be expected from his son and daughter. They represent the icy world where corruption and respectability are indistinguishable. They have no scruples, no fear, no sense of guilt. They are monsters of honesty who know how to use good means to bad ends. Their parents tried to do the opposite and failed.

The tone of theater critiques of *Frank V* ranges from neutral to negative. Reviewers of a leftist, puritanical, activist persuasion rejected the play out of hand as empty of serious social comment, as a poor imitation of Brecht's and Weill's *Die Dreigroschenoper.* Those on the right found it in bad taste, blasphemous, nihilistic. The strongest, most indignant attack calls the play unartistic, ugly, disgusting, "ein übles Machwerk" (a miserable contrived piece).[89] The aggressive component in this satire apparently far outweighs the socializing and aesthetic ones. The material and action of the play are almost too much for audiences to endure, if one is to credit reviews.

Dürrenmatt had expected that the music and songs would make the action and dialogue palatable, but he seems to have been wrong about that. The orchestra consists of a trumpet, a saxophone, drums, and piano. Paul Burkhard's numbers are set in a variety of styles, all of them light and easy to follow. Some are sweetly melodic, in the vein of *O mein Papa.* At the other extreme are more dissonant pieces in the *Agitprop* manner of Hanns Eisler's prewar music. The forms range from chorale to chanson.

The *Neue Zürcher Zeitung* sent its music expert to the opening, along with their drama reviewer. Rh., as he signed himself, felt out of place at the première and found that the music could not be analyzed in the usual critical terms. He seems disappointed that book and music failed to reinforce one another in Wagnerian fashion. The songs, he notes, had a retarding effect and did not provide "Elevation, spiritualization, mythogenesis of stage action."[90] Perhaps because the original subtitle, "Oper einer Privatbank" raised Wagnerian expectations like these, Dürrenmatt changed it in 1964 to the less ambitious "Eine Komödie mit Musik von Paul Burkhard."

A few newspaper reviews can't answer the question of whether Paul Burkhard's songs, or any music for that matter can affect an audience in the same way that the satiric fictions and comic "Einfälle" in *Der Besuch der alten Dame* do. From the available evidence it seems to have made the monstrosities of the text not more acceptable but rather, through grotesque contrast, more unnerving.[91]

In the late 1960s Dürrenmatt collaborated with a second composer, Gottfried von Einem, who also has his origins in Bern, on an operatic version of *Der Besuch der alten Dame.* It was first performed in Vienna in May of 1971. This is a full fledged opera in the late romantic tradition. Von Einem's music transforms Claire Zachanassian into a bigger-than-life, melodramatic figure like the great heroines of Strauss and Puccini. Her arias demand a voice with broad range, even when she sings lines like "Die Welt machte mich zur Hure, nun mache ich sie zu einem Bordell."

Von Einem's music is derivative and allusive. Reviewers detected reminiscences of Schumann, Massenet, Wagner, Bach, Shostakovich, and especially Mahler. One English reviewer found it primitive. William Mann of the London Times wrote scornfully: "The score of *The Visit* reminds me of film background music of 30 years ago."[92] German criticism, on the other hand, is far friendlier and finds the bitter-sweet union of book and score makes good satiric opera. Even though Dürrenmatt cut some of his most striking scenes—he reduced the length by one third—and eliminated the murder of Alfred Ill, the music made up for the loss by underlining contrasts and contradictions.

Dürrenmatt also compensated for lost dialogue by removing the final Sophoclean chorus and introducing in its stead a frenetic, demonic murder dance, or "Totentanz," by the Gülleners. The cue for the start of the dance is given by Claire's words "Der Scheck" (the check). H. H. Stuckenschmidt writes of this sequence: "This time it's a genuine opera finale, stamping, exuberant, with laugh roulades down the scale."[93]

There is no laughter whatsoever in *Der Mitmacher* (1973). In its language and dramaturgy it wastes nothing. The only music is a recording of Vivaldi's *Four Seasons,* from which first some of the allegro non molto movement of "Summer" is heard, and then later some of the largo movement from "Winter." The only reference to anything like literature is the stage direction calling for the main figure—he is called Doc—to read comic books. The play is Friedrich Dürrenmatt's end game. But whereas Samuel Beckett gives us a stalemate, Dürrenmatt works toward the worst possible end: checkmate.[94]

The plot follows roughly the same course as in *Frank V,* moving from bad to worse. The characters are more like chess figures than people. The names of the chief figures—Doc, Boss, Ann, Bill, Jack, Cop—are reminiscent of Boby, Koby, Loby, and the others in Claire Zachanassian's retinue. Like the bank employees in *Frank V,* they are all in one way or another caught up in the operation of a business somewhat like Murder Incorporated, which is run in the manner of a legitimate enterprise.

All are killed except for Doc, the accomplice, or henchman, of the title, who suffers what is for Dürrenmatt the cruellest conceivable punishment: he must go on living in the worst of all possible worlds, stripped of the last trace of human dignity, servicing the mass-producing death machine he helped to install. As others tried in vain to stop it and fell victim to it instead, so his effort to escape has only mired him deeper.

Biochemist and intellectual, Doc wants at the outset no more than just recognition of his worth and revenge on a society that valued him only so long as he brought in profits. So he offers his services to the Company. His invention, the necrodialysator, is the answer to the pollution problem that has driven the Company to the edge of bankruptcy. The machine dissolves and flushes away corpses and so provides an environmentally acceptable and legally advantageous way of handling the ever increasing volume of business.

The Company, it seems, is no different from any other corporation—except perhaps for its exceptionally rapid growth rate—in the pervasive atmosphere of universal moral "Mitmacherei," where everyone on up through the Supreme Court is an accomplice "on the take."[95] This is the basis of Dürrenmatt's satiric fiction: the world no longer as bordello, but as one great Watergate and necropolis.[96]

As the play progresses, business improves, earnings go up, and the enterprise becomes more and more respectable. Its work becomes a routine carried out by faceless employees. In the end it has, like Frank V's private bank, become so important to the nation's economic and social health that it must be nationalized.[97] Actually, *Der Mitmacher* begins at the point where *Frank V* left off and carries obsession with death to a point beyond which it would seem impossible, this side of Auschwitz and within civilized society, to go.

The only stage setting is Doc's workshop, a cellar room five levels below the ground, with water dripping from the ceiling. The dominant, insistent sound effect is the repeated flushing noise, indicating that another cadaver has been disposed of. The most prominent props are the crates in which bodies are delivered for processing. They accumulate on stage as the play moves along and production, i.e., destruction, is interrupted.

In its cool, straight-faced way, the drama seems to be treating murder as a normal business matter and at worst a pollution problem. In this regard, Dürrenmatt's ironic auctorial stance is comparable to that of Jonathan Swift and his fictive author in *A Modest Proposal*. Dürrenmatt, on the other hand, leaves no doubt where he stands on the banality and 'rationalizing of evil. The cool respectability of the Company's operation literally breaks down when Doc's refrigerating system ceases to function. During the closing scene the corpses continue to arrive. And as they decompose, the stage grows more and more a charnel house. The stench attracts flies and rats. The filth and corruption implied in the name Güllen—sewage or liquid manure—is here become pervasive and real. Doc has managed at great cost—he has necrodialysed and denied his beloved, his son, and in effect his humanity—to survive. Now he remains, the only living person in the realm of the dead.

Reviewers of the Zurich première in March, 1973, and of the Mannheim performance eight months later had only praise for the performers but found the play itself disappointing. They might have applauded a drama in this style by Beckett, but Dürrenmatt's authorship arouses expectations of a drama with organic structure, humor, and character development, like *Romulus der Große,* where spectators can empathize with the protagonist. Also, Boss's scourging mockery of intellectuals and their hypocrisy, greeted with an ovation by the opening night audience, clearly applies to critics as well and makes it hard even for the most objective of them to like the play.[98]

Conclusion
On the Satiric Complex:
Irony, the Grotesque, and Aggression

DÜRRENMATT AND THOSE CRITICS who take his self-interpretations seriously are careful to make clear and basic distinctions between his work, the theater of the absurd, and the drama of Brecht. The qualities that set Dürrenmatt apart they often sum up in the term grotesque. By trying repeatedly to define the word and to give it meaning, he has helped to give it currency among his interpreters and among literary scholars. In one of the most comprehensive investigations of the still ill-defined concept, Karl Pietzcker locates the main difference between the absurd and the grotesque in the fact that whereas the absurd seeks to hold the reader prisoner, even suffocate him in its representational world, the grotesque urges him to risk excursions beyond that world into more uncertain realms. He also argues that anticlimax, or the scheme of anticipation followed by disappointment, is a *sine qua non* of the grotesque.[1]

In the latter instance Pietzcker seems to be talking about irony. And in general, many of his criteria seem better suited to define satire than the grotesque. The confusion in terms is even more evident in the following passage from Dürrenmatt's "Über Ronald Searle," the introduction to a Searle anthology published in 1955. With a certain disdain for pedantic consistency, he moves easily among the designations grotesque, absurd, and comic while talking about one and the same thing. Yet for all the conceptual blurring, he provides a good appreciation of Searle and gives us also a very accurate account of how his own plays work.

Ronald Searle, he notes, starts from a satiric fiction or, in Dürrenmatt's words, a grotesque syllogism:

> People murder, torture, and drink; schoolgirls are people, therefore schoolgirls murder, torture, and drink. What is achieved by that? Well, what we perceive as a threat, the terrible potential in people, is brought to light, by a ploy, if you will, by a trick of the grotesque, as something absurd and simultaneously as something "omnipresent;" in this instance by eliminating time, as if the infant Hitler were being made to do all the things the mature man Hitler then carried out. So much for

satiric technique, a technique that another Englishman, Swift, mastered in the most sovereign manner. [...] today it is necessary to understand satire in any genre as a separate artistic mode which has its own laws and its own aesthetic. Satire is an exact art, precisely *because* it exaggerates, for only the person who sees the nuance and the generality at the same time *can* exaggerate.[2]

Searle is for Dürrenmatt a comedian "Komödiant") even when he is not in the least agreeable ("gemütlich"). "True comedians are never agreeable. They bite. Beware of Ronald Searle."

Dürrenmatt's remarks are, as always, forceful and clear. Nevertheless it can be a useful and instructive venture to disentangle the lines. The simplest and most practical procedure from the standpoint of this study is to fall back on Brummack's three rudiments—satire is aesthetically socialized aggression—and say that the grotesque coincides with the aggressive component and gives the satire its affective impact. Anticlimax, or the frustration of expectations, on the other hand, is a structural matter and a mode of irony. Finally, the social element is implicit in the whole and becomes apparent when we perceive the irony and construct a reading more accurate than the literal, surface one.

Satire, at least in the satiric dramas I have examined, is hard attacking irony that uses grotesque fictions and material. We can call a figure or a situation grotesque when it is uncanny, threatening, lethal, disgusting, ridiculous, and a composite of incompatibles. We may associate the term with Swift's Yahoos, the Maske family in *1913,* the citizens of Mahagonny and Güllen, or with Jack the Ripper and Lulu. It is a graphic and exaggerated embodiment of human instincts and weaknesses. Here belong the scenes where the Gülleners applaud and cheer the demand that they murder Ill and where Mahagonny's boxing fans respond to the announcement of Joe's death in the ring—"Der Mann ist tot"—with loud and prolonged laughter.[3]

These grotesqueries are not there for their own sake or merely to make the spectator shudder. The intended effect is twofold. Watching the onstage audience of Mahagonny's and Güllen's citizens respond in this perverse way the real viewer, who may identify or empathize with the actors, will be caught up short by the realization that he too is sadistically inclined. More important are the dismay and disillusionment when the grotesque agent actually kills, for the victim is often the representative of the audience's cherished beliefs and fond desires. Much of the power of grotesque effects stems from the intense involvement of the author as well as the audience. They are watching the collapse of systems of thought and belief on which they have long relied. And worse, the satire shows that the grotesque nemesis is the inevitable consequence of that very set of mind and of the forces it releases. Concretely, Wedekind's Lulu, the beautiful animal, moves gradually but surely toward her encounter with Jack the Ripper.

When they do meet, it becomes clear that they are a perfect match. In abstract terms, the death instinct will turn up behind ostensible life-oriented ideologies like vitalism, Darwinism, anarchism, as it also can be sensed by a visitor in a Marxist kibbutz. In the grotesque, the satirist has a vivid way of rudely defeating inflated expectations.

The ironic satirist lures us on with promises of human happiness in the emancipation of the flesh or of perfect togetherness. Anticipations of sensual and aesthetic resolution rise, only to be frustrated. Not merely is resolution withheld; events often take the worst imaginable turn. At all events, we note that we have been deceived by the course of events and by our own fantasies and ways of thinking.

The structural device of anticlimax, or irony of events, is discernible in the overall action of these satiric dramas and in the individual episodes as well. Along with other clues—discrepancies, contradictions, mixing of styles, and the like—it makes us apprehensive and compels us to undertake a serious rethinking of the play and of our own attitudes.

Even the moods of the times in which these dramas were written are those of frustration. Wedekind's 1890s, Sternheim's and Kaiser's prewar Germany, Brecht's waning 1920s, and Dürrenmatt's economically resurgent Europe in the Cold War are all periods when expectations of utopian freedom, of progress in human affairs, or a fresh start began to fade and hopes for changing the world began to prove illusory. In times like these, depression and *Angst* become widespread. Psychologists have noted that anger and aggression are likely to come to the fore under these circumstances. Albert Bandura has observed, for instance, that outbreaks of revolutionary violence are most likely "when a period of social or economic improvement that instills rising expectations is followed by a sharp reversal" or by the threat of recession.[4]

Since referring in the foreword to Brummack's definition—satire is aesthetically socialized aggression—I have repeatedly drawn attention to the role of aggression in the making of satire as well as to its thematic importance. Satire, particularly in its more grotesque forms, is involved in the struggle between Eros and Thanatos, or between the life instinct and the urge to destroy. In *Civilization and Its Discontents* Sigmund Freud describes the battle as follows: "This battle is the essential content of life in general, and therefore the development of culture can be termed simply the life struggle of the human species."[5] That is, the threat that brings these dramatists to speak out and reveals itself as their ultimate concern is the death instinct and its main representative, the aggressive urge.

The weapons used by the satirist are those of the enemy. The method, as Sternheim would have it, is homeopathic. And if we were to distill a quintessential plot from the plays treated in this study, it would follow the sequence of psychic events that constitute the aggression cycle as Freud perceived it and as others—Alois Becker, Alexander Mitscherlich, and Norman O. Brown—have elaborated and refined it.[6]

The close kinship of the satiric vision and the way Freud viewed culture is noted by Lionel Trilling: "Recently [...] I spoke of the modern self as characterized by its intense and adverse imagination of the culture in which it had its being, and by certain powers of indignant perception which, turned upon the unconscious portions of culture, have made it accessible to conscious thought. Freud's view of culture is marked by this adverse awareness, by this indignant perception."[7] In an earlier essay, also on Freud, Trilling provides another concise summary of Freudian ideas which is more specific and leads closer to the plot and central images of grotesque satire. Man has, he writes, "a kind of hell within him from which rise everlastingly the impulses which threaten his civilization. He has the faculty of imagining for himself more in the way of pleasure and satisfaction than he can possibly achieve."[8]

Of human fantasy, daydreams, and the danger they represent we have seen enough in all the plays considered. Claire Zachanassian's remark made in act one of Der Besuch der alten Dame, "[...] ich bin die Hölle geworden" (I have become hell), is only one of the several explicit references to hell that could be cited. But it is more important here, because it enhances our understanding of the dramas considered, to follow the aggression scenario outlined by Freud and others, to study the milieu created by aggression, and to make explicit the connections and parallels in the satiric dramas we have examined.

In situations where persons or groups suffer deprivation, real or imagined, and are forced to renounce satisfactions in order to conform to repressive social norms, there comes a time when they may begin to doubt the legitimacy of those norms. At all events, when the pressure of dammed up instinctual energy increases to a critical point, the threshold of aggression drops suddenly. The greater the frustration, the more irrational and primitive will be the discharge of emotion. The slightest irritation can then excite an outbreak of rage.[9]

Brecht's lumberjacks from the Alaskan woods, Lulu's suitors, Claire Zachanassian and the Gülleners, Master Teacher Krull in Die Kassette, Krey and the internally warring Maske family in 1913, Georg Kaiser's cashier, the repeatedly frustrated banking people in Frank V, all are either sexually or materially deprived, or both—at least by their own standards. The fact that others are more affluent, that wealth seems within reach, and the promise of gratification is in plain view but unfulfilled aggravates the problem. The resultant hostility toward civilization and toward all restraints along with the weakening of the super-ego and the loss of respect for authority lead to the sudden short circuit in the form of regression to a state of undifferentiated ego, of psychic infantilism whereby the world becomes one great Mahagonny in which pleasure is there for the taking and all urges can be satisfied without guilt.[10] Aggressive instincts, the desire to exploit others, appropriate their property, humiliate, hurt, and kill them come to the fore and may be translated into action under the right conditions. In other words, the group or individual takes refuge in the realm of imagination where magic fantasies of omnipotence occupy the psyche.[11] Sternheim's characters offer the most striking illustration of this state of mind. All the members of the Maske family as well as Wilhelm Krey in *1913* dream power and conquest of some sort. On a less ambitious scale, the Gülleners imagine themselves affluent and influential; Kaiser's cashier imagines he is creating a new world but cannot distinguish between the goal of a united mankind and his own perverse gratification. Krull's monologic ravings about what he will do once in possession of the wealth in the box would provide good source material for a psychoanalytic study of this phenomenon.

Sternheim does not let his characters take physically aggressive action. Instead he shows us the potentially dangerous and frightening workings of the unfettered paranoid imagination as it emerges in family intrigue, in the games played by high society, and in the media. We know that all will inevitably end with madness and explosive violence. But the characters are oblivious to this, and Sternheim ends his two plays before the catastrophe. This is one of the ways in which he goads his audience into thought about the consequences of what it sees on stage.

At the opposite extreme is Frank Wedekind. He reinforces the destructive urge with erotic libidinal energy. Lulu dreams of the simultaneous experiences of sex and murder. Her wish is then brutally fulfilled in her gruesome and yet comic encounter with Jack the Ripper. His deed is the realization of her fantasy of unencumbered lust and aggression. It is also the culmination of a series of aggressive and exploitative acts that include psychic murder, plain murder, extortion, and sexual enslavement.

Sternheim's characters lack the physical means to carry out their aims. Lulu, on the other hand, has in her animal magnetism the power to dominate and kill and to ignore all social restriction. Dr. Schön's might lies in his hardheaded principle of *Realpsychologie* and in his capacity to influence through the media or by the power of his rhetoric.

In most of the plays I have discussed the source of the power that makes hitherto latent omnipotence fantasies so dangerous is money. Dr. Schön is first and foremost a financier. Wealth gives Maske, Paul Ackermann, the cashier, and Claire Zachanassian the capacity to dictate at will the rules governing human relationships. It is the most efficient instrument with which to debase and harm others. Yet these dramas are not anticapitalist satires. Another instrument would serve as well. Freud makes the point in *Civilization and Its Discontents*: "Aggressiveness was not created by property. It reigned almost without limit in primitive times when property was still scanty [...]."[12]

The ultimate concern of these five dramatists is not money or the economic system but the greatest threat of all: the ways in which people come to commit aggressive acts and, more important, the ways in which they try to justify them. Once acts of violence can be made to seem morally right or morally indifferent, the controlling instances fall away. The most frightening example treated in this study is the way the Gülleners develop their system of justifications. Dürrenmatt shows us how it works from start to finish, from the first traces of moral indignation toward Alfred Ill to the elaborately staged ceremony ostensibly to celebrate democracy and justice but in fact to rationalize murder. Alois Becker writes of the process: "While expanding, wishes receive a significant offensive intensification as soon as they are granted the character of subjectively justified claims because the addition of the moral quality brings with it far-reaching consequences for the strength of the acompanying aggressive operations."[13] The Gülleners take advantage of Alfred Ill's youthful crime to make him their scapegoat and so to justify themselves. He is their most likely victim because he is associated with Claire Zachanassian, the instigator of the process and the source of their discomfort, and because he is "sufficiently removed from [her] psychologically so that restraints against aggression [are] weaker than the tendencies to attack."[14] Ill has also in the last act made himself a likely target by setting himself outside the collective and by criticizing, however tacitly, the accepted order.

Most of the protagonists in these satiric dramas can be viewed as scapegoats, whether they be the victims of group violence or whether they are the target of the satiric attack itself. The near blasphemous, rather blatant scenic and verbal allusions to the Crucifixion in the closing scenes of *Mahagonny* and *Von morgens bis mitternachts* and the more serious yet ambiguous private Gethsemane and sacrifice of Alfred Ill are not primarily meant to posit an ideal Christian alternative to the folly and evil of the present day. Paul Ackermann, the cashier, and Alfred Ill are hardly saviors. Rather, they are victims on whom the guilt and anger of the collective are focused. They are prophets of a new dispensation, but it, as well as the story of their ministry and death, are travesties of the Christian model. Paul Ackermann is closer to the Antichrist. And in all three cases, death holds no promise of a new life. It is an anticlimax and a dead end.

The close parallels to the Passion story and the verbal echoes are intended as a foil against which to contrast the incommensurable and perverse dramatic action and so achieve grotesque effects. They are also sure to arouse high expectations of religious and reverent nature whose defeat will be that much more of a shock.[15] Yet the most dangerous form of delusion in the eyes of Wedekind and the other playwrights is not the projection of guilt onto scapegoats but the development of ideologies with which to rationalize violence. This is the explosive ingredient that gives human aggression its greatest power and makes it an agent of historical cataclysms. And this is what these satirists make clear through their grotesque fictions. The phenomenon takes different guises: social Darwinism, the Western Tradition, Vitalism, but the use to which each is put remains the same.

According to Alois Becker, these elaborate rationalizing constructions are dangerous traps. Not only do they delude the attacker concerning the offensive and gratuitous nature of his action and thereby salve his conscience, but they can intimidate victims who lack the strength and independence to criticize or resist. With the history of National Socialism in mind he writes of utopian features these systems—like those of Paul Ackermann's—can assume:

> All immoderately expanding demands and claim systems contain—and contain in increasing measure—utopian traits. As the latter grow, the expansion increasingly resembles omnipotence magic in the form of intoxication with power or the certainty of future power. This aggravates, for the self as well as others, the consequences which proceed from the premises of certain prejudices in the deductions of destructive ideological systems. They are aggravated to the point where chiliastic promises exhort to radical operations in the nature of final solutions, to the "ultimate violence which should result in the annihilation of all aggression."[16]

One thinks here of the "war to end all wars" and of the depressing perception that came over Dürrenmatt in the Marxist kibbutz.

Yet however elaborate the rationalization and however vicious the act, the aggressor will derive no lasting satisfaction from his efforts. The consequence is anticlimax and frustration. Even though he may have real power over others, he is doomed to disappointment because his act will awake no resonance in its object. Hate brings no resolution. From the frustration of libidinal anticipation, from the experience of impotence grows the desire for revenge. This vicious circle is the psychological pattern of aggression. Anticlimax concludes each phase and leads into the next in the satirist's dance of death.[17]

Notes

Introduction

[1]Georgina Baum, *Humor und Satire in der bürgerlichen Ästhetik,* Germanistische Studien (Berlin: Rütten und Loening, 1959), pp. 65ff.

[2]Horst Bienek, *Werkstattgespräche mit Schriftstellern* (1962; rpt. Munich: DTV, 1965), p. 124. "Geist drückt sich entweder pathetisch oder in einer merkwürdigen, nur in diesen Zonen zu findenden, vertrottelten Witzelei aus, die offenbar, esprit sein soll. Das Komödiantische ist suspekt, wird nicht voll, nicht ernst genommen."

[3]Volker Klotz, *Dramaturgie des Publikums* (Munich: Hanser, 1976), p. 144: "[...] die unfreie Gesellschaft der kapitalistisch freien Wirtschaft bewahrt und gesichert in einem imperialistischen Staat, der außen- und innenpolitisch das Recht des stärkeren praktiziert." See also Peter Michelsen, "Frank Wedekind," in *Deutsche Dichter der Moderne,* ed. Benno von Wiese (Berlin: Erich Schmidt, 1965), pp. 49-67.

[4]Klotz, *Dramaturgie,* pp. 147-48.

[5]Wilfried Adling, "Georg Kaisers Drama *Von morgens bis mitternachts* und die Zersetzung des dramatischen Stils," *Weimarer Beiträge,* 5 (1959), 369-86. Karl-Heinz Schmidt, "Zur Gestaltung antagonistischer Konflikte bei Brecht und Kaiser: Eine vergleichende Studie," *Weimarer Beiträge,* 11 (1965), 551-69.

[6]"Über weltanschauliche und künstlerische Probleme bei Dürrenmatt," *Weimarer Beiträge,* 12 (1966), 539-65.

[7]*Ibid.,* 561, 557.

[8]Bienek, *Werkstattgespräche,* p. 130: "Der Schriftsteller kann seiner moralischen Aufgabe nur dann nachkommen, [...] wenn er Anarchist ist. Er muß angreifen aber nicht engagiert sein. Der einzige Platz, der ihm zukommt, ist der zwischen Stuhl und Bank."

[9]Robert Heilbroner, "Inescapable Marx," *New York Review,* vol. 25, No. 11 (June 29, 1978), 33-37.

[10]Wolfgang Preisendanz, "Zur Korrelation zwischen Satirischem und Komischem," in *Poetik und Hermeneutik: Arbeitserzeugnisse einer Fachgruppe,* VII, eds. W. Preisendanz and Rainer Waring (Munich: Fink, 1976), pp. 411-13.

[11]Friedrich Dürrenmatt, *Theaterschriften und Reden* (Zurich: Arche, 1966), pp. 136-37.

[12]Hans-Peter Bayerdörfer, "Sternheim: *Die Kassette,"* in *Die deutsche Komödie,* ed. Walter Hinck (Düsseldorf: Bagel, 1977), pp. 218ff.

[13]W.G. Sebald, *Carl Sternheim, Kritiker und Opfer der Wilhelminischen Ära,* Sprache und Literatur, No. 58 (Stuttgart: Kohlhammer, 1969).

[14]The introductory essay to *Psychoanalysis and the Literary Process,* ed. Frederick Crews (Cambridge, Mass.: Winthrop, 1970), p. 14.

[15]Wayne C. Booth, *A Rhetoric of Irony* (Chicago: University of Chicago Press, 1974), p. 44.

[16]Charles Witke, *Latin Satire: The Structure of Persuasion* (Leiden: Brill, 1970), p. 13.

[17]Robert C. Elliott, "The Definition of Satire," *YCGL,* 11 (1962), 20.

[18]Patricia Meyer Spacks, "Some Reflections on Satire," *Genre,* 1 (1968), 15.

[19]"Zu Begriff und Theorie der Satire," *Deutsche Vierteljahrsschrift,* Sonderheft Forschungsreferate, 45 (1971), 275-377.

[20]*The Works of John Dryden,* ed. Sir Walter Scott and revised by George Saintsbury (Edinburgh: W. Paterson, 1887), XIII, 37-38.

[21]Brummack, "Zu Begriff und Theorie [...]," p. 282.

[22]See Peter Thorpe, "Satire as Pre-Comedy," *Genre,* 4 (1971), 1-17.

[23]Ulrich Gaier, *Satire: Studien zu Neidhart, Wittenweiler, Brant und zur satirischen Schreibart* (Tübingen: Niemeyer, 1967), p. 343.

[24]Wolfgang Herles, "Die Sternheim-Renaissance auf den Bühnen der Bundesrepublik," in *Carl Sternheims Dramen: Zur Textanalyse, Ideologie-Kritik und Rezeptionsgeschichte,* ed. Jörg Schönert (Heidelberg: Quelle und Meyer, 1975), pp. 210-11.

[25]Heinrich Lausberg, *Elemente der literarischen Rhetorik,* 5th ed. (Munich: Hueber, 1976), par. 232, p. 78.

[26]See Booth, *A Rhetoric of Irony.*

[27]See Ronald Paulson, *The Fictions of Satire* (Baltimore: The Johns Hopkins University Press, 1967), pp. 9ff.

[28]Bertolt Brecht, *Stücke III* (Frankfurt: Suhrkamp, 1955), vol. I, p. 196.

[29]Karl S. Guthke, *Modern Tragicomedy* (New York: Random House, 1966), p. 70.

[30]Matthew Hodgart, *Satire,* World University Library, No. 043 (London: Weidenfeld and Nicolson, 1969), p. 31.

[31]Hodgart, p. 77.

[32]*Traumstück* (Vienna and Leipzig: Verlag "Die Fackel," 1922), p. 8.

[33]Of the critical works mentioned in this and the following paragraphs, the following have not yet been cited: Northrop Frye, *Anatomy of Criticism* (1957, rpt. New York: Atheneum, 1966); Alvin B. Kernan, *The Plot of Satire* (New Haven: Yale University, 1965); Ronald Paulson, *The Fictions of Satire* (Baltimore: Johns Hopkins, 1967); Robert C. Elliott, *The Power of Satire* (Princeton: Princeton University, 1960); Karl Pietzcker, "Das Groteske," *Deutsche Vierteljahrsschrift* 45 (1971), 197-211; Jörg Schönert, *Roman und Satire im 18. Jahrhundert: Ein Beitrag zur Poetik,* Germanistische Abhandlungen, 27 (Stuttgart: Metzler, 1969); Gerhard Hoffmann, "Zur Form der satirischen Komödie: Ben Jonsons 'Volpone'," *Deutsche Vierteljahrsschrift* 46 (1972), 1-27; Edward W. Rosenheim, *Swift and the Satirist's Art* (Chicago: University of Chicago, 1963), pp. 31, 175; Peter Uwe Hohendahl, *Das Bild der bürgerlichen Welt im expressionistischen Drama,* Probleme der Dichtung, 10 (Heidelberg: Winter, 1967).

Chapter 1

[1]M. Hodgart, *Satire,* p. 10.

[2]In a little essay entitled "Weltlage" (1913) Wedekind writes of satire as a weapon against the dominance of the military in his time: "Wie die geistige Macht vor Ausbruch der Reformation auf der höchsten Höhe ihrer Entwicklung stand, ähnlich verhält es sich heute mit der Militärgewalt. Wie sich damals die Denkfreiheit gegen die Kirche auflehnte, so lehnen sich heute internationales Menschenbewußtsein und das erwachende Solidaritätsgefühl unter den Kulturvölkern gegen die Militärherrschaft auf. In dem Kampf von heute wie in dem von vor fünfhundert Jahren werden Witz und Satire als stärkste Waffen ins Feld geführt. Witz und Satire wirken aber um so stärker, wenn sie nicht von parteiischen Schriftstellern ersonnen werden, sondern direkt aus den Verhältnissen entspringen, wie einzelne Phasen des Dreyfus-Prozesses und die Köpenickiade. Dahin gehört auch die Möglichkeit, daß der bevorstehende Weltkrieg durch die Verdauungsbeschwerden eines jungen Kriegers entfacht würde. Die Reformationsbewegung umfaßte einen Zeitraum von mehr als hundert Jahren, während die Friedensbewegung erst vor zwei Jahrzehnten einsetzte. Man wird sich deshalb wohl noch etwas gedulden müssen"—Frank Wedekind, *Prosa, Dramen, Verse,* ed. Hansgeorg Maier (Munich: Langen/Müller, n.d.), p. 938. This is Volume One of the standard two-volume edition. They will be cited hereafter in the text as I and II.

[3]London: Calder, 1977.

[4]"Aber jeder Mensch hat wohl etwas Absonderliches, das ihn vorwärts treibt, und wird eventuell durch das Verlangen, diese Absonderlichkeit zu begreifen, vorwärts getrieben. Ich gebe auch ohne weiteres zu, daß ich dieser einen [unleserlich] alles übrige verdanke," from *Der vermummte Herr: Briefe Frank Wedekinds aus den Jahren 1881-1917,* ed. Wolfdietrich Rasch, DTV 440 (Munich: DTV, 1967), p. 188.

[5]"Ich habe die Folgen, die dem Menschen aus seinen Handlungen erwachsen, nie gefälscht. Ich habe diese Folgen überall immer nur in ihrer unerbittlichen Notwendigkeit zur Anschauung gebracht" (I, 807).

[6]"[...] ein Prachtexemplar von Weib [...], wie es entsteht, wenn ein von der Natur reich begabtes Geschöpf [...] in einer Umgebung von Männern, denen es an Mutterwitz weit überlegen ist, zu schrankenloser Entfaltung gelangt."

[7]"Statt des Titels Erdgeist hätte ich gerade so gut 'Realpsychologie' schreiben können, in ähnlichem Sinn wie Realpolitik. Es kam mir bei der Darstellung um Ausschaltung all der Begriffe an, die logisch unhaltbar sind wie: Liebe, Treue, Dankbarkeit. Die beiden Hauptfiguren, Schön und Lulu, haben auch subjektiv nichts mit diesen Begriffen zu tun, sie, weil sie keine Erziehung genossen, er, weil er die Erziehung überwunden hat."

[8]See Edelgard Hajek, *Literatur und Jugendstil,* Literatur in der Gesellschaft, No. 6 (Düsseldorf: Bertelsmann, 1971); Horst Fritz, "Die Dämonisierung des Erotischen in der Literatur des Fin de Siècle," in *Fin de Siècle: Zur Literatur und Kunst der Jahrhundertwende,* ed. Roger Bauer et al., Reihe Studien zur Philosophie und Literatur des neunzehnten Jahrhunderts, No. 35 (Frankfurt: Klostermann, 1977), pp. 442-64; and especially Cl. Quiquer, "L'érotisme de Frank Wedekind," *Etudes Germaniques,* 17 (1962), 14-33.

[9]Arthur Kutscher, *Frank Wedekind* (Munich: Langen Müller, 1922), I, 36. The first printed version of *Die Büchse der Pandora* appeared in *Die Insel,* 3 (July 1902), 19-105. It contains French language dialogue in Act II and English in Act III, especially in the scenes between Lulu and her customers. Here are the play's final lines as printed:

Lulu: No, no! Have pity! The rip me up! Police!
Jack: Shut up! I have you save! *(Er trägt sie in den Verschlag.)*
Lulu: *(von innen)* O don't! Don't—No!
Jack: *(Kommt nach einer Weile zurück und setzt die Waschschale auf den Blumentisch)* It was a hard piece of work!—*(Sich die Hände waschend.)* I am a lucky dog, to find this unicum. *(Sieht sich nach einem Handtuch um.)* Not so much as a tovel in this place! It looks aw'ful poor here! *(Trocknet seine Hände am Unterrock der Geschwitz ab.)* Well! This monster is quite safe from me!—It will be all over with you in a second. *(Durch die Mitte ab.)* (p. 105)
Countess Geschwitz then delivers the curtain speech, beginning: "Lulu!—Mein Engel!"

[10]"Frank Wedekind," in *Deutsche Dichter der Moderne,* ed. Benno von Wiese (Berlin: Erich Schmidt, 1965), pp. 55-56:

"[...] der Unmittelbarkeit der Lust vermag sich die kapitalistische Gesellschaft am wenigsten als Widersacher entgegenzustellen. Unmittelbarkeit ist ein bürgerliches Ideal, das, als bloßer Trieb verstanden, gerade in einer durch nichts als Angebot und Nachfrage geregelten Welt sich noch am ehesten realisieren läßt. Hier sieht sich der Mensch, der sich aller erdenklichen Bindungen begeben hat, in seinem Verkehr mit anderen Menschen gleicherweise auf die 'elementarste' wie auf die 'abstrakteste' Vermittlung verwiesen, in denen beiden die Komplexität sozialer Kommunikation auf ein Minimum zusammengeschrumpft ist. Die Beziehung der Sexualität zum Geld stellt also keine Perversion der ersteren dar. Im Gegenteil: der Banalität des nackten Geschlechts ist die Abstraktheit der Banknote ganz angemessen."

[11]Polgar, *Ja und Nein* (Berlin: Rowohlt, 1926), Vol. I, 178. "Sein [Wedekinds] dichterischer Extrakt der Welt ist gesättigt von deren Lächerlichkeit und Elend. In der Grimasse enthüllt sich ihr wahres Antlitz."

[12]Günter Seehaus, *Wedekind und das Theater* (Munich: Laokoon, 1964), p. 346.

[13][...] das Hohnlachen der Hölle, der glänzendste Triumph der Frivolität. Die Bewegungen des Zwerchfells sind langsamer und erfolgen stoßweise. Mund und Kehle sind weit geöffnet, die Lippen aufgeworfen, so daß die Zähne ihre volle Pracht entfalten. Die Augen bleiben ruhig und kalt" (I, 900).

[14]Seehaus, p. 60: "[Das Publikum] hielt den Verfasser für naiv und glaubte, daß dieser allerhand unfreiwillige Scherze mache. So lachte es über die Dinge, die wirklich belacht sein sollen und glaubte, die Dinge seien ernst gemeint [...]."

[15]Seehaus, p. 346: "Aber es kommt ja sehr auf die Tonart des Lachens an. Es darf nicht das befreite, glückliche Lachen herausklingen, sondern eben das verkürztere, verkrampftere, das der bizarren Tragi-Komödie entspricht."

[16]Seehaus, p. 342: "Gerade so wie *Frühlings Erwachen* übergrotesk schloß, sollte sich auch der 'Erdgeist' auf seinen letzten Seiten zu einer komischen Verzerrung steigern, durch die dann die Tragik vollständig aufgehoben wurde und die Schwere der Handlung possenhaft erschien [...]."

[17]Diebold, *Anarchie im Drama,* 4th ed. (Berlin, 1928), quoted in Seehaus, p. 386.

[18]The following is extracted from Seehaus, p. 411 passim.

[19]See Frank Kermode, *The Romantic Image* (1957, rpt. New York: Vintage, 1964), Ch. IV.

[20]"Heilmittel und Gift unterscheiden sich nur durch die Art ihrer Verwendung" (I, 465).

[21]"Die komödiantischen Grotesken Frank Wedekinds," in *Das deutsche Lustspiel,* ed. Hans Steffen (Göttingen: Vandenhoeck und Ruprecht, 1969), II, 92: "Totentanz der Sinnenlust."

[22]Peter Thorpe, "Satire as Pre-Comedy," *Genre* 4 (1971), 1-17.

[23]Heinrich Mann, "Erinnerung an Frank Wedekind," in *Sieben Jahre: Chronik der Gedanken und Vorgänge* (Berlin: Zsolnay, 1929), p. 84: "Vor die Rampe treten und sprechen."

[24]See Frank Hartwig's edition of Wedekind's *Marquis von Keith,* Komedia, No. 8 (Berlin: de Gruyter, 1965), pp. 114-15.

[25]Seehaus, p. 366: "Wedekind liebte im Leben wie auf dem Theater wohl gebaute Perioden in einem zuweilen fast feierlichen Deutsch bei stets gemessener Haltung, wie sie Hoteldirektoren beim Empfang illustrer Gäste pflegen [...], um dann plötzlich mit Sarkasmen und gut geschliffenen Antithesen dazwischen zu feixen. Das Gegenteil von naturalistischem

Sprechstil. Wenn seine Sätze aber wie in einem realistischen Drama gesprochen werden, so klingen sie alle papiern, oder wie auf Stelzen, zwischen die sich fast unfreiwillig allerhand Sarkasmen verirrt haben."

[26]*Satire*, p. 342: "Die Satire kämpft also gegen das, mit dem das Bewußtsein nicht fertig wird, gegen eine pure Macht und Plage [...]; gegen eine Lücke im System der Reihen, durch die das Chaos einbricht *(horror vacui);* gegen ein Sein, das sich jeder Funktionalisierung widersetzt [...]; gegen das Wirkliche überhaupt, sofern es jeden Versuch zur Aneignung vereitelt."

[27]In *To Damascus,* published 1898, three years after *Erdgeist,* August Strindberg uses the word in an altogether negative sense to signify woman as the demonically carnal seducer, in contrast to the spiritually inclined male: "Ich habe in der Frau einen Engel gesucht, der mir seine Schwingen leihen sollte, und ich fiel in die Arme eines Erdgeistes, der mich unter den Polstern erstickte, die er mit den Federn seiner Flügel gestopft hatte.—Ich suchte einen Ariel und fand einen Caliban. Wenn ich in die Höhe wollte, zog mich die Frau herab [...]" (Quoted in Horst Fritz, "Die Dämonisierung des Erotischen [...]," p. 450; see note 8.

[28]*The. Greek Myths,* Penguin Books, Nos. 1026-27 (1955), I, 35, 114-45; II, 349, 352.

[29]*Ibid.,* 145.

[30]*Ibid.,* I, 190; see also J.J. Herzog, *Realencyclopädie für protestantische Theologie und Kirche* (Leipzig, 1889) under the heading "Lilith."

[31]See Peter Wapnewski, *Der traurige Gott: Richard Wagner in seinen Helden,* 2nd ed. (Munich: Beck, 1980), pp. 230ff.

[32]This is the view of Wilhelm Emrich. See below and note 47.

[33]A. G. Lehman, "Pierrot and Fin de Siècle," in Ian Fletcher, ed., *Romantic Mythologies* (New York: Barnes and Noble, 1967), p. 214; and Day Dick, *Pierrot* (London: Hutchinson, 1960), p. 178.

[34]Lehman, p. 224 et passim; Dick, p. 181.

[35]Robert F. Storey, *Pierrot: A Critical History of a Mask* (Princeton University Press, 1978), p. 125.

[36]Storey, p. 97.

[37]R. Peacock, "The Ambiguity of Wedekind's Lulu", *Oxford German Studies* 9 (1978), 109-10.

[38]*Dictionary of National Biography* (New York: Macmillan, 1895), Vol. 44, p. 155.

[39]Sol Gittleman, *Frank Wedekind,* TWAS, No. 55 (New York: Twayne, 1969), p. 66.

[40]*Frau Lou: Nietzsche's Wayward Disciple* (Princeton University Press, 1968), p. 55 et passim.

[41]*Frau Lou,* p. 135.

[42] *Frau Lou,* p. 183: "Er ist schon erzogen."

[43] *Die Zeit,* 9 January 1970, Overseas Edition.

[44] Seehaus, pp. 382-83.

[45] "Incitements to Passion," *TLS,* October 3, 1975, pp. 1136-37.

[46] Here belong Klaus Völker, *Wedekind,* Friedrichs Dramatiker des Welttheaters, no. 7 (Velber: Friedrich, 1965), pp. 19-20; Sol Gittleman, *Frank Wedekind,* TWAS, No. 55 (New York: Twayne, 1969), p. 19: Karl Kraus, *Literatur und Lüge* (Munich: Kosel, 1958), pp. 9-21.

[47] Among these are Wilhelm Emrich, "Frank Wedekind—Die Lulu-Tragödie," in *Protest und Verheißung,* 2nd ed. (Frankfurt: Athenäum, 1963), pp. 206-22; Peter Michelsen, "Frank Wedekind," in *Deutsche Dichter der Moderne,* ed. Benno von Wiese (Berlin: Erich Schmidt, 1965), pp. 49-67; Arthur Kitscher, *Frank Wedekind* (Munich: Langen/Müller, 1922), vol. I, 368; Gertrud Milkereit geb. Becher, *Die Idee der Freiheit im Werke von Frank Wedekind* (diss., Cologne, 1957); Wolfdietrich Rasch, "Sozialkritische Aspekte in Wedekinds dramatischer Dichtung: Sexualität, Kunst und Gesellschaft," in Helmut Kreuzer, ed., *Gestaltungsgeschichte und Gesellschaftsgeschichte, Festschrift für Fritz Martini* (Stuttgart: Metzler, 1969), pp. 409-26.

[48] See Alfred Kerr, *Die Welt im Drama,* ed. G. F. Hering, 2nd ed. (Cologne: Kiepenheuer, 1964), pp. 229-246; Alfred Polgar, *Ja und Nein* (Berlin: Rowohlt, 1926), Vol. I, 175-76; Max Spalter, *Brecht's Tradition* (Baltimore: Johns Hopkins, 1967), p. 124; Paul Böckmann, "Die komödiantischen Grotesken Frank Wedekinds," in Hans Steffen, ed., *Das deutsche Lustspiel* (Göttingen: Vandenhoeck & Ruprecht, 1969), Vol. II, 79-102; and Heinrich Mann, "Erinnerungen an Frank Wedekind," in *Sieben Jahre: Chronik der Gedanken und Vorgänge* (Berlin: Zsolnay, 1929), pp. 75-95.

[49] *Frank Wedekinds Dramen: Jugendstil und Lebensphilosophie,* Germanistische Abhandlungen, no. 23 (Stuttgart: Metzler, 1968).

[50] Dürrenmatt, "Bekenntnisse eines Plagiators," *Theaterschriften und Reden* (Zurich: Arche, 1966), p. 245: "Sein Problem, das Geschlechtliche, steht heute nicht mehr im Mittelpunkt leider. Es wäre sicher angenehmer als der kalte Krieg. Noch hat man es nicht gelernt, in Wedekind Komödien zu sehen, daher läßt er die meisten kalt: sie nehmen ihn ernst, falsch ernst. Man sieht ihn immer noch als wilden Sexualreformer und wertet seine Aussagen mit Wahr oder Falsch; man sollte endlich dahin kommen, in ihm nicht ein Verhältnis zu der Wirklichkeit zu sehen, sondern eine Wirklichkeit, nicht so sehr *was* er widerspiegelt, sondern *wie* er die Dinge widerspiegelt."

[51] *Ibid.,* p. 135.

[52] Seehaus, p. 196.

[53] Gaier, *Satire,* p. 449.

[54] In 1899 Wedekind pictured himself as the "dumme August" in real life. "Dieses ewige

Beinahe, das ist das Verhängnis, das Charakteristische meiner Natur. Ich war beinah verheiratet, wäre beinah Schauspieler geworden [...]" (*Der vermummte Herr*, pp. 114-15).

[55]"Erinnerung an Frank Wedekind," see note 23:

"Wenn im Jahre 1900 jemand so schrieb, als sei es 1914: wer sollte den mit offenen Armen empfangen! Eine Welt nackten Kampfes hinstellen, während man sich doch noch vollauf gesittet glaubte! Alles anders, drohender auffassen, als man sich selbst damals auffaßte; alles entkleiden, zuerst von den schönen Worten, den sittlichen Vorwänden, endlich beinahe vom Fleisch! Noch dazu auf dem Theater, wo man sich so gern in behaglichem oder rührendem Leben liebevoll gespiegelt sieht!

"Dies war nun die Sendung des dramatischen Dichters Frank Wedekind."

[56]Seehaus, p. 17: "Es gibt unter den lebenden deutschen Dichtern wohl keinen, der so vollkommen Ausdruck der Denk- und Gefühlsweise unserer Zeit wäre wie Frank Wedekind."

[57]Sternheim, *Gesamtwerk* (Neuwied: Luchterhand, 1976), X/1, pp. 481-82. "Deutschland war durch ihn [...] fortgesetzt auf dem wirklich Laufenden. Seine Prominenten wurden ihm [dem einfachen Mann] gesalzen und gepfeffert noch einmal angerichtet bis er vor ihnen das Kotzen bekam, die Staatsmänner, [die] Max Reinhardts, Paul Cassirer, die Mentalitäts- und Bildfälscher, die Dirnen, Zuhälter, Päderasten haute volée standen pudelnackt vor dem einfachen Mann aus dem Volk, daß er die Angst vor den 'Gespenstern' völlig verlor und der Dichter Befreier noch das jauchzende Lachen erlebte [...]."

[58]Chapter 2, pp. 71-74.

[59]I refer to *Geschlecht und Charakter*, 20th ed. (Vienna and Leipzig: Braumüller, 1920). This sentence paraphrases material on p. 108.

[60]Weininger, pp. 140ff., 185, 234: "Undine die seelenlose Undine, ist die platonische Idee des Weibes."

[61]Weininger, pp. 243, 251, 255, 256, 292: "[...] ihren Trieben Lauf lassend und sie wie im Trotz befriedigend, fühlt sie sich als Herrscherin und die tiefste Selbstverständlichkeit ist ihr, daß sie Macht habe."

[62]Weininger, p. 292.

[63]Weininger, pp. 295-96.

[64]Weininger, p. 299: "[...] denn alles Leben, das sie hat, will sie in diesem Moment [des Orgasmus] konzentriert, zusammengedrängt wissen. Weil dies nicht gelingen kann, darum wird die Prostituierte in ihrem ganzen Leben nie befriedigt, von allen Männern der Welt nicht."

[65]Weininger, p. 304: "Sie will vernichtet werden und vernichten. Sie schadet und zerstört."

[66]Weininger, pp. 455-58.

[67]See Wesley V. Blomster, "The Documentation of a Novel: Otto Weininger and *Hunde-jahre* by Günter Grass," *Monatshefte*, 61 (1969), 122-38.

[68]See Carl Schorske, *Fin de Siècle Vienna: Politics and Culture* (New York: Knopf, 1980), pp. 223ff.

[69]Schorske, pp. 322ff.

[70]See George Mosse, *The Crisis of German Ideology* (New York: Grosset and Dunlap, 1964), pp. 113-15.

[71]Mosse, p. 114. Mittgart, or more often Midgard and Mithgarthr, is in Germanic mythology the region inhabited by humans and their gods, i.e., the Earth.

[72]Quoted in Fritz Bolle, "Darwinismus und Zeitgeist," *Zeitschrift für Religions- und Zeitgeschichte,* 14 (1962), 143-78; here, 171-72.

[73]Moeller-Bruck, *Der neue Humor,* Die moderne Literatur in Einzeldarstellungen, no. 11 (Berlin/Leipzig, 1902), pp. 43-44: "Man sehe sich an, wie die Handlungen einsetzen, unter welchen antiidealistischen Bedingungen und wie folgerichtig sie schließen: was dazwischen liegt, ist regelmäßig ein mustergiltiges Beispiel unserer vitalsten Triebe, im Gastrologischen, Sexuellen usw., und hat deren Sinn [...]."

[74]*Aktuelle Dramaturgie* (Berlin: Schmiede, 1924), pp. 71-72. Ulrich Gaier—*Satire,* p. 336—says of the satirist's relation to reality, "[...] er fühlt sich von der Wirklichkeit bedrängt und bedrückt." In his "Pariser Tagebuch"—*Werke in drei Bänden,* ed. Manfred Hahn (Berlin/Weimar: Aufbau, 1969), III, 317f.—Wedekind tells how in the early 1890s he once suffered a nervous collapse with loss of speech and muscular control after watching Marcel Herwegh tyrannize his 76-year-old mother Emma, the widow of the poet and a person of whom Wedekind was very fond.

[75]Though conceived as a single three-act piece, *Schloß Wetterstein* appeared first as three one-act plays: *In allen Sätteln gerecht* [Ready for Anything], *Mit allen Hunden gehetzt* [Wily as a Fox], and *In allen Wassern gewaschen* [Too Clever by Half].

[76]These lines represent the last of Wedekind's efforts to revise the speech and so placate the censor while preserving the sense of the play's denouement. The Berlin police censor remained adamant, however, and the play waited until 1919 for its first production in Germany.

[77]*Der vermummte Herr: Briefe,* p. 132.

[78]Hellmut Rosenfeld, *Der mittelalterliche Totentanz,* 2nd ed. (Cologne: Böhlau, 1968), pp. 304-05, 51.

[79]"Die schöne Melusine" is the ambiguous title heroine of a fifteenth-century chapbook. Though each Saturday the lower part of her body takes the form of a dragon's tail and though each of her children has a weird physical deformity, she is nevertheless a powerful, virtuous, and beautiful noblewoman. Her happy marriage to a human is ruined when on a Saturday her husband, overcome with curiosity and breaking his vow, peers at her through a hole in the door.

[80]I, 956-57: "Lulu was Salomé. Dr. Schön was Pastor Rosmer of Rosmersholm."

Chapter 2

[1]Jörg Schönert, ed. *Carl Sternheims Dramen* (Heidelberg: Quelle und Meyer, 1975), p. 31. Portions of this chapter appeared in Donald H. Crosby and George C. Schoolfield, eds., *Studies in the German Drama: A Festschrift in Honor of Walter Silz* (Chapel Hill: University of North Carolina Press, 1974).

[2]"Nicht Ironie und Satire also, die als meine Absicht der Reporter festgestellt hatte und die Menge nachschwatzte, sondern vor allgemeiner Tat aus meinen Schriften schon die Lehre: daß Kraft sich nicht verliert, muß auf keinen überkommenen Rundgesang doch auf seinen frischen Einzelton der Mensch nur hören, ganz unbesorgt darum, wie Bürgersinn seine manchmal brutale Nuance nennt," from Sternheim's preface to *Die Hose,* dated 1918, reprinted in Carl Sternheim, *Gesamtwerk,* ed. Wilhelm Emrich (Neuwied: Luchterhand, 1963f.), I, 24. Unless otherwise noted, further references to Sternheim's writings cite this edition by volume and page number.

[3]*Säkularausgabe,* XII, 194. Ideologically inspired scholars—e.g., Wilhelm Emrich in his introduction to Carl Sternheim's *Gesamtwerk* vol. I—insist that Sternheim overtly states his ideal and point to passages with the ring of pronouncement. But they overlook others that contradict them. See also W. G. Sebald, *Carl Sternheim: Kritiker und Opfer der Wilhelminischen Ära,* Sprache und Literatur, no. 58 (Stuttgart, Kohlhammer, 1969).

[4]Carl Sternheim, *Gesamtwerk,* VI, 53. Silvio Vietta—in Vietta and Kemper, *Expressionismus,* Uni-Taschenbücher, no. 362 (Munich: Fink, 1975), pp. 100-02—backs Sternheim on this point. He argues that the comedies are decidedly "ideologiekritische Satiren" and that to come forth in the last scene with a "positive anthropology" would be to compromise his critical position by resorting to a new ideology.

[5]See Ulrich Gaier, *Satire,* p. 135.

[6]"[...] ich hatte keinen 'Standpunkt,' [...] als daß ich in jedem das Besondere antippte; ihm in Bezug auf sein Unvergleichliches ohne Werturteil gerecht wurde! Ich mußte erkennen, nicht 'entlarven,' mich nicht als 'Satiriker' über sie 'lustigmachen'; zeigen, wie wesentlich traurig, komisch, heldisch, überlegen jeder an sich war!"

[7]Burghard Dedner, "Aufklärungskomödien im 'Massenzeitalter': Über Carl Sternheims Beziehungen zum Publikum," *JDSG,* 19 (1975), 284-305.

[8]"Das moderne Gefühl: Ich kann auf keine andere Weise mich auszeichnen, als wenn ich als Mitmensch besonders gut angepaßt bin, zerstörte jedes Bedürfnis der Isolation, indem im Gegenteil Vorstellung derer, mit denen ich ringend lebe, vom Kampf ums Dasein unzertrennlich, ja dessen Voraussetzung ist."

[9]"Der Mensch in gewaltigen, unentrinnbaren Naturmechanismus gefesselt, ohne Rest eigener Aktion im Entscheidenden, betäubt sich innerhalb starrer Scharniere durch Fessellosigkeit, die ohne Beispiel ist."

[10]Nowadays prestige connotes standing in the eyes of people, power, glory. In earlier times it signified illusion or deception and translated Latin "praestigiae," which means

conjurer's tricks. The same ambiguity is inherent in Sternheim's use of the word "das Ansehen."

[11]"Hinter noch so forscher Geste, keckem Wort hob als lächelnder Schatten sich steil eine eherne Wirklichkeit, die es zum Witz, zur Metapher schlug. Nichts mehr zu gestalten hatte im Grunde ja der Mensch, nur aufzupassen und sich Ereignendes mit einem Schlagwort zu prägen."

[12]"Ein Dichter wie Molière ist Arzt am Leibe seiner Zeit. Des Menschen sämtliche, ihm von seinem Schöpfer gegebene Eigenschaften blank und strahlend zu erhalten, ist ihm unabweisbar Pflicht. Zur Erreichung seines hohen Zieles bedient er sich wie der medizinische Helfer der allopathischen oder homöopathischen Methode. Er kann den Finger auf die bedenkliche Stelle des Menschtums legen und den Helden eine dagegen mit Einsetzung seines Lebens eifernde Kampfstellung einnehmen lassen (Wesen der Tragödie), er kann aber auch die aufzuweisende Eigenschaft in den Helden selbst senken und ihn mit fanatischer Lust von ihr sinnlos besessen sein lassen (Wesen der Komödie). Der Eindruck auf den Zuschauer ist in beiden Fällen der gleiche: ihn überwältigt zum Schluß die Sehnsucht nach einem schönen Maß, das der Bühnenheld nicht hatte, zu dem er selbst aber durch des Dichters Aufklärung nunmehr leidenschaftlich gewillt ist.

[13]"Ich entfachte zu keiner Erziehung; im Gegenteil warnte ich vor Kritik göttlicher Welt durch den Bürger und machte ihm Mut zu seinen sogenannten Lastern, mit denen er Erfolge errang, und riet ihm, meiner Verantwortung bewußt, Begriffe, die einseitig nach sittlichem Verdienst messen, als unerheblich und lebensschwächend endlich aus seiner Terminologie zu entfernen [...]. Im Grund aber hoffte ich, der Arbeiter sähe statt des ihm frisiert hingesetzten Mannes des *Juste Milieu* daraus endlich den wahren und echten Jakob ein; hinter dessen literarischem Entgegenkommen und geschminkten Mätzchen seine wirkliche, noch allmächtig lebendige, brutale Lebensfrische und messe an ihr als an formidabler Wirklichkeit statt an verblasenen Theorien Wucht bevorstehender Entscheidung, der ich mit dem einzigen Verlangen gegenüberstand, es möchte sich aus ihr, gleichviel auf welcher Seite, der Zeit Wahrhaftigkeit offenbaren."

[14]One notable exception is Hellmuth Karasek whose *Carl Sternheim*, Friedrichs Dramatiker der Weltliteratur (Velber bei Hannover: Friedrich, 1965) makes a convincing case for the opposite view and accentuates the negative.

[15]Sebald, *Carl Sternheim, Kritiker und Opfer* [...]

[16]Sebald, pp. 17, 26, 38, 39, 43. Sternheim's dramaturgical thinking is in fact dialectic, but not in a political or ideological sense. Sebald has in mind dialectical materialism, which demands a positive twist, no matter what. See Friedrich Dürrenmatt, *Monstervortrag über Gerechtigkeit und Recht* (Zurich: Arche, 1969), p. 95.

[17]See Hodgart, *Satire*, p. 14.

[18]"Sieben Komödien schrieb ich von 1908-1913. Die letzte, die des Vorkriegsjahres Namen trägt, zeigte, wohin, in aller Einfalt womöglich, des Bürgers Handel gediehen war. Vom Dichter gab es nichts, nur noch von Wirklichkeit hinzuzusetzen. Trotz vielfacher

öffentlicher Darstellung und Verbreitung durch Druck hatte niemand bemerkt, wohin mit meinem Werk mein Wille ging."

[19]Wedekind, mit dem ich in meinem Haus in Höllkriegelskreuth bei München und anderswo zusammengetroffen bin, ist mir stets [...] auch in persönlichem Verkehr als der einzige zu ähnlichen Zielen der Kunst entschlossene erschienen."

[20]Published Berlin and Leipzig, 1913.

[21]See Alvin Kernan, ed. *Modern Satire* (New York: Harcourt, Brace, 1962), pp. 177-78.

[22]Ronald Paulson, *The Fictions of Satire* (Baltimore: The Johns Hopkins University Press, 1967), p. 79. See also Gerhard Hoffmann, "Zur Form der satirischen Komödie: Ben Jonsons *Volpone,*" *Deutsche Vierteljahrsschrift,* 46 (1972), 14.

[23]See W. H. Auden, *The Dyer's Hand* (London: Faber and Faber, 1963), p. 384.

[24]Jacobsohn, *Jahre der Bühne* (Reinbek: Rowohlt, 1965), p. 86.

[25]See W. Wendler, *Carl Sternheim* (Bonn: Athenäum, 1966), p. 24.

[26]If Krull had looked at the pertinent scenes of Goethe's *Faust, Part II,* he would have been disappointed. They contain an attack on the idea of bank notes.

[27]See *Gesamtwerk,* X/1, 226.

[28]"[...] alles Falsche, Abzulehnende, das inzwischen aufgetreten war, hatte sich in Deutschlands Hauptstadt besonders breitgemacht. Eine Mischung von Kleinbürgern, Proletariern wurde in der Welt 'Volk,' dem die doppelte Katastrophe zu Ende des vorigen Jahrhunderts, Darwin, Einstein, die Maschine, das Genick gebrochen hatte; *auf dem eine Oberschicht hauste, die es sich [...] gutgehen ließ.* Aber auch in ihr war keine Absicht hervorzuragen mehr [...]; auf andere Weise *machte sie Mimikry;* welches Schutzmittel Darwin im entfesselten Kampf ums Dasein in der Natur bewiesen hatte."

[29]"[...] ein Artist voller Widerwillen gegen verdorbene Luft mit der unbezwinglichen Neigung, Götzen anzurempeln, die Leerheit von Attrappen zu erweisen."

[30]"Sie sind wie tobsüchtige Maschinen, die gegeneinander und in ihr Verderben rasen. Der Humor, der davon kommt, hat deutlich sadistische Züge. Vernichtung wird vorge-zeichnet und geliebt.
"*1913* ist gewiß nicht die beste seiner Strampel-Komödien. Hier gießt er satirische Säure aus mit doppelter Hand. Die Lauge des Spottes spritzt über die Dummheit der Materialisten, über die Matadoren des Wirtschaftswunders vor dem ersten Weltkrieg."

[31]"Sternheim's prophetisches Gemüt roch, wohin der Hase lief. Das Stück, auch wo es Gelächter schafft, macht Gänsehaut. Es gruselt einen vor diesem bösen, klaren Blick."

[32]"Unter Albert Steinrücks Regie, ihm selbst in der Hauptrolle des Krull [und den Schauspielern] in den übrigen Rollen brachen—nachdem schon in den ersten Zügen das Publikum deutlich gezeigt hatte, diese Aufführung ginge über alles, was ihm je auf dieser Bühne zugemutet war, hinaus—während des letzten Aktes solche Sturmszenen aus, daß

unter Pfeifen und Johlen man harte Gegenstände nach den Schauspielern auf der Bühne warf; der eiserne Vorhang niedergelassen werden mußte, *Gegner und Zustimmende in dem Saal der Mozart-Festspiele handgemein wurden.*"

[33]I, 586; and Klaus Hagedorn, *Carl Sternheim: Die Bühnengeschichte seiner Dramatik,* Diss. Cologne 1961 (Cologne, 1976), pp. 68-70.

[34]*Süddeutsche Zeitung,* 1/2 July, 1961.

[35]See Arno Paul, *Aggressive Tendenzen des Theaterpublikums: Eine strukturell-funktionale Untersuchung über den sog. Theaterskandal anhand der Sozialverhältnisse der Goethezeit.* Diss. FU Berlin 1969 (Munich: Schön, 1969), esp. 287-88.

[36]See Wolfgang Grothe, "Dramatiker im ideologischen Niemandsland: Bemerkungen anläßlich der Carl-Sternheim-Gesamtausgabe," *Studia Neophilogica,* 41 (1969), 339, 345.

[37]Gerhard Ritter, *Staatskunst und Kriegshandwerk* (Munich: Oldenbourg, 1960), II, pp. 117ff.

[38]"Sicher ist, daß die Deutschen sich jetzt im Klange ihrer Sprache militarisieren; wahrscheinlich ist, daß sie, eingeübt militärisch zu sprechen, endlich auch militarisch schreiben werden. Denn die Gewohnheit an bestimmte Klänge greift tief in den Charakter:—man hat bald die Worte und Wendungen und schließlich auch die Gedanken, welche eben zu diesem Klange passen," Nietzsche, *Werke,* ed. Karl Schlechta (Munich: Hanser, 1955), II, 111.

[39]"Abends Sternheims *1913* in den Kammerspielen. Sternheim hat mit starker dramatischer und komischer Kraft die entscheidenden Faktoren in der Struktur des deutschen Volkes vor dem Kriege herausgestellt. Krai ist [Gustav] Stresemann in seiner Werdezeit, der 'teutsche' Jüngling mit poetischem Ehrgeiz, der durch die reiche Fabrikantentochter 'korrumpiert' wird, nicht durch eine Kokotte, wie es konventionell geschieht. Ein starkes und tiefes Stück." Kessler, *Tagebücher 1918-1937* (Frankfurt: Insel, 1961), p. 396.

[40]Quoted by Robert Wohl in *The Generation of 1914* (Harvard University Press, 1979), p. 49.

[41]"Die Geschichte kennt keinen Staatsmann, der sich so ausdauernd und eindringlich mit der öffentlichen Meinung und ihrer Bedeutung beschäftigt hätte, wie Fürst von Bülow," from *Das Wilhelminische Deutschland: Stimmen der Zeitgenossen,* Fischer Bücherei, no. 611 (Frankfurt: Fischer, 1965).

[42]Winfried Baumgart, *Deutschland im Zeitalter des Imperialismus (1890-1914),* 3rd. ed., Deutsche Geschichte: Ereignisse und Probleme, Ullstein Buch no. 3844 (Frankfurt/Berlin/Vienna: Ullstein, 1979), pp. 119, 149.

[43]Fritz Fischer, *Germany's Aims in the First World War* (New York: Norton, 1967), pp. 16f.

[44]Das alldeutsche Gedankengut ist ein Gemisch aus dem von Ernst Haeckel popularisierten Sozialdarwinismus, aus den Lehren Paul de Lagardes vom Volkstum und Friedrich

Tatzels vom Lebensraum, aber auch aus Nietzsches Ideen vom 'Übermenschen,' vom 'Herrenvolk,' vom 'Willen zur Macht' [...] überhaupt aus allen möglichen damals greifbaren Gedankensplittern der Lebensphilosophie, des Voluntarismus, des Irrationalismus und des Materialismus. Die Linie, die von hier zum Gedankenwust des Natinalsozialismus führt, ist unverkennbar." Baumgart, *Deutschland,* p. 167.

[45]See Willi Boelcke, *Krupp und die Hohenzollern: Aus der Korrespondenz der Familie Krupp, 1880-1916* (Berlin: Rütten und Loening, 1956), pp. 112-13.

[46]Peter de Mendelssohn, *Zeitungsstadt Berlin* (Berlin: Ullstein, 1959), pp. 505-07.

[47]*Zeitungsstadt Berlin,* 151ff.

[48]"Passierte [...] doch einmal das Unwahrscheinliche, das Unvernünftige, blieb es in den Zeitungen unerwähnt und existierte also gar nicht. Längst hatte der Jounalist erkannt, daß das, wovon er nicht sprach, in Hirnen der Berliner auch nicht vorhanden war. Jibt's ja jarnich!"

[49]Published in Berlin and Leipzig by Teubner.

[50]See Max Weber, *Gesammelte Aufsätze zur Religionspsychologie,* 5th ed. (Tübingen: Mohr. 1963), p. 17.

[51]Max Stirner (pseudonym for Kaspar Schmidt), *Der Einzige und sein Eigentum* (Leipzig: Reclam, 1892), pp. 17, 223, 422.

[52]Hannah Arendt, *On Violence* (New York: Harcourt Brace, 1970), p. 54.

[53]Richard Hofstadter, *Social Darwinism in American Thought: 1860-1915* (Philadelphia: University of Pennsylvania Press, 1945).

[54]"Der Krieg hat dem Wandervogel rechtgegeben, hat seine tiefe nationale Grundidee los von allem Beiwerk stark und licht in unsere Mitte gestellt. Wir müssen immer deutscher werden. Wandern ist der deutscheste aller Triebe, ist unser Grundwesen, ist der Spiegel unseres Nationalcharakters überhaupt." Cited from Karl O. Paetel, *Jugend in der Entscheidung, 1913-1933-1945* (Bad Godesberg: Voggenreiter, 1963), p. 26.

[55]"In dieser Romantik treten, wie in der alten, teils anarchistisch-subjektivistische Züge hervor, die von Nietzsche zur höchsten Macht gebracht und modern darwinistisch begründet worden sind, teils die Sehnsucht nach Gemeinschaft und mystischer Willenseinheit," Sarason, p. 547.

[56]"Wer den hohen Ernst einer nicht fernen Zukunft absichtlich verschleiern will, weil er davon 'Abschwächung der Konjunktur' befürchtet, der versündigt sich namenlos schwer am deutschen Volke, der ist des Hochverrats am deutschen Volke zu zeihen. Den großen Entscheidungskampf werden wir nur bestehen, wenn wir in ihn nicht nur in vollster militärischer, sondern auch in höchster seelischer Bereitschaft eintreten [...].
. . . .
Die Hand bis zum letzten Augenblick am Pfluge, aber das Schwert locker und scharf zur Seite, so wollen wir Deutsche der Zukunft entgegengehen, so allein ist's rechte Deutsche

Art." Quoted in Lothar Werner, *Der Alldeutsche Verband, 1890-1918: Ein Beitrag zur Geschichte der öffentlichen Meinung in Deutschland in den Jahren vor und während des Krieges,* Historische Studien, no. 278 (Berlin: Ebering, 1935), p. 195.

[57]*New York Review,* 3 April 1975, pp. 11-17.

Chapter 3

[1]Bertolt Brecht, *Stücke III* (Frankfurt: Suhrkamp, 1964), vol. I, 210, 233. Cited hereafter by page number alone.

[2]Friedrich Dürrenmatt, *Komödien I* (Zurich: Arche, 1967), p. 325, cited hereafter by volume and page number.

[3]Georg Kaiser, *Von morgens bis mitternachts,* in *Werke,* ed. Walther Huder (Berlin: Propylaen, 1971), I, 515. Cited hereafter by volume and page number alone.

[4]German audiences must be aware that Frau Ill's pious sounding saw is in fact only the first half of the Berlin axiom: "Geld allein macht nicht glücklich. Man muß es auch besitzen." Or worse: "Geld allein macht nicht glücklich, sagte der Jude, man muß es zu dreißig Prozent ausleihen"—Karl Friedrich Wilhelm Wander, ed., *Deutsches Sprichwörter-Lexikon* (Darmstadt: Wissenschaftliche Buchgesellschaft, 1964), vol. I, col. 1479.

[5]*The Idea of a Theater* (1949, rpt. New York: Anchor-Doubleday, 1953), p. 31. See also Alvin B. Kernan, *Modern Satire* (New York: Harcourt, Brace and World, 1962), pp. 177-78. I have added to his two-beat rhythm of purpose and passion a third which is implicit in it.

[6]"*Von morgens bis mitternachts* ist dem Deutschen Theater in Berlin, dem Schauspielhaus in Düsseldorf, dem Neuen Theater in Frankfurt a.M. verboten, in München kämpfen die Kammerspiele noch um seine Freigabe, Wien hat noch keinen Bescheid."

[7]"Als ich mir mit den Komödien eine unerträgliche, faule, vergiftete Atmosphäre gereinigt hatte, schrieb ich *Die Bürger von Calais.*"

[8]"Angreifer in Bewußtheit auf Zuständliches mit Stoff und Form des Zuständlichen."

[9]"Die Menschen sind alle schlecht aus Genußgier, fühlt der Beamte. Und Sie, Herr Held? Wer hat seine zwei Töchter, wer seine Frau unglücklich gemacht, wer seiner Mutter den Tod bereitet? hä?" Alfred Kerr, *Die Welt im Drama,* ed. Gerhard F. Hering, 2nd ed. (Cologne: Kiepenheuer und Witsch, 1964), p. 258.

[10]"Die Tragödie eines Mannes mit einer Primanerphantasie." Kessler, *Tagebücher 1918-1937* (Frankfurt: Insel, 1961), entry of January 31, 1919, p. 116.

[11]Ernst Schürer, *Georg Kaiser,* TWAS (New York: Twayne, 1971); Wilhelm Steffens, *Georg Kaiser* (Velber: Friedrich, 1969).

[12]Denis Calandra, "Georg Kaiser's *From Morn to Midnight:* The Nature of Expressionist Performance," *Theatre Quarterly,* 4, (1976), no. 21, 48ff.

[13]"Nun, eine Analyse der Hitlerschen Reden wird zeigen, [...] ob [...] gerade der gespreizte Schriftstil, ein [...] Bürokraten-Deutsch in Verbindung mit Kolportage-Elementen die braune Rhetorik geprägt hat." Walter Jens, *Von deutscher Rede* (Munich: Piper, 1969), p. 31.

[14]*Hochland*, 15 (1917/18), no. 3, 357-60.

[15]See Christopher Booker, *The Neophiliacs* (Boston: Gambit, 1970).

[16]*Schriften zum Theater* (Frankfurt: Suhrkamp, 1963), II, 1918-1933, 113-14.

[17]See his long and brilliant review of the Leipzig world première in *Der Scheinwerfer*, III, Essen, 13 April 1930, reprinted in Monika Wyss, ed., *Brecht in der Kritik* (Munich: Kindler, 1977), p. 111.

[18]Patty Lee Parmalee, *Brecht's America* (Miami University Press, 1981), p. 177.

[19]"Der Name Mahagonny bezeichnet lediglich den Begriff einer Stadt. Es ist aus klanglichen phonetischen Gründen gewählt worden. Die geographische Lage spielt keine Rolle." Arnolt Bronnen, *Tage mit Brecht* (Munich: Desch, 1960), pp. 143ff.; and Parmalee, pp. 154, 184.

[20]For the contradictory statements on sensuality see pp. 190, 215; on winning and losing, pp. 225-26 and 234.

[21]The "Benares Song" is still in the opera libretto but has been cut from the text as printed in Brecht's collected works.

[22]"In Leipzig bekommt man Bücher, Pelze, Fluchtgedanken, und zur Messezeit kein Zimmer, in Mahagonny Whisky, sangbare Ironien, Huren, einschmeichelnd formulierte Hinweise auf die menschliche Natur und Ordnung, so wie Bitterkeiten von verschiedenem Geschmack [...]." From Monika Wyss, ed., *Brecht in der Kritik*, p. 108. Originally in *Das Tagebuch*, 22 March 1930, Berlin.

[23]"Die Stadt Mahagonny ist eine Darstellung der kapitalistischen Welt, entworfen aus der Vogelperspektive der klassenlosen Gesellschaft." *Brecht in der Kritik*, p. 110.

[24]"Je undeutlicher, irrealer die Realität durch die Musik wird—es entsteht ja ein Drittes, sehr Komplexes, an sich ganz Reales, von dem ganz reale Wirkungen ausgehen können, das aber eben von seinem Gegenstand, von der benutzten Realität, völlig entfernt ist—, desto genußvoller wird der Gesamtvorgang [...]," *Schriften zum Theater*, II, pp. 113-14.

[25]Gottfried Wagner, *Weill und Brecht: Das musikalische Zeittheater* (Munich: Kindler, 1977), p. 169.

[26]Wagner, *Weill und Brecht*, p. 170; *Stücke III*, vol. I, 177.

[27]*Weill und Brecht*, 194, 203, 206ff.

[28]*The New Yorker*, 6 January 1973, p. 61.

[29]See Helmut Kindler's introduction to Monika Wyss, *Brecht in der Kritik*, pp. xxiiff.

[30]*Brecht in der Kritik*, p. 108f.

[31]Herbert Ihering, *Von Reinhardt bis Brecht* (Hamburg: Rowohlt, 1967), p. 321.

[32]*Brecht in der Kritik*, p. 121.

[33]Cited from Manfred Voigts, *Brechts Theaterkonzeptionen: Entstehung und Entwicklung bis 1931* (Munich: Fink, 1978), p. 158.

[34]*Stücke III*, vol. I, 253-54. John xix. 28.

[35]"Zerrissenheit durch Zerrissenheit wiederzugeben," reprinted in Günther Rühle, ed., *Theater für die Republik 1917-1933* (Frankfurt: Fischer, 1967), p. 61.

[36]Ernst Schürer, ed., *Georg Kaiser, Von morgens bis mitternachts, Erläuterungen und Dokumente*, Reclams Universalbibliothek, no. 8131 (Stuttgart: Reclam, 1975), pp. 58-59.

[37]"Die Aufführung in den Kammerspielen [wurde] von dem aufgerüttelten Publikum durch Rufe, Lachen und Zischen unterbrochen, durch stürmischen Beifall dem Schluß zu hinaufgehoben zu der Besonderheit eines Theaterereignisses." Taken from a newspaper clipping dated 3 May 1917 in the holdings of the Georg Kaiser Archiv of the Akademie der Künste, Berlin (West).

[38]"Die krassen Effekte wurden vom Publikum mit Pfeifen und Johlen beantwortet, man geriet in lebhafte persönliche Auseinandersetzungen, bot sich Ohrfeigen an und beteiligte sich am Spiel. Der Regisseur Hollaender erschien am Schluß und erklärte, er werde dem Dichter von der lebendigen Aufnahme des Stückes Bericht erstatten." Unsigned and undated clipping from the Kaiser Archiv.

[39]"Das [...] Stück fand ein unruhiges, immer stürmischer bewegtes Publikum. Man klatschte, zischte, pfiff auf Hausschlüsseln Katzenmusik. Man schrie, ballte die Fäuste und sagte sich Grobheiten." Ernst Schürer, *Erläuterungen und Dokumente*, p. 63.

[40]Jacobsohn, *Jahre der Bühne* (Hamburg: Rowohlt, 1965), p. 175.

[41]"Pallenberg spielt und die Leute möchten lachen. Aber sie stutzen, wenn der unheimliche geduckte Blick des bärtigen Männchens hin und her wandert; und eiskalt wird ihnen, als es auf seinen schwachen Beinen durchs Hotelzimmer der Dame geht und rechthaberisch zu toben beginnt. Nichts Grelles. Nichts Burleskes. Ein bitterer, menschenferner Ernst, der alle Komikerspäße verleugnet, eine lauschende Angst, die in der Heilsarmee–Szene wild zuckt und so ergreift, als wäre dieser Büßer Moissi, nicht Pallenberg [...]" From a newspaper review signed P. W., in the Kaiser Archiv. Alexander Moissi (1880-1935) acted in Max Reinhardt's Deutsches Theater, Berlin, and played big tragic roles: Hamlet, Romeo, Tasso.

[42]"Man sah einen Betrogenen und Enterbten, der jählings erwacht, der aber dann sofort einer Art Besessenheit und Wahnwitz verfällt und maniakalisch dahinrast. Ein hohläugiges, hageres, zerklüftetes Gesicht, ausgezehrte Hände mit spinnendürren Fingern, ein

vertragener, schlotterig sitzender Rock charakterisieren das Äußere. Aus dem Innern aber schrie ein heiserer hungriger Jammer in harten ruckhaften Tönen." Newspaper review dated 15 April 1918 and signed F.S.-s., in the Kaiser Archiv.

⁴³Review by K. E., Kaiser Archiv.

⁴⁴"[...] ins Denk-Spiel sind wir eingezogen und bereits erzogen aus karger Schau-Lust zu glückvoller Denk-Lust." *Werke,* IV, 545.

⁴⁵Anton Kaes, "Rezeption und Innovation: Zur Wirkungsgeschichte des deutschen Expressionismus in Amerika," Diss. Stanford 1973, pp. 138, 127.

⁴⁶See several reviews in the Kaiser Archiv, esp. Hans Schwab-Felisch in the *Frankfurter Rundschau,* 22 October 1974; and Ulrich Schreiber in the same paper, 11 October 1974.

⁴⁷Walter Laqueur, *Weimar: Die Kultur der Republik,* tr. Otto Weith, Ullstein Buch, no. 3383 (Frankfurt: Ullstein, 1977), p. 282.

⁴⁸"Indem man die ratio schlechterdings verdammte, 'den Geist unter das Leben hinabdrückte' (Th. Mann), öffnete man der subjektiven Willkür weltanschaulicher Setzungen Tür und Tor, schlimmer noch: man öffnete bewußt das Ventil der Triebe und Leidenschaften, und fand es in der Nachfolge Sorels grandios, diesen Trieben und Leidenschaften mythische Bilder und Symbole vor Augen zu stellen, die sich an die Stelle des denkenden Geistes setzten. Die Abdankung des Geistes vor den Mächten der Tiefe charakterisiert darum im eigentlichen Sinne die Situation. Damit werden aber, wenn die gesellschaftlichen Verhältnisse in Unruhe geraten, die ordnenden und kulturschöpfenden Funktionen des Geistes an die dunklen Mächte des Lebens verraten. Wer den Irrationalismus predigt, muß damit rechnen, daß das Unvernünftige und Böse die Macht gewinnen kann. Wer dem Leben keinerlei Schranken von Vernunft und Sitten auferlegen will, muß gewärtig sein, daß das Leben in seiner inhumansten Form die Macht an sich reißt und dann so schnell nicht wieder abgibt." Kurt Sontheimer, *Antidemokratisches Denken in der Weimarer Republik: Die politischen Ideen des deutschen Nationalismus zwischen 1918 und 1933* (Munich: Nymphenburg, 1962), p. 64.

⁴⁹"Die ganze Zeit bietet das Bild eines Narkotikers, der immer stärkere Dosen eines Reizmittels bedarf, um die erschlaffenden Sinne, die abgestumpften Nerven erneut aufzupeitschen." Gunter Martens, *Vitalismus und Expressionismus,* Studien zur Poetik und Geschichte der Literatur, no. 22 (Stuttgart: Kohlhammer, 1971), p. 100. The essay cited is Karl Holl, "Der Wandel des deutschen Lebensgefühls im Spiegel der deutschen Kunst seit der Reichsgründung," *Deutsche Vierteljahrsschrift,* 4 (1926), 548-63.

⁵⁰"Im Hagel der Tatsachen erstirbt die Verwunderung, der Respekt vor dem Ereignis, die Empfänglichkeit, und gleichzeitig erhöht sich die Begierde nach neuen Tatsachen, nach Steigerungen. Wird die Begierde nicht gesättigt, so tritt eine verzweifelte Erschöpfung ein, [...] die dem Menschen seine eigene Lebenszeit hassenswert erscheinen läßt und daher Langeweile genannt wird.

"Mechanisch betrachtet ist die Langeweile das Warnungssignal, das dem Menschen in die Ohren bläst: er sei zeitweilig ausgeschaltet aus dem allgemeinen Werben und Walten, und ihn zum Zwang der Arbeit oder des Genusses antreibt." Walter Rathenau, *Zur Kritik der Zeit* (Berlin: Fischer, 1912), p. 90.

[51]Fritz Stern, *The Politics of Cultural Despair* (Berkeley: University of California, 1961), pp. 290-92, 268.

[52]Booker, *The Neophiliacs* (Boston: Gambit, 1970).

[53]Booker, pp. 61, 66, 69, 70.

[54]Booker, p. 361.

[55]*Bilder und Zeichnungen* (Zurich: Diogenes, 1978).

[56]"Alle sind gegen den Turm und dennoch kommt er zustande." Friedrich Dürrenmatt, *Komödien I* (Zurich: Arche, 1957), p. 263; cited hereafter by volume and page number.

[57]"Die Abderiten lachten jetzt selbst über ihre Torheit, als einen Anstoß von fiebrischer Raserei, der nun, Gottlob!, vorüber sei." *Geschichte der Abderiten,* Fischer Bücherei Exempla Classica, no. 37 (Frankfurt: Fischer, 1961), p. 253.

[58]*Abderiten,* p. 123.

[59]Friedrich Dürrenmatt, *Gesammelte Hörspiele* (Zurich: Arche, n.d.), p. 68.

[60]*Hörspiele,* p. 82.

[61]*Hörspiele,* p. 85. See also *Der Verdacht* (Einsiedeln: Benziger, 1953), p. 107: "Der Mensch selbst wünscht seine Hölle herbei."

[62]"Der Trost, daß auch das Zusammenbrechen aller Dinge Gnade ist, ja, daß es die Engel selbst sind, die töten, ist der Gewißheit gewichen, daß der Mensch aus eigenem Antrieb ein Inferno der Elemente zu entfesseln vermag, das man einst nur Gottes Zorn zuzuschreiben wagte; und Grausamkeiten werden verübt, die jene des Teufels mehrfach übertreffen. So ist Ereignis geworden, was Offenbarung war, aber es ist nicht mehr ein Kampf um Gut und Böse, so gern dies jede Partei auch darstellt. Die Menschheit ist als ganze schuldig geworden, ein jeder will mit den Idealen auch die Kehrseite retten: die Freiheit und die Geschäfte, die Gerechtigkeit und die Vergewaltigung. Der Mensch, der einst vor der Hölle zitterte, hat sich ein Diesseits errichtet, das Höllen aufweist, die Schuldige und Unschuldige [...] gleicherweise verschlingen [...]." Dürrenmatt,*Theaterschriften und Reden* (Zurich: Arche, 1967), pp. 40-41.

[63]"[...] die Beschaffenheit, die leider den Menschen anhaftet in all ihrer Widerborstigkeit, Wildheit, Trägheit, Bequemlichkeit, in all ihrer Habgier und Machtgier, aber auch in all ihrem Unbewußten." Dürrenmatt, "Über Toleranz," in *Lesebuch* (Zurich: Arche, 1978), p. 274.

[64]*Theaterschriften und Reden,* pp. 29, 45.

[65]"Der Schriftsteller kann seiner moralischen Aufgabe nur dann nachkommen, [...] wenn er Anarchist ist. Er muß angreifen und nicht engagiert sein." From Horst Bieneck, *Werkstattgespräche mit Schriftstellern* (1962, rpt. Munich, DTV, 1965), p. 130.

[66]"Die heutige Menschheit gleicht einer Autofahrerin. Sie fährt immer schneller, immer rücksichtsloser ihre Straße. Doch hat sie es nicht gern, wenn der konsternierte Mitfahrer 'Achtung!' schreit und 'Hier ist eine Warnungstafel,' 'Jetzt sollst du bremsen,' oder gar 'Überfahre nicht dieses Kind.' Sie haßt es, wenn einer fragt, wer denn den Wagen bezahlt oder das Benzin und das Öl geliefert habe, oder wenn er gar ihren Führerschein zu sehen verlangt. Ungemütliche Wahrheiten könnten zutage treten. Der Wagen wäre vielleicht einem Verwandten entwendet, das Benzin und das Öl aus den Mitfahrern selber gepreßt und gar kein Öl und Benzin, sondern unser aller Blut und unser aller Schweiß, und der Führerschein wäre möglicherweise gar nicht vorhanden; es könnte sich gar herausstellen, daß sie zum ersten Mal fährt. Dies wäre freilich peinlich, fragte man nach so naheliegenden Dingen. So liebt sie es denn, wenn man die Schönheit der Landschaft preist, durch die sie fährt, das Silber eines Flusses und das Glühen der Gletscher in der Ferne, auch amüsante Geschichten liebt sie ins Ohr geflüstert. Diese Geschichten zu flüstern und die schöne Landschaft zu preisen ist einem heutigen Schriftsteller jedoch oft nicht mehr so recht mit gutem Gewissen möglich. Leider kann er aber auch nicht aussteigen, um der Forderung nach reinem Dichten Genüge zu tun, die da von allen Nicht-Dichtern erhoben wird. Die Angst, die Sorge und vor allem der Zorn reißen seinen Mund auf." *Theaterschriften und Reden*, pp. 129-30.

[67]*Theaterschriften und Reden*, p. 128.

[68]Bieneck, *Werkstattgespräche*, p. 125; *Theaterschriften und Reden*, pp. 132ff.; *Der Verdacht* (Einsiedeln: Benziger, 1953), pp. 23, 40; *Theaterprobleme* (Zurich: Arche, 1955), p. 59; *Friedrich Dürrenmatt: Gespräch mit Heinz Ludwig Arnold*, ed. H. L. Arnold (Zurich: Arche, 1976), p. 15.

[69]"Anmerkungen zur Komödie," *Theaterschriften und Reden*, p. 135.

[70]"So sind die grotesken Reisen des Gulliver gleich einer Retorte, in der durch vier verschiedene Experimente die Schwächen und die Grenzen des Menschen aufgezeigt werden. Das Groteske ist eine der großen Möglichkeiten, genau zu sein. Es kann nicht geleugnet werden, daß diese Kunst die Grausamkeit der Objektivität besitzt, doch ist sie nicht die Kunst des Nihilisten, sondern weit eher der Moralisten, nicht die des Moders, sondern des Salzes. Sie ist eine Angelegenheit des Witzes und des scharfen Verstandes [darum verstand sich die Aufklärung darauf], nicht dessen, was das Publikum unter Humor versteht, einer bald sentimentalen, bald frivolen Gemütlichkeit. Sie ist unbequem aber nötig." *Theaterschriften und Reden*, pp. 136-37.

[71]Northrop Frye, *Anatomy of Criticism* (1957, rpt. New York: Atheneum, 1966), p. 238.

[72]"Denn eine Gesellschaft, wie auch ihre Ordnung beschaffen sein mag, wird nicht vom Einzelnen bedroht, sondern von sich selbst." *Der Mitmacher: Ein Komplex* (Zurich: Arche, 1976), p. 146.

[73]Erna K. Neuse, "Das Rhetorische in Dürrenmatts *Der Besuch der alten Dame:* Zur Funktion des Dialogs im Drama," *Seminar,* 11 (1975), 225-241; this is one of the very best studies on Dürrenmatt. Also informative on the question of rhetoric and in general is Hans-Jürgen Syberberg, *Zum Drama Friedrich Dürrenmatts: Zwei Modellinterpretationen zur Wesensdeutung des modernen Dramas,* 3rd ed. (Munich: Uni-Druck, 1974).

[74]Jürgen Brummack, "Zu Begriff und Theorie der Satire," *Deutsche Vierteljahrsschrift,* Sonderheft Forschungsreferate, 45 (1971), 347.

[75]*Standard Edition of the Complete Psychological Works of Sigmund Freud,* tr. and ed. James Strachey (London: Hogarth, 1961), XXI, 81.

[76]Friedrich Dürrenmatt, *Die Wiedertäufer* (Zurich: Arche, 1967), p. 81.

[77]*Porträt eines Planeten* (Zurich: Arche, 1971), p. 10.

[78]"Die wirkliche Geschichte ist eine Geschichte der Kollektive und der Machtkämpfe, die diese Kollektive gegeneinander und untereinander austrugen." From "Gespräch 1971," *Dramaturgisches und Kritisches* (Zurich: Arche, 1972), pp. 269, 275.

[79]"[...] gegen einen solchen Dialog sind telegrafierende Schatten die puren Wortverschwender." *Die Zeit,* 16 March 1973.

[80]"Das Publikum läßt sich nur bezwingen, indem man es überlistet. Die Regisseure sollten daher jedes Stück kulinarisch und revolutionär zugleich inszenieren, eine Aufgabe, die sogar bei den Klassikern lösbar ist. Wer heute die Wahrheit sagen will, kann es im Osten und im Westen nur auf eine listige Weise sagen, und die Wahrheit ist immer revolutionär." *Dramaturgisches und Kritisches,* p. 152.

[81]"Ich versuche dramaturgisch immer einfacher, immer sparsamer zu werden, immer mehr auszulassen, nur noch anzudeuten." "Ich schreibe meine Stücke nicht mehr *für* Schauspieler, ich komponiere *mit* ihnen." *Porträt eines Planeten,* p. 10. Italics mine.

[82]*Zusammenhänge* (Zurich: Arche, 1976), p. 139.

[83]"Wir müssen schließlich begründen, warum es hienieden so blutig zugeht, der Verdacht käme sonst auf, es mache uns am Ende Vergnügen." *Zusammenhänge,* p. 219.

[84]"Was mich damals streifte an diesem sinnlosen Abend in der scheinbar so perfekten Welt eines Kibbuz, war der Anhauch dessen, was wir alle befürchten, daß nämlich nach all dem Planen, nach all den Bemühungen, nach all dem Einlenken, nach all den Kompromissen, nach all dem Blutvergießen, nach all den Revolutionen und Kriegen, nach all dem Scheitern und Gelingen der Friede als Friede nicht auszuhalten sei, eine um so bangere Befürchtung, weil sie nur durch den Frieden widerlegt oder bestätigt werden könnte. Dem Kampf einen Sinn zu geben, ist leicht, weil wir uns vorlügen, dieser Sinn des Kämpfens liege im Frieden; mit dieser Lüge legen wir den Sinn in ein Ziel außer uns, wir legen es in unseren Gegner und damit ins Unerreichbare [...]." *Zusammenhänge,* p. 211. See also "Über Toleranz" in Dürrenmatt, *Lesebuch,* p. 289.

[85]Friedrich Dürrenmatt, *Komödien II* (Zurich: Arche, n.d.), p. 199. Cited hereafter in the text by volume and page number alone.

[86]Bieneck, *Werkstattgespräche*, p. 125.

[87]"Das Erträgliche ist in diesem Stück, in *Frank V,* das Verlogene, die Ausrede, die spezifisch poetische Atmosphäre, in die das Stück getaucht ist. Im *Frank* singen die Menschen, wenn sie lügen [...]." Bieneck, p. 127.

[88]*Theaterschriften und Reden,* pp. 85-86.

[89]Anonymous column in *Die Tat,* 23 May 1959, two months after the première.

[90]"Überhöhung, Entwirklichung, Mythisierung der szenischen Vorgänge," from the *Neue Zürcher Zeitung,* 20 March 1959.

[91]I read reviews by the following: Hg. in the *Neue Zürcher Zeitung,* 20 March, 1959; ebs. in *Die Tat,* 23 March, 1959; m.sch. in *Radio und Fernsehen,* 14 (1959); Walter Fabian in *Volksrecht,* 28 March, 1959; Joachim Kaiser in the *Süddeutsche Zeitung,* 21/22 March, 1959; -oe- in *Tagesanzeiger* (Zurich), 21 March 1959; and -nn. in *Neue Zürcher Nachrichten,* 21 March, 1959.

[92]In the issue of 1 June, 1973. The review deals with a performance in English translation at the Glyndebourne Opera Festival.

[93]"Diesmal ist es ein echtes Opernfinale, stampfend, übermütig, mit Lach-Rouladen die Tonleiter herunter." From a review of the Berlin performance published in the *Frankfurter Allgemeine Zeitung,* 6 March, 1972. See also Stuckenschmidt's review of the Vienna première in the *Frankfurter Allgemeine Zeitung,* 25 May, 1971. Further, Brünhilde Sonntag, "Wie sich die alte Dame veränderte," *Opernwelt,* 13 (1972), no. 2, 45-47; and Andreas Briner, "Zu Gottfried von Einems Dürrenmatt-Oper *Der Besuch der alten Dame,"* in Karl S. Weimar, ed., *Views and Reviews of Modern German Literature,* Festschrift for Adolf C. Klarmann (Munich: Delp, 1974), pp. 251-56. Two reviews of the Glyndebourne production are in the archives of the Reiss AG, Basel.

[94]*Der Mitmacher: Ein Komplex* (Zurich: Arche, 1976), p. 161.

[95]*Mitmacher,* p. 181.

[96]*Mitmacher,* p. 187.

[97]*Mitmacher,* p. 65.

[98]*Mitmacher,* p. 53. The comments on the reviews are based on those by ebs in *Die Tat,* 12 March, 1973; sda in the same issue; Friedrich Luft in *Die Welt,* 20 March, 1973; Hellmuth Karasek in *Die Zeit,* 16 March, 1973; I.V. in the *Neue Zürcher Zeitung,* 10 March, 1973; Günther Rühle in the *Frankfurter Allgemeine Zeitung,* 2 November 1973; Peter Iden in the *Frankfurter Rundschau,* 3 November, 1973; and Hans Bayer in the *Frankfurter Abendpost,* 6 November, 1973.

Conclusion

[1]Karl Pietzcker, "Das Groteske," *Deutsche Vierteljahrsschrift,* 45 (1971), 202f., 199f.

[2]"Die Menschen morden, foltern und trinken, Schoolgirls sind Menschen, also morden, foltern und trinken Schoolgirls. Was wird damit erreicht? Nun, das Bedrohliche, die schreckliche Möglichkeit im Menschen wird durch einen Dreh, wenn man will, durch einen Kniff der Groteske, als etwas Absurdes und gleichzeitig als etwas 'Allgegenwärtiges,' ans Tageslicht gebracht; hier, indem Zeit eliminiert wird, als würde man etwa den Säugling Hitler alle jene Dinge vollbringen lassen, die der Mann Hitler dann vollbrachte. Dies zur satirischen Technik, zu einer Technik, die ja am vollendetsten ein anderer Engländer, Swift, beherrscht hat. [...] es ist heute nötig, die Satire in jeder Gattung als eine eigene Kunstart zu begreifen, die ihre eigenen Gesetz besizt und ihre eigene Ästhetik. [...] Die Satire ist eine exakte Kunst, gerade *weil* sie übertreibt, denn nur wer die Nuance und das Allgemeine zugleich sieht, *kann* übertreiben." "Das sind die echten Komödianten nämlich nie. Die beißen. Achtung vor Robert Searle." *Theaterschriften und Reden*, pp. 289-90.

[3]Brecht, *Stücke III* (Frankfurt: Suhrkamp, 1964), vol. I, 223.

[4]Albert Bandura, *Aggression: A Social Learning Analysis* (Prentice Hall, 1973), 171-72. See also Dürrenmatt's account of how his hopes for a fresh start and a new Europe after World War II were dashed in "Über Toleranz," *Lesebuch* (Zurich: Arche, 1978), pp. 271-72.

[5]"Dieser Kampf ist der wesentliche Inhalt des Lebens uberhaupt, und darum ist die Kulturentwicklung kurzweg zu bezeichnen als der Lebenskampf der Menschenart." Sigmund Freud, *Studienausgabe*, Conditio Humana (Frankfurt: Fischer, 1974), vol. IX, 249 (Chapter Six).

[6]Alexander Mitscherlich, *Die Idee des Friedens und die menschliche Aggressivität: Vier Versuche,* Bibliothek Suhrkamp, no. 233 (Frankfurt: Suhrkamp, 1970); Alexander Mitscherlich, ed., *Bis hierher und nicht weiter: Ist die menschliche Aggression befriedbar?* suhrkamp taschenbuch, no. 239 (Frankfurt: Suhrkamp, 1974); Alexander Mitscherlich, *Massenpsychologie ohne Ressentiment: Sozialpsychologische Betrachtungen,* suhrkamp taschenbuch, no. 76, 2nd ed. (Frankfurt: Suhrkamp, 1975); Norman O. Brown, *Life Against Death: The Psychoanalytical Meaning of History* (Middletown: Wesleyan University, 1959); Sigmund Freud, *Das Ich und das Es und andere metapsychologische Schriften,* Fischer Taschenbuch, no. 680 (Frankfurt: Fischer, 1978).

[7]Lionel Trilling, *Freud and the Crisis of our Culture* (Boston: Beacon, 1955), p. 39.

[8]Trilling, "Freud and Literature," in *The Liberal Imagination* (New York: Viking, 1950), p. 57.

[9]Alexander Mitscherlich, "Aggression—Spontaneität—Gehorsam," in *Bis hierher und nicht weiter,* p. 79.

[10]Freud, *Studienausgabe,* IX, 240f.

[11]Alois Becker, "Der operative Aspekt menschlicher Aggression," in Mitscherlich, ed., *Bis hierher und nicht weiter,* p. 27.

[12]*Standard Edition,* ed. and tr. James Strachey (London: Hogarth, 1961), vol. XXI, 113 (Chapter Five).

[13]"Eine bedeutende offensive Verschärfung erhalten in Expansion begriffene Wünsche, sobald ihnen der Charakter subjektiv rechtmäßiger Ansprüche zuwächst, weil das Hinzukommen der moralischen Qualität [...] weitreichende Konsequenzen für die Stärke der mit ihr verknüpften aggressiven Operationen nach sich zieht." *Bis hierher und nicht weiter,* p. 28.

[14]Leonard Berkowitz, *Aggression: A Social Psychological Analysis,* McGraw Hill Studies in Psychology (New York: McGraw Hill, 1962), p. 122.

[15]See Gunter G. Sehm, "Moses, Christus und Paul Ackermann: Brechts *Aufstieg und Fall der Stadt Mahagonny,"* in John Fuegi, et al., eds., *Brecht Jahrbuch 1976* (Frankfurt: Suhrkamp, 1976), pp. 83-100; Jenny C. Hortenbach, "Biblical Echoes in Dürrenmatt's *Besuch der alten Dame,"* *Monatshefte,* 57 (1965), 145-61. Eli Pfefferkorn, "Dürrenmatt's Mass Play," *Modern Drama,* 12 (1969), 30-37.

[16]"Alle unmäßig expandierenden Ansprüche und Anspruchsysteme enthalten—und enthalten in zunehmendem Maße—utopische Züge. Indem sich diese anreichern, nähert sich die Expansion immer mehr der Allmachtsmagie in Form des Machtrausches oder der Gewißheit kommender Machtfülle. Dadurch verschärfen sich die fremd- und selbstdestruktiven Konsequenzen, die aus den Prämissen bestimmter Vorurteile in den Deduktionen einer *Vernichtungsideologik* hervorgehen. Sie steigern sich in dem Maße, in dem chiliastische Verheißungen zu radikalen Operationen vom Charaker der Endlösungen, zur *'letzten* Gewalt, die dann den Zustand der Vernichtung *aller* Gewaltsamkeit bringen würde,' aufrufen." *Bis hierher und nicht weiter,* p. 31; the short quote is taken from Max Weber, *Gesammelte Aufsätze zur Wissenschaftslehre* (Tübingen: Mohr, 1922), p. 177.

[17]See Alexander Mitscherlich, "Aggression—Spontaneität—Gehorsam," in *Bis hierher und nicht weiter,* p. 88.

Bibliography

Adling, Wilfried. "Georg Kaisers Drama *Von morgens bis mitternachts* und die Zersetzung des dramatischen Stils." *Weimarer Beiträge* 5 (1959): 369-86.

Adorno, Theodor. Review of the première of *Mahagonny*. In *Der Scheinwerfer* 3. Essen, April, 1930.

Arendt, Hannah. *On Violence*. New York: Harcourt Brace, 1970.

Auden, Wystan Hugh. *The Dyer's Hand*. London: Faber and Faber, 1963.

Bandura, Albert. *Aggression: A Social Learning Analysis*. Englewood Cliffs: Prentice Hall, 1973.

Barraclough, Geoffrey. "A Farewell to Hitler." *New York Review*. 3 April, 1975. Pp. 11-17.

Baum, Georgina. *Humor und Satire in der bürgerlichen Ästhetik*. Germanistische Studien. Berlin: Rütten und Loening, 1959.

Baumgart, Winfried. *Deutschland im Zeitalter des Imperialismus (1890-1914)*. 3rd edition. Ullstein Buch, no. 3844. Frankfurt: Ullstein, 1979.

Bayer, Hans. Review of performance of *Der Mitmacher*. *Frankfurter Abendpost*. 6 November 1973.

Bayerdörfer, Hans-Peter. "Sternheim: *Die Kassette*." In *Die deutsche Komödie*. Edited by Walter Hinck. Düsseldorf: Bagel, 1977.

Berkowitz, Leonard. *Aggression: A Social Psychological Analysis*. McGraw Hill Studies in Psychology. New York: McGraw Hill, 1962.

Bieneck, Horst. *Werkstattgespräche mit Schriftstellern*. 1962. Reprint. Munich: DTV, 1965.

Binion, Rudolph. *Frau Lou: Nietzsche's Wayward Disciple*. Princeton: Princeton University Press, 1968.

Blomster, Wesley P. "The Documentation of a Novel: Otto Weininger and *Hundejahre* by Günter Grass." *Monatshefte* (1969): 122-38.

Böckmann, Paul. "Die komödiantischen Grotesken Frank Wedekinds." In *Das deutsche Lustspiel*. Edited by Hans Steffen. Vol. 2. Göttingen: Vandenhoeck und Ruprecht, 1969.

Boelcke, Willi. *Krupp und die Hohenzollern: Aus der Korrespondenz der Familie Krupp, 1880-1916*. Berlin: Rütten und Loening, 1956.

Bolle, Fritz. "Darwinismus und Zeitgeist." *Zeitschrift für Religions- und Zeitgeschichte* 14 (1962): 143-78.

Booker, Christopher. *The Neophiliacs*. Boston: Gambit, 1970.

Booth, Wayne C. *A Rhetoric of Irony*. Chicago: University of Chicago Press, 1974.

Brecht, Bertolt. *Schriften zum Theater*. Vol. 2. Frankfurt: Suhrkamp, 1963.

——————————. *Stücke III*. Vol. 1. Frankfurt: Suhrkamp, 1964.

Briner, Andreas. "Zu Gottfried von Einems Dürrenmatt-Oper *Der Besuch der alten Dame.*" In *Views and Reviews of Modern German Literature.* Festschrift für Adolf C. Klarmann. Edited by Karl S. Weimar. Munich: Delp, 1974.

Bronnen, Arnolt. *Tage mit Brecht.* Munich: Desch, 1960.

Brown, Norman O. *Life Against Death: The Psychoanalytical Meaning of History.* Middletown: Wesleyan University Press, 1959.

Brummack, Jürgen. "Zu Begriff und Theorie der Satire." *Deutsche Vierteljahrsschrift* 45 (1971). Sonderheft Forschungsreferate: 275-377.

Calandra, Denis. "Georg Kaiser's *From Morn to Midnight:* The Nature of Expressionist Performance." *Theatre Quarterly* 4 (1976), no. 21: 48ff.

Conrad, Peter. "Incitements to Passion." *Times Literary Supplement.* 3 October 1975: 1136-37.

Crews, Frederick, ed. *Psychoanalysis and the Literary Process.* Cambridge, Mass.: Winthrop, 1970.

Cyprian, M. F. Review of the première of *Von morgens bis mitternachts. Hochland* 15 (1917/18), no. 3: 357-60.

Dedner, Burghard. "Aufklärungskomödien im Massenzeitalter: Über Carl Sternheims Beziehungen zum Publikum." *Jahrbuch der deutschen Schillergesellschaft* 19 (1975): 284-305.

de Mendelssohn, Peter. *Zeitungsstadt Berlin.* Berlin: Ullstein, 1959.

Deutsches Sprichwörterlexikon. Edited by Karl Friedrich Wilhelm Wander. Darmstadt: Wissenschaftliche Buchgesellschaft, 1964.

Dick, Day. *Pierrot.* London: Hutchinson, 1960.

Dictionary of National Biography. New York: Macmillan, 1895.

Diebold, Bernhard. *Anarchie im Drama.* 4th Edition. Berlin: Keller, 1928.

Dryden, John. *Works.* Edited by Sir Walter Scott. Revised by George Saintsbury. Vol. 13. Edinburgh: W. Paterson, 1887.

Dürrenmatt, Friedrich. *Bilder und Zeichnungen.* Zurich: Diogenes, 1978.

––––––––––––. *Dramaturgisches und Kritisches.* Zurich: Arche, 1972.

––––––––––––. *Friedrich Dürrenmatt: Gespräch mit Heinz Ludwig Arnold.* Edited by Heinz Ludwig Arnold. Zurich: Arche, 1976.

––––––––––––. *Gesammelte Hörspiele.* Zurich: Arche, n.d.

––––––––––––. *Komödien I.* Zurich: Arche, 1967.

––––––––––––. *Komödien II.* Zurich: Arche, n.d.

––––––––––––. *Lesebuch.* Zurich: Arche, 1978.

––––––––––––. *Der Mitmacher.* Zurich: Arche, 1976.

––––––––––––. *Monstervortrag über Gerechtigkeit und Recht.* Zurich: Arche, 1969.

––––––––––––. *Porträt eines Planeten.* Zurich: Arche, 1971.

––––––––––––. *Theaterprobleme.* Zurich: Arche, 1955.

––––––––––––. *Theaterschriften und Reden.* Zurich: Arche, 1967.

––––––––––––. *Der Verdacht.* Einsiedeln: Benziger, 1953.

––––––––––––. *Die Wiedertäufer.* Zurich: Arche, 1971.

––––––––––––. *Zusammenhänge.* Zurich: Arche, 1976.

Elliott, Robert C. "The Definition of Satire." *Yearbook of Comparative and General Literature* 11, (1962).

———. *The Power of Satire.* Princeton: Princeton University Press, 1960.

Emrich, Wilhelm. *Protest und Verheißung.* 2nd edition. Frankfurt: Athenäum, 1963.

Fabian, Walter. Review of performance of *Frank V. Volksrecht,* 28 March 1959.

Fischer, Fritz. *Germany's Aims in the First World War.* New York: Norton, 1967.

Freud, Sigmund. *Das Ich und das Es und andere metapsychologische Schriften.* Fischer Taschenbuch, no. 680. Frankfurt: Fischer, 1978.

———. *Standard Edition of the Complete Psychological Works.* Edited by James Strachey. Vol. 21. London: Hogarth, 1961.

———. *Studienausgabe.* Conditio Humana. Vol. 6. Frankfurt: Fischer, 1974.

Fritz, Horst. "Die Dämonisierung des Erotischen in der Literatur des Fin de Siècle." In *Fin de Siècle: Zur Literatur und Kunst der Jahrhundertwende.* Edited by Roger Bauer et al. Reihe Studien zur Philosophie und Literatur des neunzehnten Jahrhunderts, no. 35. Frankfurt: Klostermann, 1977: 442-64.

Frye, Northrop. *Anatomy of Criticism.* 1957. Reprint. New York: Atheneum, 1966.

Gaier, Ulrich. *Satire: Studien zu Neidhart, Wittenweiler, Brant und zur satirischen Schreibart.* Tübingen: Niemeyer, 1967.

Gittleman, Sol. *Frank Wedekind.* Twayne World Authors, no. 55. New York: Twayne, 1969.

Graves, Robert. *The Greek Myths.* 2 vols. Penguin Books, nos. 1026-27. 1955.

Grothe, Wolfgang. "Dramatiker im Niemandsland: Bemerkungen anläßlich der Carl-Sternheim-Gesamtausgabe." *Studia Neophilologica* 41 (1969): 339-345.

Guthke, Karl. *Modern Tragicomedy.* New York: Random House, 1966.

Hagedorn, Klaus. *Carl Sternheim: Die Bühnengeschichte seiner Dramatik.* Ph.D. dissertation. Cologne, 1961. Published Cologne, 1976.

Hajek, Edelgard. *Literatur und Jugendstil.* Literatur in der Gesellschaft, no. 6. Düsseldorf: Bertelsmann, 1971.

Heilbroner, Robert. "Inescapable Marx." *New York Review,* 29 June 1978: 33-37.

Herbort, Heinz Josef. Review of a performance of the opera *Lulu. Die Zeit.* Overseas edition. 9 January 1970.

Herles, Wolfgang. "Die Sternheim-Rennaissance auf den Bühnen der Bundesrepublik." In *Carl Sternheims Dramen: Zur Textanalyse, Ideologiekritik und Rezeptionsgeschichte.* Edited by Jörg Schönert. Heidelberg: Quelle und Meyer, 1975.

Hodgart, Matthew. *Satire.* World University Library, no. 043. London: Weidenfeld and Nicolson, 1969.

Hoffmann, Gerhard. "Zur Form der satirischen Komödie: Ben Jonsons *Volpone.*" *Deutsche Vierteljahrsschrift* 46 (1972): 1-27.

Hohendahl, Peter Uwe. *Das Bild der bürgerlichen Welt im expressionistischen Drama.* Probleme der Dichtung, no. 10. Heidelberg: Winter, 1967.

Holl, Karl. "Der Wandel des deutschen Lebensgefühls im Spiegel der deutschen Kunst seit der Reichsgründung." *Deutsche Vierteljahrsschrift* 4 (1926): 548-63.

Hortenbach, Jenny C. "Biblical Echoes in Dürrenmatt's *Besuch der alten Dame*." *Monatshefte* 57 (1965): 145-61.

Iden, Peter. Review of a performance of *Der Mitmacher*. *Frankfurter Rundschau*, 3 November 1973.

Ihering, Herbert. *Aktuelle Dramaturgie*. Berlin: Schmiede, 1924.

——————. *Von Reinhardt bis Brecht*. Hamburg: Rowohlt, 1967.

Jacobsohn, Siegfried. *Jahre der Bühne*. Hamburg: Rowohlt, 1965.

Jens, Walter. *Von deutscher Rede*. Munich: Piper, 1969.

Kaes, Anton. "Rezeption und Innovation: Zur Wirkungsgeschichte des deutschen Expressionismus in Amerika. Ph.D. dissertation. Stanford University, 1973.

Kaiser, Georg. *Werke*. Edited by Walther Huder. Berlin: Propyläen, 1971.

Kaiser, Joachim. Review of a performance of *Die Kassette*. *Süddeutsche Zeitung*, 1/2 July, 1961.

——————. Review of a performance of *Frank V*. *Süddeutsche Zeitung*, 21/22 March 1959.

Karasek, Hellmuth. *Carl Sternheim*. Friedrichs Dramatiker des Welttheaters. Velber: Friedrich, 1965.

——————. Review of performance of *Der Mitmacher*. *Die Zeit*, 16 March 1973.

Kernan, Alvin B., ed. *Modern Satire*. New York: Harcourt Brace, 1962.

——————. *The Plot of Satire*. New Haven: Yale University Press, 1965.

Kermode, Frank. *The Romantic Image*. 1957. Reprint. New York: Vintage, 1964.

Kerr, Alfred. *Die Welt im Drama*. 2nd edition. Edited by Gerhard F. Hering. Cologne: Kiepenheuer und Witsch, 1964.

Kessler, Harry Graf. *Tagebücher 1918-1937*. Frankfurt: Insel, 1961.

Klotz, Volker. *Dramaturgie des Publikums*. Munich: Hanser, 1976.

Kraus, Karl. *Literatur und Lüge*. Munich: Kösel, 1958.

——————. Traumstück. Vienna: Verlag "Die Fackel," 1922.

Kühne, Erich. "Über weltanschauliche und künstlerische Probleme bei Dürrenmatt." *Weimarer Beiträge* 12 (1966): 539-65.

Kutscher, Arthur. *Frank Wedekind*. Vol. 1. Munich: Langen Müller, 1922.

Laqueur, Walter. *Weimar: Die Kultur der Republik*. Translated by Otto Weith. Ullstein Buch, no. 3383. Frankfurt: Ullstein, 1977.

Lausberg, Heinrich. *Elemente der literarischen Rhetorik*. 5th edition. Munich: Hueber, 1976.

Lehman, A.G. "Pierrot and Fin de Siècle." In *Romantic Mythologies*. Edited by Ian Fletcher. New York: Barnes and Noble, 1967.

Luft, Friedrich. Review of a performance of *Der Mitmacher*. *Die Welt*, 20 March 1973.

Mann, Heinrich. *Sieben Jahre: Chronik der Gedanken und Vorgänge*. Berlin: Zsolnay, 1929.

Mann, William. Review of a performance of the opera version of *The Visit*. *London Times*, 1 June 1973.

Martens, Gunter. *Vitalismus und Expressionismus*. Studien zur Poetik und Geschichte der Literatur, no. 22. Stuttgart: Kohlhammer, 1971.

Michelsen, Peter. "Frank Wedekind." In *Deutsche Dichter der Moderne*. Edited by Benno von Wiese. Berlin: Erich Schmidt, 1965.

Milkereit, Gertrud. "Die Idee der Freiheit im Werke von Frank Wedekind." Ph.D. dissertation, University of Cologne, 1957.

Mitscherlich, Alexander, ed. *Bis hierher und nicht weiter: Ist die menschliche Aggression befriedbar?* Suhrkamp Taschenbuch, no. 239. Frankfurt: Suhrkamp, 1974.

Mitscherlich, Alexander. *Die Idee des Friedens und die menschliche Aggressivität: Vier Versuche*. Bibliothek Suhrkamp, no. 233. Suhrkamp, 1970.

——————————. *Massenpsychologie ohne Ressentiment: Sozialpsychologische Betrachtungen*. Suhrkamp Taschenbuch, no. 76. 2nd edition. Frankfurt: Suhrkamp, 1975.

Moeller-Bruck, Arthur. *Der neue Humor*. Die moderne Literatur in Einzeldarstellungen, no. 11. Berlin and Leipzig, 1902.

Mosse, George. *The Crisis of German Ideology*. New York: Grosset and Dunlap, 1964.

Neuse, Erna K. "Das Rhetorische in Dürrenmatts *Besuch der alten Dame:* Zur Funktion des Dialogs im Drama." *Seminar* 11 (1975): 225-41.

Nietzsche, Friedrich. *Werke*. 3 vols. Edited by Karl Schlechta. Munich: Hanser, 1955.

Paetel, Karl O. *Jugend in der Entscheidung: 1918-1933-1945*. Bad Godesberg: Voggenreiter, 1963.

Parmalee, Patty Lee. *Brecht's America*. Columbus: Miami University Press, 1981.

Paul, Arno. *Aggressive Tendenzen des Theaterpublikums: Eine strukturell-funktionale Untersuchung über den sog. Theaterskandal anhand der Sozialverhältnisse der Goethezeit*. Ph.D. dissertation, Freie Universität Berlin, 1969. Munich: Schön, 1969.

Paulson, Ronald. *The Fictions of Satire*. Baltimore: The Johns Hopkins University Press, 1967.

Pfefferkorn, Eli. "Dürrenmatt's Mass Play." *Modern Drama* 12 (1969): 30-37.

Polgar, Alfred. *Ja und Nein*. Vol. 1. Berlin: Rowohlt, 1926.

Porter, Andrew. Review of a performance of *Mahagonny*. *The New Yorker*, 6 January 1973.

Preisendanz, Wolfgang. "Zur Korrelation zwischen Satirischem und Komischem." In *Poetik und Hermeneutik: Arbeitserzeugnisse einer Fachgruppe*. Vol. 7. Edited by W. Preisendanz and Rainer Waring. Munich: Fink, 1976.

Quiquer, Cl. "L'érotisme de Frank Wedekind." *Etudes Germaniques* 17 (1962): 14-33.

Rasch, Wolfdietrich. "Sozialkritische Aspekte in Wedekinds dramatischer Dichtung: Sexualität, Kunst und Gesellschaft." In *Gestaltungsgeschichte und Gesellschaftsgeschichte*. Festschrift für Fritz Martini. Edited by Helmut Kreuzer. Stuttgart: Metzler, 1969.

Rathenau, Walter. *Zur Kritik der Zeit*. Berlin: Fischer, 1912.

Ritter, Gerhard. *Staatskunst und Kriegshandwerk*. Vol. 2. Munich: Oldenbourg, 1960.

Rosenfeld, Hellmut. *Der mittelalterliche Totentanz*. 2nd edition. Cologne: Böhlau, 1968.

Rosenheim, Edward. *Swift and the Satirist's Art*. Chicago: University of Chicago Press, 1967.

Rothe, Friedrich. *Frank Wedekinds Dramen: Jugendstil und Lebensphilosophie*. Germanistische Abhandlungen, no. 23. Stuttgart: Metzler, 1968.

Rühle, Günther. Review of a performance of *Der Mitmacher*. *Frankfurter Allgemeine Zeitung,* 2 November 1973.

―――――――――, ed. *Theater für die Republik.* Frankfurt: Fischer, 1967.

Sarason, D., ed. *Das Jahr 1913: Ein Gesamtbild der Kulturentwicklung.* Berlin and Leipzig: Teubner, 1913.

Schiller, Friedrich. *Über naive und sentimentalische Dichtung.* In Säkularausgabe, vol. 12.

Schmidt, Karl-Heinz. "Zur Gestaltung antagonistischer Konflikte bei Brecht und Kaiser: Eine vergleichende Studie." *Weimarer Beiträge* 11 (1965): 551-69.

Schmidt, Kaspar [Max Stirner]. *Der Einzige und sein Eigentum.* Leipzig: Reclam, 1892.

Schönert, Jörg. *Roman und Satire im 18. Jahrhundert: Ein Beitrag zur Poetik.* Germanistische Abhandlungen, no. 27. Stuttgart: Metzler, 1969.

Schorske, Carl. *Fin de Siècle Vienna: Politics and Culture.* New York: Knopf, 1980.

Schürer, Ernst, ed. *Georg Kaiser, Von morgens bis mitternachts: Erläuterungen und Dokumente.* Reclams Universalbibliothek, no. 8131. Stuttgart: Reclam, 1975.

Schürer, Ernst. *Georg Kaiser.* Twayne World Authors. New York: Twayne, 1971.

Schwab-Felisch, Hans. Review of a performance of *Von morgens bis mitternachts. Frankfurter Rundschau,* 22 October 1974.

Sebald, W. G. *Carl Sternheim: Kritiker und Opfer der Wilhelminischen Ära.* Sprache und Literatur, no. 58. Stuttgart: Kohlhammer, 1969.

Seehaus, Günter. *Wedekind und das Theater.* Munich: Laokoon, 1964.

Sehm, Gunter G. "Moses, Christus und Paul Ackermann: Brechts *Aufstieg und Fall der Stadt Mahagonny.*" *Brecht Jahrbuch* 1976: 83-100.

Sonntag, Brunhilde. Review of a performance of the opera version of *Der Besuch der alten Dame. Opernwelt* 13 (1972), no. 2: 45-47.

Sontheimer, Kurt. *Antidemokratisches Denken in der Weimarer Republik.* Munich: Nymphenburg, 1962.

Spacks, Patricia Meyer. "Some Reflections on Satire." *Genre* 1 (1968): 13-30.

Spalter, Max. *Brecht's Tradition.* Baltimore: The Johns Hopkins University Press, 1967.

Stern, Fritz. *The Politics of Cultural Despair.* Berkeley: The University of California Press, 1961.

Sternheim, Carl. *Das Gesamtwerk.* Edited by Wilhelm Emrich. Neuwied: Luchterhand, 1963-76.

Storey, Robert F. *Pierrot: A Critical History of a Mask.* Princeton: Princeton University Press, 1978.

Stuckenschmidt, H. H. Reviews of two productions of the opera version of *Der Besuch der alten Dame. Frankfurter Allgemeine Zeitung,* 6 March and 25 May 1971.

Syberberg, Hans-Jürgen. *Zum Drama Friedrich Dürrenmatts: Zwei Modellinterpretationen zur Wesensdeutung des modernen Dramas.* 3rd edition. Munich: Uni-Druck, 1974.

Thorpe, Peter. "Satire as Pre-Comedy." *Genre* 4 (1971): 1-17.

Trilling, Lionel. *Freud and the Crisis of our Culture.* Boston: Beacon, 1955.

―――――――――. *The Liberal Imagination.* New York: Viking, 1950.

Vietta, Silvio and Hans-Georg Kemper. *Expressionismus.* Uni-Taschenbücher, no. 362. Munich: Fink, 1975.

Voigts, Manfred. *Brechts Theaterkonzeptionen: Entstehung und Entwicklung bis 1931.* Munich: Fink, 1978.

Völker, Klaus. *Wedekind.* Friedrichs Dramatiker des Welttheaters. Velber: Friedrich, 1965.

Wagner, Gottfried. *Weill und Brecht: Das musikalische Zeittheater.* Munich: Kindler, 1977.

Wapnewski, Peter. *Der traurige Gott: Richard Wagner in seinen Helden.* 2nd edition. Munich: Beck, 1980.

Weber, Max. *Gesammelte Aufsätze zur Religionsgeschichte.* 5th edition. Tübingen: Mohr, 1963.

Wedekind, Frank. *Die Büchse der Pandora.* In *Die Insel* 3 (July, 1902): 19-105.

───────────────. *The Lulu Plays and Other Tragedies of Sex.* Translated by Stephen Spender. London: Calder, 1977.

───────────────. *Der Marquis von Keith.* Edited by Frank Hartwig. Komedia, no. 8. Berlin: de Gruyter, 1965.

───────────────. *Prosa, Dramen, Verse.* Edited by Hansgeorg Maier. 2 vols. Munich: Langen Müller, n.d.

───────────────. *Der vermummte Herr: Briefe Frank Wedekinds aus den Jahren 1881-1917.* Edited by Wolfdietrich Rasch. DTV, no. 440. Munich: Deutscher Taschenbuch Verlag, 1967.

───────────────. *Werke in drei Bänden.* 3 vols. Edited by Manfred Hahn. Berlin and Weimar: Aufbau, 1969.

Weininger, Otto. *Geschlecht und Charakter.* 20th edition. Vienna and Leipzig: Braumüller, 1920.

Wendler, Wolfgang. *Carl Sternheim.* Bonn: Athenäum, 1969.

Werner, Lothar. *Der Alldeutsche Verband, 1890-1918: Ein Beitrag zur Geschichte der öffentlichen Meinung in Deutschland vor und während des Krieges.* Historische Studien, no. 278. Berlin: Ebering, 1975.

Wieland, Christoph Martin. *Die Abderiten.* Fischer Bücherei Exempla Classica, no. 37. Frankfurt: Fischer, 1961.

Witke, Charles. *Latin Satire: The Structure of Persuasion.* Leiden: Brill, 1970.

Wohl, Robert. *The Generation of 1914.* Cambridge: Harvard University Press, 1979.

Wyss, Monika, ed. *Brecht in der Kritik.* Munich: Kindler, 1977.

Index